SOX AND THE *City*

SOX AND THE *City*

A Fan's Love Affair with the
White Sox from the Heartbreak
of '67 to the Wizards of Oz

Updated Edition

RICHARD ROEPER

CHICAGO
REVIEW
PRESS

Library of Congress Cataloging-in-Publication Data
Roeper, Richard, 1959–
    Sox and the city : a fan's love affair with the White Sox from the heartbreak
of '67 to the Wizards of Oz / Richard Roeper.
        p. cm.
    ISBN-13: 978-1-55652-679-4
    ISBN-10: 1-55652-679-2
    1. Chicago White Sox (Baseball team)—History. 2. Chicago White Sox
(Baseball team)—Anecdotes. 3. Baseball fans—Illinois—Chicago. I. Title.

    GV875.C58R64 2006
    796.357'640977311—dc22

                                                              2006010392

Cover and interior design: Scott Rattray
Front cover image: © Terrence Fogarty 2004, www.terrencefogarty.com

Published by Chicago Review Press, Incorporated
814 North Franklin Street
Chicago, Illinois 60610
ISBN-13: 978-1-55652-679-4
ISBN-10: 1-55652-679-2
Printed in the United States of America
5 4 3 2 1

For my father

Contents

Acknowledgments

Thanks to Robert and Margaret Roeper, Lynn and Nick Zona, Bob and Colleen Roeper, Laura Roeper, Sam Saunders, Laura LeQuesne, John LeQuesne, Emily Roeper, Caroline Roeper, and Bobby Roeper.

Thanks also to Bill Adee, Grace Adee, Leslie Baldacci, John Barron, Anna Butler, Michael Cavoto, Richard Cavoto, Susan Carlson, Michelle Carney, Jennifer Ciminillo, John Cruickshank, Darcie Divita, Don Dupree, Roger and Chaz Ebert, Laura Emerick, Robert Feder, Wendy George, Amanda Kammes, Drew Hayes, Don Hayner, Susanna Homan, Steve Huntley, Jon and Liz Kaplan, John Kiehle, Tim King, David Kodeski, Rick Kogan, Janet LaMonica, Todd Musburger, Brian Musburger, Steve Pallotto, David Plummer, Phil and Jennie and Zachary Rosenthal, the Shempster, Nancy Stanley, Neil Steinberg, Ken Swanborn, Gwynne Thomas, Christy Van House, Jenniffer Weigel, Joyce Winnecke, and the Wisers: Paige, Jim, Audrey, and Jack.

To Annabelle: Kisses.

A dugout curtain call for Mark Liptak of White Sox Interactive and *White Sox Encyclopedia* author Richard C. Lindberg—Sox fans who have forgotten more about the history of the team than I will ever know of it.

To my assistant, Lia, her husband, Sam, and their son, Konstantinos Papadopoulos: Ευχαριστώ!

Thanks to Luis Aparicio, Dick Allen, Harold Baines, Magglio Ordonez, and Tadahito Iguchi.

Big thanks to my editor, Yuval Taylor.

Great thanks to Sheree Bykofsky and Janet Rosen. You always believe.

Introduction

For most of my lifetime, the Chicago White Sox have been the second team in the Second City. Whenever I'm on the road and mention that I'm from Chicago, the automatic assumption is that I'm a Cubs fan. People start waxing rhapsodic about the glories of Wrigley Field (the most overrated venue in all of sports) and the trials and tribulations of the Cubbies—the most romantic, the most lovable, the most endearing losers, ever. Maybe this year will be the year when the Cubs finally end that drought of, what is it, 754 years without a World Series appearance? That's the kind of crap I have to hear.

Finally, I have to cut them off and say, "Actually, I'm a Sox fan."

"You're a Red Sox fan?" they say.

"Uh, no. White Sox. I'm a White Sox fan."

"Oh."

That's all they ever say: "Oh." It's as if I'd said, "Actually, I'm more of a fan of Frisbee Football featuring three-legged dogs." There's just no quick reaction to the fact that I'm a White Sox fan. Prior to 2005, if there *was* a response, it's usually a mention of the movie *Eight Men Out* and the infamous 1919 Black Sox, the only professional team in the history of sports to conspire to throw a championship series. Pete Rose got kicked out of baseball after he had played for two decades and been a manager. Eight guys on the Sox were thrown out of the game while they still had careers.

Great. Thanks for bringing that up.

Forget about the Curse of the Bambino or the Bartman ball or any of that nonsense. If ever a team should get cursed, it wouldn't be because they sold the greatest player in the game to another team, or a fan reached out and interfered with a foul ball. It would be payback for *deliberately losing the World Series.*

Cubs fans and Red Sox fans wear their allegiances on their sleeves. They've always been proud of their long history of glorious failures, like parents who apologize for the failures of their grown children long after it's the rational thing to do. The Cubs and Red Sox didn't just fall short for all those decades; they fell short in a romantic fashion. They lost with style, with drama, with heartbreak.

The White Sox mostly just lost in front of half-empty stadiums. On the South Side of Chicago and in the south suburbs, we didn't write poems about it or make movies about it. We were just pissed off about it.

By the early part of this century, Sox fans were so frustrated that we started participating in the action. One fan ran onto the field and tackled an umpire. Another idiot streaked across the outfield. Yet another ran onto the field and was hauled down by security. He lost his pants in the process, revealing a pair of red-white-and-blue boxer shorts.

And then there were the Ligues, the heavily tattooed father-and-son tag team that jumped over the first base railing and attacked the first base coach for the Kansas City Royals. They were featured on every newscast and in every newspaper in the country—snarling at the camera like perps on a particularly white-trashy episode of *Cops.*

You heard "Cubs fan" and you thought of some diehard yuppie geek with a pencil and a scorecard, or some tanned babe in the bleachers, flashing a lot of leg as she soaked up the sun. You heard "White Sox fan" and you thought of a father-and-son team that looked like they could have been extras in *The Devil's Rejects.*

In 1959, the White Sox were in the World Series against the Los Angeles Dodgers—and my mother was nine months pregnant with me. The Sox won Game 1, 11–0, and for one fleeting evening it seemed as if they would be World Series champions for the first time since World War I.

Six days after the Dodgers won Game 6 and clinched the Series, I was born in Little Company of Mary Hospital in Evergreen Park, just south of the city limits and smack-dab in the middle of White Sox country.

Before the Sox would make it to the World Series again, 14 teams would be added to the major leagues, and the country would go through the war in Vietnam, the assassinations of two Kennedys and Martin Luther King, the moon walk, the resignation of Richard Nixon, the end of the Cold War, the invention of the Internet, the Persian Gulf War, the impeachment of Bill Clinton, the dawn of a new millennium, the tragedy of 9/11, the war in Iraq, the Boston Red Sox winning the World Series, and Brad Pitt dumping Jennifer Aniston for Angelina Jolie.

I went to my first White Sox game in 1966, when I was six years old. The Sox played the Yankees—and lost. Over the next four decades I would attend approximately 1,000 games, seeing many more losses than victories, and witnessing every season end with the Sox relegated to the sidelines, as the Yankees or the Cardinals or the A's, or even the friggin' Diamondbacks or the Marlins, celebrated a world championship.

In all those years, I went to maybe 10 Cubs games. That's the way it works in Chicago—either you're a Cubs fan or you're a White Sox fan. There's no in-between. If you say that you're a fan of both teams, it means you're not a fan at all. You're a Bi-Soxual.

I was born a Sox fan. I can't change that reality any more than I can change my Irish–German heritage. If you grew up on the South Side or in one of the south suburbs of Chicago, you were identified by your neighborhood parish, your ethnic background—and your team allegiance.

Grinder Rule #1: Once a Sox fan, always a Sox fan.

In *Sox and the City*, I will celebrate the championship season of 2005—and recall my adventures, heartbreaks, and moments of elation as a Sox fan from the mid-1960s to the present. We'll start with the scariest portion of the stretch drive of 2005, and then cut back and forth between the magic of '05 and the various hopes, dreams, heartbreaks, and head-shaking moments I've experienced over the last four decades. (The structure will be like *Pulp Fiction*, without Uma Thurman and the blood.)

As a diehard fan, I've listened to hundreds of games on the radio and watched thousands on the tube. And I was there in person when:

- Mickey Mantle went deep against the Sox to surpass Lou Gehrig on the all-time home run list.
- Bill Melton got thrown out of a game for throwing a punch.
- Dick Allen hit a homer into the center field bleachers and Harry Caray nearly caught it in his oversized net.
- The South Side Hit Men took first place in 1977.
- The throng at Disco Demolition stormed the field and caused the cancellation of the second game of a doubleheader.
- The 1983 team clinched the division to put the Sox in the postseason for the first time since 1959.
- Old Comiskey closed.
- New Comiskey opened.
- The 1993 Sox tried to concentrate on the playoff game against the Blue Jays, even as the park buzzed with news that Michael Jordan was quitting the Bulls.
- A.J. reached on a "dropped" third strike against the Angels; Dye went deep on Clemens in the 1st inning of Game 1 of the Series; Konerko put the Sox in the lead in Game 2 with a grand slam; and Podsednik won that game with his walk-off homer in the cold mist.

And I was there a thousand other times, for Sunday afternoon doubleheaders and Saturday night fireworks games, for weekday games attended by 2,000 fans, for playoff games when you couldn't find an empty seat to save your life.

Whether you're a casual Sox supporter and you go to maybe a game a year, or you're a diehard maniac who knows the names of the two cowboys who appeared in the Falstaff Beer commercials for the Sox in the 1970s,* *Sox and the City* is meant for you—the White Sox fan.

---

*Gabe and Walker. But then, you probably knew that.

SOX AND THE *City*

In a Choke Hold

September 20, 2005

You've got to be kidding me.

You have *got to be kidding me*!

It's supposed to be a done deal by now. The Chicago White Sox are supposed to be the 2005 American League Central Division champions. They're not supposed to be involved in a damn race to the wire. It was over in August! I was there. I remember. If this division chase was an *American Idol* audition, we're already out in the lobby, holding a "golden ticket," jumping around and telling our loved ones that we're going to Hollywood for the real competition—the elimination round. Now you're telling us, in essence, that Simon is having second thoughts and is wondering if, in fact, we're "quite dreadful," that Randy might change his vote and say, "Sorry, dog," that even Paula might be changing her mind, such as it is. *No-no-no-no-no-no.* Sox fans are already scouting possible playoff opponents and pitching matchups, baby. We're not ready to go back—to walk through that door and reenter the regular season.

Let's put it this way: I've already given away my tickets to the final regular-season home weekend games against Minnesota. Back in February, when the treasured box of season tickets (and parking passes) arrived in the mail and I sat down with my buddy Phil for the annual ritual of mapping out the schedule and carving up the thick brick of ducats, those Minnesota games loomed huge. At that point, we hoped against hope that come September 24 and 25, the Sox and Twins would be duking it out for the AL Central title. That would mean the season would have mattered. But by the end of July, the Twins were treading water around the .500 mark, while the Sox had a record that looked like it belonged to the 1955 Dodgers or the 1961 Yankees or the 1976 Reds. The Twins? Irrelevant.

Sixty-nine and thirty-six. On August 1, the Sox were 69–36—as in nearly twice as many wins as losses. They were so far ahead it was like Secretariat in the Belmont. You couldn't even *see* the other horses.

Blinded by the shining light of a 15-game lead heading into the final two months of the season, I started dishing out my season tickets as casually as if they were free passes to the next *Deuce Bigalow* movie. If you walked under my balcony in late summer, there was a 35 percent chance you'd get hit in the head with a couple of tickets and a parking pass. Sure, I kept a few games for myself, figuring I'd want to enjoy the rarefied air of a late-season Sox game that was meaningless—not for the usual out-of-contention reasons, but because they were so far ahead that a loss wouldn't even sting. Enjoy the fireworks, slap high-fives with fellow diehards, check out this Brandon McCarthy kid to see if he's the real deal. Take a Yankee-like victory lap, if you will.

But those last games against the Twins? I figured they'd be about as meaningful as a third date with Wilmer Valderrama.

And then.

And then the Sox turned into the .500 club everyone had expected them to be at the beginning of the season, and the Indians started winning games in clumps of four and five. From August 1 through September 20, the Tribe went an ungodly 33–11, systematically trimming the Sox' lead from 15 games to 12 to 10 to 8½ to 5½. Now, on September 21, the morning after a 7–5 Cleveland victory over the Sox at U.S. Cellular Field, the ChiSox lead is down to 2½ games.

Making us even more anxious is the fact that the Sox are just four ahead of the Yankees for the wild card. One more rough week, and the Sox won't just be out of first place—they'll be out of the playoffs all together.

Now, here's one of the six million differences between White Sox fans and Red Sox fans (not to mention Cubs fans). We're not sitting around saying, "Here we go again." We're not lamenting that the Sox are blowing a big lead, because we're not used to their *having* a big lead. We're practical, big-picture fans. We keep saying things like "Hey, if you had told us on Opening Day that we'd have a 2½ game lead in the division with 13 games to go, ya think we wouldn't have taken that deal?"

There's also this. Even as we've enjoyed this amazing season filled with comeback wins and one-run squeakers and "How did we win that game?" specials, many of us have been quietly acknowledging that on paper, the 2005 edition White Sox are not the best team we've ever seen. Surely, the 1993 and 1994 teams, not to mention the 2000 squad, had more talent on the roster. Maybe the only fan in the city who has absolutely no doubt in his mind that the Sox are the best team in baseball in 2005 is Ken "Hawk" Harrelson, who has become the biggest homer in the history of broadcasting.* (Kind of ironic, given that some 20 years earlier, Hawk's criticisms of players and management led to Jerry Reinsdorf's taking Hawk out of the broadcast booth and giving him the general manager's job, and what a disaster that was.)

I love the Hawkeroo. I love his blind enthusiasm and his Sox passion. I love his arsenal of terrible clichés. I love the way he talks about the game as if he's mastered every nuance you can imagine, and if only the players would listen to him, they'd all be Hall of Famers. (Even though his own career was mostly mediocre, save the one season in which he led the American League in RBIs. Harrelson finished with a lifetime average of just .239.) I love the way he announces the games as if he's a Little League dad, and every single player on the roster is his own son. Whenever his announcing partner, Darrin Jackson, talks about the talent level of the Angels or the Yankees or the A's, Hawk butts in with something like "I'll tell you what, I like this ball club right here. I'll take our guys over anybody else in EITHER league. I'd go to war with these guys. I'd go to Mars with these guys. Besides, D. J., you're forgetting about the Ozzie factor. Ozzie's got the guys playing Ozzie Ball like nothing I've ever seen. I have never seen a manager so liked and so respected by his team, and I've been in this game in one capacity or another for nearly 150 years . . ."

According to the Hawk, Joe Crede is the best defensive third baseman in the game, and probably the best since Brooks Robinson. Bobby Jenks throws as hard as anyone since Sudden Sam McDowell. Jim Thome is the strongest guy he's seen since Frank Howard. (Nearly all of Hawk's

---

*A homer is a media person who is blindly loyal to the home team.

references are from his own playing days.) Paulie Konerko is the best "lead by example" guy since John F. Kennedy. Scott Podsednik is worth about 14 runs a game with his ability to distract a pitcher.

Ozzie? Smartest human being since Einstein. And the East Coast media probably overrated Einstein anyway.

Unlike, say, Vin Scully, who prided himself on objectivity and would never scream, "Get the ball!" if it got away from the catcher, Hawk makes no bones about his allegiance to the White Sox. The minute someone is traded or let go by the Sox, Hawk never talks about him again. (Have you heard him even mention Jerry Manuel's name in the last few years?) As soon as a new player joins the club, Hawk welcomes him with open arms and talks about how he always loved this guy. At the end of an inning, Harrelson will say, "Going into the 7th, it's the Tigers four, with the good guys coming to bat and we need two to tie." If Paulie gets rung up on a called strike three in a clutch situation with two outs, Hawk won't even describe the pitch. He'll just stew in silence before finally saying, "Home plate umpire Jim Sox-Hater continues to have a very wide strike zone, at least when we're batting, so we go into the bottom of the 8th with the good guys still trailing by two. Mercy!"

So there's the Hawk, and there's the rest of us—and the rest of us are stunned but not shocked by the events of the last six weeks. The Sox going a couple of games under .500 over a 45-game stretch? That's not a surprise. It's the 2005 Indians playing like the 1995 Indians—that's what's making the difference. They're the hottest team in baseball by far, and we want them to stop that, right now.

Monday night's game had all the ingredients of a classic Sox comeback. Freddy Garcia was down 4–0 to Cleveland ace Kevin Millwood after 4½ innings, but after Casey Blake botched an Aaron Rowand line drive to right in the bottom of the 5th, the near-capacity crowd got behind the Sox. The guys started stringing together hits, with Paulie Konerko knotting it up at four with a two-run double that had the ballpark shaking with excitement. (We don't need no stinkin' "Make Some Noise!" sign to tell us when to make noise.) When Carl Everett smacked a two-out solo homer in the bottom of the 7th to give the Sox a 5–4 lead, it seemed as if they had put the Indians back on the canvas. We'll win this one, the lead will be 4½, the Tribe faithful will be muttering about that Blake error in the 5th, and we'll go for the knockout punch over the next two nights. By the end of the week, the Sox will be up by six or seven games, and we'll go back to talking about whether we'd rather play the Angels, the A's, the Red Sox, or the Yankees in the first round of the playoffs.

Enter Damaso Marte, master of the ill-timed walk.

I'm not talking about the way he walks, though that's a bit funky as well. I'm talking about the way he *walks batters at the worst possible time.* Sox fans still shudder when we talk about the July 4, 2004, game against the Cubs at Wrigley Field. A Sunday night game on ESPN—so the whole country was able to tune in for our misery. It was 1–1 in the 9th and the bases were loaded with Cubbies when Ozzie Guillen brought in Marte to relieve Shingo Takatsu, who was a folk hero on the South Side for about 12 minutes. (Shingo's entrances were always accompanied by a gong sound effect, which would have seemed slightly racist if Shingo himself hadn't voiced his approval. Through a translator.)

As usual, Marte had great stuff—a quick fastball, a dipping curve—and he quickly went ahead 0–2 on Todd Walker.

As usual, Marte then proceeded to nibble at the corners and aim the ball. Walker worked the count full, and with the Cubbie yuppies going wild, Marte threw a 58-footer that would have been too low for Verne Troyer in a crouch.

Ball four. Cubs win. A walk-off walk, of all things.

Cubs 2, Sox 1. Happy Fourth of July.

Now, in a much bigger game some 14 months later, Marte walked the dangerous Travis Hafner and yielded a double to Victor Martinez before striking out Ben Broussard. Ozzie then brought in new fan favorite, Bobby Jenks, he of the doublewide body and the 100 mph fastball—but Jenks gave up a two-run single to Aaron Boone, or as Red Sox (and now White Sox) fans like to call him, Aaron *!@#ing Boone.

The Indians added an insurance run in the top of the 9th. In the bottom of the inning, the Sox had two on with two out and Konerko at the plate, and the crowd rose as one in anticipation of a season-highlight moment. As we used to say in the 1970s, "Oh, for the Long One." But

Paulie popped it up, bending over in disbelief and clutching his helmet a moment after the ball left his bat.

Cleveland 7, White Sox 5. The lead is now 2½ games.

Everybody is talking about the Sox. In a bad way.

In the *Sun-Times*, longtime Sox watcher Jay Mariotti feared the worst. The headline over Jay's column: NOW PLAYING IN CHICAGO: CHOKE-JOB THEATER.

Jay figures it's all over. He's got the Sox in a body bag. "A mood that started as concern has passed through a panic state and is headed toward a familiar feeling of doom and white-flag resignation. . . . Four months of euphoria have descended into a deathly hush, largely because a front office protected its payroll and chemistry instead of acquiring bats and a closer . . . it should be obvious by now that the Indians are a much better team and are worthier of the American League Central title."

Geez. Why bother to play the last two weeks of the season?

Even before Monday's game, Salon.com's terrific sports observer, King Kaufman, had reminded Sox fans that things were getting historically bad: "The Chicago White Sox are on the verge of an epic collapse, a historic pratfall, unless they get their act together in a hurry."

Magazines and newspapers were trotting out the dreaded list of the worst collapses in baseball history:

- The 1951 Brooklyn Dodgers, who led the Giants by 13 games on August 11 but fell into a tie, and then lost to the Giants in a one-game playoff on Bobby Thomson's "shot heard 'round the world."
- The 1964 Philadelphia Phillies, who had a 6½-game lead over the Cardinals with 12 to play, but lost 10 straight and finished a game out.
- The 1978 Boston Red Sox, who led the Yankees by 6½ on September 1, blew the whole lead, then won eight straight to finish the season tied with the Yanks—only to lose the playoff on Bucky Dent's pop fly/homer.
- The 1993 San Francisco Giants, who led the Braves by nine games on August 12, but finished one game out.

And, oh, yeah, the 1969 Cubbies, who had a nine-game lead over the Mets on August 16, but blew it down the stretch.

We never hear about that one in Chicago.

Things would get worse before they'd get better. The Sox would come back to take the second game against Cleveland, 7–6, but they lost the rubber match 8–0, and the next night they dropped an extra-inning heartbreaker to the Twins while the Indians pounded on the hapless Royals.

Heading into the next-to-last weekend of the season, the lead was down to 1½ games. By Saturday night, the Sox could be looking up at Cleveland in the standings. Within a week they could be out of the race.

Here's the thing about all those bitter disappointments that they still talk about in Philadelphia and San Francisco and Bah-ston: No team, ever, had blown a 15-game lead in the last two months of the season,

If the Sox blow this thing, it will be the biggest collapse in the history of baseball.

The Mick Goes Deep

July 29, 1966

It looked like a glorified pop-up leaving Mickey Mantle's bat. I'd never seen anyone hit a ball so high, but it didn't seem like it was going to go that *deep*. Ken Berry, a natural center fielder and one of the best of his time, was playing right field that night in order to make room in center for speedy rookie sensation Tommie Agee, touted by some observers as the closest thing to Willie Mays the Sox organization had ever seen. As the ball started wafting to right-center, I figured maybe Berry would catch it on the edge of the warning track.* He'd gracefully drift back and camp under the ball, like I'd seen him do on black-and-white TV.

---

*I'm not James Frey and this isn't *A Million Little Pieces,* so I'm not asking you to believe that I remember exactly what I was wearing, what I ate, and what I was feeling on a certain night more than 40 years ago, nor am I going to give you verbatim conversations from my childhood. What I do know beyond a doubt is that the first White Sox game I ever attended was on July 29, 1966. The accounts of this game, and of subsequent games and seasons you'll find in this book, are based on my recollections, conversations with friends and family members, and research materials that reinforced my memories and provided additional details. I knew that Mantle and Maris played in that long-ago game against the White Sox and that the Yankees prevailed in a pitchers' duel, but only after consulting the *Baseball Almanac* (Triumph Books, 2002) and other sources was I able to accurately report the attendance figures, the starting pitchers, and the exact sequence of scoring. Also, I'm leaving out the story about the time I personally met Batman and Robin in the summer of '66, because upon further review, I'm fairly certain I made that up.

Ken Berry would have no problem making the play. After all, he was good field, no hit.

That is to say, he was on the White Sox.

In the summer of 1966, I was seven years old. I had a crew cut, and I was quite a bit shorter than I am today, mostly due to my being a child. My brother was nine—and maybe he'd been to a big league game before, but this was my first, and it was a hell of an in-person introduction to the game: White Sox–Yankees on a Friday night, with 30,000-plus fans at ·Comiskey Park, a magical place that had previously existed only on the radio, in box scores, and in grainy images on the Motorola 19-inch TV in our basement. Neither team was going to win the pennant that year, but the Sox were a solid ball club, and the Yankees, while on a downslide, still featured some of the key names from their early championship teams from the early 1960s. The starting lineup for the Yanks that night included World Series–familiar names like Mantle, Maris, Elston Howard, and Bobby Richardson (I remember seeing him on a Wheaties box), along with young guys, such as Joe Pepitone and Tommy Tresh, who were sure to be perennial All-Stars for the Bronx Bombers in the very near future. (Or so the Yankees thought at the time. Turns out that Pepitone had a Hall of Fame personality and an All-Star haircut, and Tresh had a comic book name—but neither was all that good.)

You know that song "Summer in the City" by the Lovin' Spoonful? It still is played on commercials and on TV shows whenever some oldies-loving, imagination-impaired director wants to convey that it's, you know, warm in the city in the middle of the summer. "Hot town, summer in the city, back of my neck getting dirty and gritty, been down, isn't it a pity . . ." This was the summer of "Summer in the City." On Friday, July 29, 1966, it was the No. 1 song on the WLS "Silver Dollar Survey." Other big hits of the time included "Paperback Writer" by the Beatles, "Hanky Panky" by Tommy James & the Shondells, "Wild Thing" by the Troggs, and "Mother's Little Helper" by the Rolling Stones. These songs ENDURED, people. Even the schmaltzy hit of the summer was classic schmaltz: "Strangers in the Night" by the Chairman of the Board.

The top-rated TV shows of the time were *Bonanza*, *The Red Skelton Show*, and *The Andy Griffith Show*. My mom drank Fresca and Tab; my dad smoked L&Ms. Lyndon Johnson was president. We were sinking to our necks in the quagmire of the Vietnam War. Richard J. Daley was the mayor of Chicago. And racial tensions were simmering everywhere.

I grew up in a two-newspapers-a-day family. We took the *Chicago Daily News* and the *Chicago Sun-Times*, occasionally the *Chicago American*, never the *Tribune*. (We must have known something.) Walter Cronkite gave us the national news and Fahey Flynn delivered the local news every night. Johnny Carson peppered the late-night airwaves with jokes about hippies and Doc Severinsen's wardrobe. Not that I understood all that at the time. At the age of seven I didn't know about the double-entendre name of the Lovin' Spoonful, or what the Stones were singing about in "Mother's Little Helper." I didn't grasp the significance of Martin Luther King Jr. or those anti-war marches. I was a kid. Baseball, I knew. I loved to play catch with my dad or my brother, I loved to play "running bases" with the neighbor kids, and I loved to play in pick-up games. I couldn't wait to turn eight so I'd be eligible to play in the "minors" of the Dolton-Riverdale Little League, where I'd be able to wear a uniform. They kept score on a real scoreboard, and they started every game with a brand-new baseball that was so white it was almost a color unto itself. I knew I'd play for the A's. My brother played for the A's, and they always tried to put brothers on the same team so families didn't wear out the tires on the station wagon driving kids to different games on different nights.

Although I was born at Little Company of Mary Hospital in Oak Lawn, and I spent the very early stages of my life on the South Side, I grew up in the south suburb of Dolton, first in a ranch house at 152nd and Dorchester and then in a bungalow on 156th and Maryland. The latter was a dead-end street populated almost entirely by large Catholic families that had made the pilgrimage—some called it White Flight—from the South Side as soon as the neighborhoods started changing. "Changing." That's the code word everybody used to describe the complicated realities of black families moving in and white families moving out. What "changing neighborhood" meant was that a nearly all-white area was on its way to becoming 95 percent black, save for a few stalwarts who were too stubborn, too poor, or too eccentric to leave.

Nearly every single one of the squat brick bungalows on Maryland Avenue was populated by Catholic families that belonged to St. Jude the

Apostle parish, which was only a couple of blocks north but was officially situated in the neighboring suburb of South Holland. (First there was the heavily Dutch town of Holland, Michigan. Then came South Holland, Illinois, also heavily Dutch, and just about the least progressive town in the south suburbs. The sale of liquor was prohibited throughout the village, and businesses weren't allowed to open on Sunday. You half-expected to see Amish-looking families plodding down 159th Street in a horse-and-buggy.) The families in my neighborhood were Irish, Italian, German, Polish, Croatian. They had lived on streets such as Cottage Grove and Drexel and Ingleside and Ellis on the South Side—and now they were in different houses on the same streets, but instead of it being 71st and Cottage Grove, it was 154th and Cottage. Years later, they'd move farther south, to Tinley Park and Orland Park and Frankfort, or to the east and Indiana. You kept migrating until you wound up in Florida, or dead.

My dad worked for the Illinois Central Railroad. He caught the train at the Ivanhoe Station and rode downtown every day. In later years, my mother would work at the bookstore at Thornton Community College (now South Suburban College), but in the 1960s she had enough work to do at home, what with four children between the ages of six and 10. (Talk about a full-time job. I believe my mother turned on the washer and put in a load of clothes in 1965 and didn't turn it off until around 1982.) Not that a four-kid family was unusual at the time. In fact, we were about average for the block. There were 10 kids living in the house across the street, and a family down the street had 12 children. (That poor mom. Nothing like being pregnant for 108 months.) In St. Jude's annual yearbook, some of the family photos had to be shown with a wide-angle lens so the entire brood could fit into the frame. Ah, the rhythm method of birth control!

Our house was a redbrick bungalow with three bedrooms, one bathroom, a small living room, a smaller kitchen, and a "half-finished," wood-paneled basement that included a laundry room. (Picture the basement in *That 70s Show*, minus the dope and Mila Kunis.) We had a one-car garage to house the Dodge Polara, a fenced-in backyard, a driveway that consisted of two long strips of concrete separated by a narrow patch of grass, and a small front lawn with an Elm tree so mighty the roots always seemed to be on the verge of busting through the grass and the concrete.

The front "porch" was really just four concrete steps and a little landing that led to the door.

The going rate for one of these cozy bungalows at the time was $17,000. You hear that figure now and you chuckle, but look at it this way: Jack Lamabe was a pitcher for the White Sox, and his salary for the 1966 season was also 17 grand.

What were your entertainment options as a kid in the mid-1960s? Weekly trips to the Dolton Public Library to check out Hardy Boys books and Mel Martin sports novels. Basic television—the three networks plus WGN, and the fuzzy images on the UHF stations. (I hated *The Munsters,* loved *The Dick Van Dyke Show.*) Pop music on the 45-rpm portable player (the first single I ever bought was "Bend Me, Shape Me" by the American Breed) and on the AM radio, most notably WLS and WCFL. Street games, like monkey in the middle and kick the can.

And sports. You played sports, you watched sports, you listened to sports, you read about sports, you talked about sports. In 1966, the big four sports in the Chicago area were baseball, football, basketball, and hockey, in that order. We didn't really start getting into that new NBA franchise, the Bulls, until the 1970s, when they had guys like Norm Van Lier, Chet Walker, Bob Love, and Jerry Sloan, and they were tough enough to compete with (though never ultimately beat) the Knicks and the Lakers and the Bucks.

We played street hockey in regular shoes on the mashed-down snow/ice or even on the frozen Little Calumet River. We played ice hockey at venues such as the Dutch Masters rink in South Holland (until it burned to the ground one night). We followed the Blackhawks on the radio and TV—and we were thrilled when Bobby Hull made a personal appearance at the St. Jude's Sports Spectacular Banquet one year. Really, though, it was mostly about football from September through November, basketball from November through February, and baseball from the moment the ground started peeking through the snow in March until it got so cold in October that even the most casual lob would sting in your glove like a Joe Frazier jab.

I played football and basketball. Not all that well, mind you, but I played, and I kept playing through my teenage years. But I *lived and breathed* baseball. So it was with everybody in the neighborhood. Baseball was king in nearly every household.

Of course, there were two pro baseball teams in Chicago, but only one team in my house: The White Sox. Nobody in my family was a Cubs fan. Nobody. Not a single cousin or uncle or eccentric aunt who rooted for the Cardinals because she dated Stan Musial's brother-in-law in the '50s. None of that nonsense.

When there was a family picnic, the Sox game would be blaring on the tinny portable radio, which was situated on the table somewhere between the giant vat of potato salad, the Jays potato chips, and the hot dog buns. My uncles and great-uncles and older cousins would gather their lawn chairs in a semicircle and camp out near the radio, offering their own running commentary as they listened to the likes of Bob Elson and Red Rush and Milo Hamilton (yes, THAT Milo Hamilton) broadcasting the games on WCFL, WMAQ, and later on such obscure stations as WTAQ in LaGrange and WEAW in Evanston, the only stations that could be bothered to broadcast the Sox circa 1972. (Harry Caray had an audience of about 117 on the radio when he first came to town and teamed up with the immortal Ralph Faucher.) The beers my uncles sipped were Hamm's, Stroh's, Schlitz. You needed a church key to punch a couple of drinking holes in the top of the can, and there was a steel strip running down the side. It actually took a bit of strength to crush one of those beer cans. Three decades later, I'd occasionally stop in at a place called the House of Beer on Division Street. They had more than 100 brands of beer from around the world, but I'd always order a Schlitz or an Old Style or a Pabst, as a tribute to those family picnics.

This was the state of the White Sox franchise in the mid-1960s: they were good, but never quite good enough. They always had pitching and speed and defense, they knew how to execute the fundamentals—but their offense was anemic and their star power was nonexistent.

In 1963, probably the first year I had any conscious knowledge of the game of baseball and the fact that I'd been born with a virtual *Sox* logo tattooed on my forehead, the White Sox were a stellar 94–68. In the modern era, that'd be good enough for a division championship or a wild-card berth. In '63, it meant they finished 10½ games behind the Yankees. The Sox had a solid pitching staff, but their home run leader was Al Smith (the guy who was victimized by the falling cup of beer in 1959) with a grand total of 16. The entire team hit 92 dingers for the year.

When fans talk about the 1964 season, it's all about the National League, with the Philadelphia Phillies blowing that 6½ lead to the Cardinals in the final week of the season—but there was a hell of a pennant race in the American League as well, and the Sox were in the thick of it until (you know it's coming) the bitter end. The late, great Al Lopez was known for his gentlemanly demeanor, but as Richard Lindberg recounts in *The White Sox Encyclopedia** or as I like to call it, the New Testament), Lopez could also hold a grudge. In 1964 he feuded with a number of players, including Go-Go Sox favorite Jim Landis, who was benched by Lopez after demanding 50 bucks from General Manager Ed Short for a Sox-related TV appearance. Lindberg reports that Bill Gleason, the *Chicago American* columnist who found later local fame in Chicago on *The Sportswriters* show on radio and TV, held a "Jim Landis Night" at Comiskey Park on June 10, 1964, at which Lopez was hung in effigy in the parking lot and Landis was given a trophy. (Can you imagine a sports columnist for one of the Chicago papers holding a "Juan Uribe Night" or whatever in 2006, complete with a hanging of Ozzie in effigy? How fast would the columnist get canned?) Lopez reacted by having no reaction. Minnie Minoso was in the starting lineup that night, and Landis remained on the bench.

Controversies aside, the Sox raced off to a 31–14 mark and were in the race from wire to wire, running neck-and-neck with the Yankees and the Baltimore Orioles. The Yankees won the first 11 head-to-head matchups against the Sox, but on August 20, the ChiSox knocked out Whitey Ford in the 3rd inning and completed a four-game home sweep that left the Sox at 75–47 and the Yanks at 69–50. (The Orioles were sandwiched in between at 74–47). I was just a little dude, too young to play "Don't Break the Ice" without breaking the ice, but my designated team for life had a very real shot at getting into the World Series for the second time in five years.

Sporting lore has it that when the Yankees boarded the team bus after that Sunday afternoon loss to the Sox, a utility infielder named Phil Linz took out his harmonica and played "Mary Had a Little Lamb." Manager Yogi Berra tried to throttle Linz, and somehow that incident is given

---

*Temple University Press, 1997

credit for waking up the Yankees and sending them on their way to a sustained pennant drive. By September 25, the Sox had fallen four games back. As most of the nation's baseball fans focused on the Phillies and the Cardinals, the Sox made a heroic sprint for the finish, winning their last nine games—but the damn Yankees won 13 of their last 14.

The final standings:

Team	W	L	Pct.	GB
New York	99	63	.611	—
White Sox	98	64	.605	1
Baltimore	97	65	.599	2

In 1965 the Sox jumped out to another fast start, going 23–8 in the first month and a half of the season, and the Yankees fell into their worst funk in years. Unfortunately for Sox fans, who thought this might be our year, the Minnesota Twins were loaded with stars such as Harmon Killebrew, Tony Oliva, and Mudcat Grant. Their shortstop, Zoilo Versalles, had a career year and became perhaps the least famous guy to ever win the Most Valuable Player Award. The Sox finished in second place at 95–67, a full seven games behind the Twins.

Once again, the Sox were good. Just not good enough.

By late July of 1966, the Sox didn't even have dreams of winning the AL pennant. Their new manager was Eddie Stanky, whose nickname was "the Brat." (Now you know where the hip-hopper known as Da Brat got the name. Or maybe not.) Stanky had a personality that made Billy Martin seem like Mister Rogers. He was forever battling with his players, the opposition, the umpires, fans, and the media (including Brent Musburger, then a columnist for the *Chicago American* and later a national fixture on TV). Nobody disputed Stanky's knowledge of the game, but everybody questioned his ability as a leader. Jerkiness will take you only so far. As usual, the Sox had some good arms in the starting lineup and plenty of speed and defense, but their offense sucked in a way that 21st-century fans can't imagine. The team average was a paltry .231. First baseman Tommy McCraw hit .229, and second baseman Al Weis hit .155 with zero homers and nine RBIs in nearly 200 at-bats. Weis was pla- tooned with Jerry Adair, who hit .243 with four homers. (Nice produc- tion out of that second base slot.) The team had a grand total of 87 homers, with only rookie Tommie Agee (22) and John Romano (15) in double figures.

Imagine pitching for a team like that. You think Roger Clemens didn't get any offensive support from the Astros in the 2005 regular season? Take a look at what the White Sox starters had to work with. Tommy John, still pitching with his own left arm, had an earned run average of 2.62 and he tossed five complete game shutouts—yet he finished just 14–11. Joel Horlen had an ERA of 2.43, and he was under .500 at 10–12. Gary Peters led the league with a sparkling 1.98 ERA, a half-run a game better than Horlen's second-best league mark—and Peters was only 12–10.

If you were a starting pitcher on the 1966 White Sox and you gave up three runs, you were in serious jeopardy of losing the damn game.

The Sox averaged only about 12,000 fans per game in '66, so I'm sure it wasn't that hard for my father to get tickets, even for a Friday night game in July against a Yankees team that still had plenty of marquee value despite the fading record. No doubt we gave ourselves plenty of time to make the 20-minute drive from Dolton to 35th and Shields, and I'm sure we were well in place long before the game started.

Comiskey was so much bigger and so much greener and so much LOUDER than I could have possibly imagined. When the stadium was built in 1910, the publicists crowned it the Baseball Palace of the World, but the unofficial nickname for the park was *The World's Largest Out- door Tavern*. To this day, I can see the giant cloud of cigarette smoke that hovered above the park on muggy summer nights, and I can hear the roars and shouts that would break out in some distant corner of the stands when the inevitable brawl would start up, usually late in the game when the Sox were behind. The game would come to a halt as the play- ers patiently waited for the off-duty Chicago cops to break up the fight and haul away the offenders.

Here's one of the beauteous wonders of the Internet: the *Baseball Almanac* is available online (www.baseball-almanac.com), and with a key- stroke here and a keystroke there, you can find the box scores for virtually every major league baseball game since 1960. You say you were born on May 17, 1965? Well, the Sox defeated the Kansas City Athletics that day, 13–2. Floyd Robinson, Pete Ward, and Ken Berry hit home runs, and Gary Peters went the distance to improve his record to 4–2. (Imagine right now that someone who was actually born on May 17, 1965 is reading this book. "Holy *!@#! What is this thing, interactive? Honey, Roeper's White Sox book knows my birthday!!!") Perusing the box score of the first game I ever saw in person, a number of names leapt out:

- There's the Mick, of course. Mickey Mantle. He was only 34 at the time, but as we later learned, 34 in Mickey Mantle years was like 44 in regular baseball player-years. When Mantle joined the Yankees at 19, he possessed arguably the most impressive array of physical tools in the history of the game. He was one of the strongest AND one of the fastest athletes the scouts had ever seen. If not for the booze, the broads, and the injuries, Mantle might have hit 800 homers. In '66, though, Mantle was only three years away from retirement. He struggled so much at the plate in his final four seasons that his career average dipped below .300.

  Mantle was the biggest name in the game at the time, even bigger than Willie Mays, who was perhaps the only player who had more natural talent. Only after Mantle's retirement, with the publication of Jim Bouton's *Ball Four* (Macmillan, 1970; Bulldog, 2001), did the public first hear about Mickey's lecherous, boozing ways. Decades later, the great Mickey Mantle would wind up in a hospital, hoping for a new liver and lamenting what he'd done to his body and to his life.

- Also in the lineup for the Yankees was Roger Maris (played by Barry Pepper in Billy Crystal's excellent docudrama *61** on HBO), who never came close to matching his stunning season of 1961, when he set the record that would last until the late 1990s, when Mark McGwire and Sammy Sosa downed all those milkshakes and gobbled all those Flintstones vitamins that made them so strong and mighty. (Ahem.) Maris must have loved playing the Sox, given that in his record-setting season, Sox pitchers yielded a whopping 13 of his 61 homers. One of the great offshoots of the 1998 home run race was that Maris got his due for his '61 season. A shame he wasn't around to experience all that appreciation, but at least his family was there, front and center, on the night when McGwire broke the mark. Say what you will about McGwire and his refusal to even talk about whether he ever took steroids; he was nothing but class when dealing with the Maris family. Nineteen sixty-six was Maris's last season as a Yankee. He would hit just .233 with only 13 home runs.

- The first baseman for the White Sox that night was "Moose" Skowron, who as of this writing remains a fixture at Sox games and often appears at team functions as one of the team's goodwill ambassadors, along with Billy Pierce and Minnie Minoso. (God bless the Sox and many other major league teams for embracing their alumni with unprecedented enthusiasm in recent years.) When Skowron's name was called, the crowd would bellow "Moooooooose"—and of course the radio guys would remind us, "They're not booing, they're saying 'Moooooooose.'" Skowron would be in his 10th season in the majors, and the play-by-play guy would still be telling us, "They're not booing, they're saying 'Moooooooose.'" All right, we GET IT. To this day, radio and TV analysts provide us with similar reminders whenever some player named "Lou" or "Duke" steps up to the plate. Moose played in eight World Series with the Yankees, collecting five championship rings and pounding out eight homers and knocking in 29 runs, and he was with the Sox for only two full seasons and parts of two others—but he's a Chicago guy through and through. He was a star fullback at Weber High School a half-century ago, and he's got a bar named Call Me Moose in Cicero, across the street from the Hawthorne Race Track. There are all kinds of Moose memorabilia on the wall, and if the Sox aren't playing on a particular evening, they'll pop in an old highlight tape of one of Moose's World Series appearances.

You gotta love the Moose. When my dad introduced himself to Skowron at a White Sox event in 2005 and mentioned that he had attended Mount Carmel High School on the South Side, the 75-year-old Skowron said, "We kicked the *!@# out of you guys," as if the homecoming game had been three months ago and not in the 1940s.

- The starting pitcher for the Yankees was Al Downing, a solid left-hander who had a 20-win season and made an All-Star team, but will forever be known as the guy who (as a Los Angeles Dodger) yielded Hank Aaron's 715th home run in front of a crowd of some 55,000-plus in Atlanta—a crowd that did not include Commissioner Bowie Kuhn, who attended a dinner in Cleveland that night and sent Monte Irvin as baseball's official representative. I guess Kuhn was holding back and waiting for a truly important record to be in jeopardy before he could be bothered to show up. Some pitchers who have given up record-breaking homers have shunned the attendant publicity, but Downing always seemed fine with it. He and Aaron have even signed some memorabilia together. A baseball inked by Downing and Aaron fetches about $350 on the open market.

- Sox pitcher Joel Horlen was a pinch runner in the game. You don't see pitchers doing a lot of pinch running any more. When they're not pitching, they're wearing jackets, adhering to some 80-year-old superstition about the arm tightening up on the sidelines, even if it's 97 degrees.

- And I love this: The shortstop for the White Sox that night was none other than Lee Elia. Elia's entire major league playing career consisted of 80 games with the White Sox in 1966 and 15 games with the Cubs in 1968—but he will forever have a plaque in the Sound Bite Hall of Fame for his meltdown in 1983, when he was the manager of the Cubbies and he blew his stack in a postgame press conference. At the time, the Cubs were still playing day games only, and they'd just suffered another one-run loss to fall to 5–14 on the season. Here's what Elia had to say about fans who seemed to show up for the sole purpose of heckling his players. (WARNING: The following passage is rated NC-17.)

> I'll tell you one fucking thing, I hope we get fucking hotter than shit, just to stuff it up them 3,000 fucking people that show up every fuckin' day. Because if they're the real Chicago fuckin' fans, they can kiss my fuckin' ass right downtown, and print it! They're really, really

behind you here. My fucking ass. What the fuck am I supposed to do, go out there and let my fuckin' players get destroyed every day and be quiet about it? For the fuckin' nickel-dime people who turn up? The motherfuckers don't even work. That's why they're out at the fuckin' game. They oughta go out and get a fuckin' job and find out what it's like to go out and earn a fuckin' living. Eighty-five percent of the fuckin' world is working. The other fifteen percent come out here. A fuckin' playground for the cocksuckers. Rip them motherfuckers! Rip them fuckin' cocksuckers like the fuckin' players. We got guys bustin' their fuckin' ass, and them fuckin' people boo. And that's the Cubs? My fuckin' ass. They talk about the great fuckin' support the players get around here. I haven't seen it this fuckin' year.

Everybody associated with this organization have been winners their whole fuckin' life. Everybody. And the credit is not given in that respect . . . It'll take more than a 5 and 13 or 5 and 14 to destroy the makeup of this club. I guarantee you that. There's some fuckin' pros out there that wanna play this game. But you're stuck in a fuckin' stigma of the fuckin' Dodgers and the Phillies and the Cardinals and all that cheap shit. All these motherfucking editorials . . . it's sickening. It's unbelievable. It really is. It's a disheartening fuckin' situation that we're in right now. Five and fourteen doesn't negate all that work. We got 143 fuckin' games left. What I'm tryin' to say is don't rip them fuckin' guys out there. Rip me. If you wanna rip somebody, rip my fuckin' ass. But don't rip them fuckin' guys 'cause they're givin' every-thing they can give. But once we hit that fucking groove, it will flow . . .

Unfortunately for Elia, the media not only took him up on his ultimatum and printed it (with expletives deleted, of course), the electronic media played it, and played it, and played it.

And played it.

Leading the charge was the wildly popular radio duo of Steve Dahl and Garry Meier, who made a shortened version of the Elia rant a permanent entry in their on-air jukebox. I have to admit, I laughed my head off every time I heard it back in the day—but now, I think, Poor Lee Elia. A quarter-century later, this career baseball man is still most closely identified not with anything he did as player, not with any strategy he came up with as a coach or a manager for the Cubs or the Phillies or the Blue Jays or the Yankees or the Devil Rays or the Orioles, but with a five-minute tantrum at a lonely press conference in the spring of 1983.

Listening to an audio file of the rant, it's not as funny as I remember. There's something slightly sad, and even a little noble, about Elia pouring his heart out, Marine-style, in an effort to protect his players. Amid all those expletives and non sequiturs, Elia seemed sincerely wounded by those heartless Cubs fans. In his own way, he was trying to protect his players.

If you look at the Wikipedia, the people's online encyclopedia, as a kind of first draft of your life history—a living obituary—for Lee Elia, there's as much written about his tirade as there is about the rest of his life. In the summer of 1966, however, he was a 28-year-old infielder who was finally getting his chance to play in the big leagues some eight years after signing his first pro contract. I wish I could tell you that Elia and second baseman Jerry Adair worked some double play magic that night against the Yankees, or that Elia hit one of his three career home runs to propel the Sox to a come-from-behind victory, but the box score tells me he took an 0-for-4 collar and was a nonfactor in the game.

Mickey Mantle was another story.

♩   ♩   ♩

It looked like a glorified pop-up leaving Mickey Mantle's bat. I'd never seen anyone hit a ball so high, but it didn't seem like it was going to go that deep . . .

We were sitting far down the first base line, closer to the warning track than the infield. It was the top of the 4th inning. A journeyman named Bruce Howard was on the mound for the White Sox (the kids on Maryland Avenue had nicknamed him "Snicker and Sneer" in honor of the strange facial pose he struck for one of his Topps baseball cards), and there was no score when the mighty Mickey uppercut the ball and sent it on an impossibly high arc out to right-center.

That ball just kept carrying and carrying and carrying—until it landed in the seats.

Home run, Mantle. Home run, Yankees. Sox down, 1–0.

It was Mantle's 14th home run in 24 games—perhaps the last great hot streak of his career. It also was career blast number 494 for Mantle, and that number was a lot more impressive in 1966 than it is today. The sky-high homer put the Mick one ahead of the great Lou Gehrig and into sole ownership of sixth place on the all-time home run list. Mantle would retire with 536 home runs, behind only Willie Mays and Babe Ruth at the time. Even today he stands in 14th place—and a couple of players ahead of him don't deserve to be mentioned in the same breath. (Hello, Rafael Palmeiro.)

Even though the Sox outhit the Yankees 10–6 in that game, they wound up on the short end of a 2–1 score.

I was 0–1 lifetime as a fan. Some 40 years and 1,000 ball games later, I still can't guarantee you that I'm over the .500 mark.

To hear it from Cubs fans, they've always been the oppressed party rooting for the perpetual underdog, but let's take a look at what it meant to be a kid and a White Sox fan in the 1960s.

It's not as if I inherited a storied franchise. The White Sox record book circa 1966 was just sad. They had one MVP (Nellie Fox) and one Cy Young Award winner (Early Wynn), both coming in the pennant-winning year of 1959. There were quite a few Rookie of the Year winners, including Minnie Minoso and Luis Aparicio, but most of the Sox top rookie honorees (e.g., Pete Ward and Tommie Agee) never became bona fide stars.

In 1965 the Sox had the 17th pick in the draft. Still on the board: Johnny Bench, Nolan Ryan, Craig Nettles, and Sal Bando. Chicago selected Ken Plesha, and we all know how that worked out. Wonder what happened to those other guys?

The last Sox player to win a batting title was Luke Appling in 1943. A home run champ? Are you kidding me? The all-time single season home run record for the Sox was 29, held jointly by the nearly immortal Gus Zernial and the even-closer-to-immortal Eddie Robinson. After more than six decades of White Sox baseball, not a single Sox player had ever cracked the 30-homers mark. Not once! The CAREER home run leader in a Sox uniform was Minnie Minoso with 135, followed by Sherman Lollar with 124. If you managed to hit 50 or 60 home runs in your career with the Sox, it was good enough to get you on the leader board.

Throughout the 1960s, exactly two White Sox players had 100-plus RBI seasons: Minnie Minoso with 105 RBIs in 1960, and Floyd Robinson with 109 in 1962. The leading home run hitter for the decade was Pete Ward with 97. Ninety-seven. Who did he think he was, Home Run Baker?

Granted, the Sox had some great pitching and solid defense in the 1960s—but when you're seven, eight, nine years old and you're just learning the game, and there are guys named Mantle and Mays and Killebrew and Aaron and Banks and Robinson smacking the ball all over the place for other teams, you're not all that thrilled about your team mastering the art of the 2–1 victory.

Not to mention the heartbreak of the 2–1 defeat. At a family gathering in the summer of 2005, my father talked of a Joel Horlen masterpiece in 1963 that went terribly wrong in the 9th inning. When I looked into the details of the game, it was remarkable to see how closely my dad's memories jibed with the actual events.

On July 29, 1963—exactly three years to the day before my first major league game—the Sox were in Washington to take on the Senators, who eventually left the nation's capital and became the Rangers. For years there was no baseball in Washington, but now they've got the Nationals, who used to be the Expos, who were formed in 1969 and named after Expo '67, which was a kind of funky world's fair type of deal. In front of a "crowd" of fewer than 5,000, Horlen breezed through a less-than-ferocious Washington lineup that included Don "The Blazer" Blasingame, Lawrence Sidney "Bobo" Osborne, Don "Popeye" Zimmer (yes, *that* Don Zimmer), Charles "Chuck" Hinton, and Jim "I Never Got a Nickname" King. In the meantime, the powerful Sox bats staked Horlen to a lead of, well, 1–0. When King led off the 9th with a groundout to Nellie Fox, Horlen was just two outs away from a no-hitter.

The next batter was Chuck Hinton, the very definition of a perfectly decent ballplayer. Just good enough to be a semiregular player, but never good enough to make an All-Star team. (Eleven seasons in the bigs, a .264 career average, 113 homers, 443 RBIs.) Hinton hit a clean single up the middle that skipped past Horlen, and the no-hitter was gone.

One out, one on, Sox up 1–0.

Next, Horlen retired Bobo Osborne.

Two outs, one on, Sox up 1–0.

Up to the plate stepped one Don Lock, the pride of the Municipal University of Wichita. Although Lock finished with a career average of just .238, he actually had a couple of pretty good power years with the Senators, hitting 27 homers in '63 and 28 homers in '64.

You know what happened next. Horlen served up a cookie, and Lock blasted a two-run home run.

Joel Horlen had been two outs from a no-hitter, and one out from a complete-game one-hitter. With one pitch, he lost the shutout and the game.

Senators 2, White Sox 1.

Four years later, the Sox were in the midst of one of the most heated pennant races in the history of baseball. Those annoying Boston Red Sox fans remember it as the season of the "Impossible Dream" (I guess they were big fans of *Man of La Mancha*), though I don't how you can go with the whole dream-underdog-miracle theme when you've got a Triple-Crown MVP in Carl Yastrzemski and a Cy Young Award winner in Jim Lonborg. *Oooh, your team had the most talent. You were such a crazy dreamer to think your team had a shot at the pennant. Why, it was nearly impossible.* The Twins and Tigers had strong teams and stayed near the top throughout the year—as did the White Sox, who held first place from early June until mid-August, and stayed in contention until the end.

The bitter end.

This is the White Sox team I remember best from my early days as a fan. They had some of the coolest uniforms in Sox history. The home uni's were white with navy pinstripes, with *SOX* in script on the left chest, and the player's number on the right chest. The road uniforms were a nifty shade of powder blue (the better to be seen on color TV), the road hats an even sharper shade of blue. *Chicago* was spelled in script across the chest of those road uniforms, with *White Sox* etched into the underline. The logo was not unlike the one used by the band named Chicago for their *Chicago Transit Authority* debut album of 1969, and the 1,345 self-titled *Chicago* albums that followed in the years, decades, and centuries to follow.

For the World Series games in 2005, I wore my navy wool replica 1967 jacket, with that *Chicago* logo on the front. The jacket had been 4–0 in the regular season, and it remains undefeated on the strength of the Sox wins in Game 1 and Game 2. I plan to wear that jacket on my wedding day, which might explain why I've never been married.

In the summer of 1967, WCFL and WLS were constantly playing a song by some hippie named Scott MacKenzie, singing, "If you're going to San Francisco, be sure to wear some flowers in your hair." Movies like *Bonnie and Clyde* and *The Dirty Dozen* were playing at the downtown theaters and the suburban drive-ins. I wouldn't turn eight until October, so I was still a year away from organized-ball eligibility, but I spent a lot of time watching my brother and my friends play at the Dolton-Riverdale Little League fields, and I spent even more time thumbing through my collection of baseball cards (some of them slightly tinted by the powder from the wad of bubblegum that came with each pack) and playing "against the steps."

What, you never played against the steps? Often it was the only game in town for a kid who was too young to play in Little League or even in the pickup games on the street or at the park down the block. All you needed to play against the steps was a glove, a rubber ball from the Ben Franklin store, and some steps. Our front porch had four steps, and a sidewalk leading to the curb and the street. You stood halfway between the steps and the curb, and you wound up and fired away, trying to hit the corner of one of the steps so you'd get a nice line drive or fly ball. Most times, though, you'd hit the vertical, flat part of the steps, which means you'd get a weak grounder, or a horizontal section of the steps, resulting in a "foul ball" that would bounce away from you. Whenever that happened, you just hoped the ball wouldn't smash through a pane of glass in the door or bounce off the railing and get lost in the bushes.

I played entire games against the steps, pretending I was Joel Horlen mowing down the Red Sox or even facing the Cardinals in the World Series. (Talk about your impossible dream). After I got three outs, I'd become Lonborg or Bob Gibson or Luis Tiant, emulating their deliveries as I faced the White Sox lineup, with guys like Wayne Causey, Ron Hansen, and J. C. Martin at the plate.

Even against the steps, the Sox rarely scored.

On June 12th, two nights after the Sox claimed sole possession of first place, they lost to the Senators 6–5 in a 22-inning marathon that took six hours and 38 minutes. It was the longest night game in American League history. Leave it to the Sox to manage only five runs in 22 innings.

Talk about Hitless Wonders. Even for a pitching-rich era, the Sox were unbelievably terrible at the plate. The team batting average in '67 was .225. Take a look at some of the stats for the BEST hitters on the team:

Player	AB	HR	RBI	Avg.
Tommy McCraw	453	11	45	.236
Don Buford	535	4	32	.241
Pete Ward	467	18	62	.233
Tommie Agee	529	14	52	.234

Buford's .241 average tied Ken Berry for the team lead among regulars. Think about that: You're at a game and your team is trying to rally, and you're thinking, "If only we could get enough guys on base to give Don Buford another turn at the plate—he's hitting .241!" I've had to look up a lot of numbers while working on this book, but one of the stats I was absolutely certain about before looking it up was Don Buford's .241 average in 1967. For the last two decades, I've been telling incredulous younger fans that the Sox were once so anemic with the bats that nobody on the team hit as high as .242. They never believe me, but there you have it.

These guys were spectacularly, historically bad on offense. If you couldn't crack a lineup filled with .225 hitters, you really couldn't complain about the manager playing favorites. On the bench, the Sox had such weapons as Jerry Adair, who hit .204, Jimmy "Don't You Know Me, Mary!" Stewart at .167, Jim King, who hit .120, Dick Kenworthy, with an average of .111, and Bill Voss at .091.

Sneaky little Eddie Stanky, always looking for an edge, reportedly froze baseballs in the clubhouse refrigerator before home games. If his men couldn't hit the ball out of the infield anyway, might as well make it tougher on the likes of Yaz and Boog Powell, right?

In true South Side fashion, Stanky felt the media didn't give the Sox enough credit—even though he happened to agree with the consensus that the punchless Sox were hardly the most electrifying team in the league. This led to his infamous declaration: "We're last in homers, we're last in hitting and we're last in war and peace, but we're first in guts and determination."

The Sox did have the pitching. A team ERA of 2.45 and some 24 team shutouts, with Gary Peters, Joel Horlen, and Tommy John leading the way. Jim Lonborg won the Cy Young Award that year, but Joel Horlen might have been the best pitcher in baseball. He was lights-out all year long, going 19–6 with a 2.06 ERA and six shutouts.

On Sunday, September 10, 1967, in the heat of a four-team pennant race, Horlen took the mound for the first game of a doubleheader against the Detroit Tigers, who had a formidable lineup that included future Hall of Famers Al Kaline and Eddie Mathews, along with Norm Cash (who hit .361 for the Tigers and won the batting title in 1961, two years after the White Sox had given up on him), Willie Horton (the terrific hitter, not the convict used in the infamous political ad), and Bill Freehan. The White Sox shocked the Tigers, the crowd of 23,625, and themselves by scoring five runs in the 1st inning, with the big blow a triple by Wayne Causey.

Giving Joel Horlen a five-run lead in 1967 was like walking up to Muhammad Ali and saying, "Hit me just once, on the chin. I can take it." You were done. It was over. As WGN-TV's Jack Brickhouse got increasingly excited, Horlen set down the Tigers in rapid fashion with just a hit batsman here and a walk there. Horlen took the no-hitter into the 9th with a 6–0 lead. Tigers second baseman Dick McAuliffe was the Last Tiger Standing, and he hit a slow roller to shortstop Don Hansen, who gunned down McAuliffe with a step to spare. It was the 20th groundout of the game for the crafty Horlen, and it gave him a no-hitter some four years after the heartbreak of Washington in '63.

In Game 2 of the doubleheader, Cisco "Was a Friend of Mine" Carlos, Hoyt Wilhelm, and Bob Locker teamed up to blank the Tigers 4–0. A few days later, on September 13, Gary Peters walked 10 Cleveland Indians but gave up only one hit in 11 innings, leaving with the score knotted at zero. (How 'bout those White Sox bats!) Rocky Colavito finally managed to knock in a run in the 17th for a 1–0 win.

On Thursday, September 14, while I was in my second grade class at St. Jude the Apostle and just about every other White Sox fan was either at work or in school, the Sox hosted the Indians in front of 4,314. Unbelievably, ridiculously, astonishingly, they played *another* game that went into extra innings with neither side scoring. Cisco Carlos, only recently called up from the minors, followed his scoreless stint from the Sunday doubleheader with a 10-inning masterpiece in which he gave up just five hits and walked nobody. Somehow, the Sox managed to load the bases with two outs in the bottom of the 10th, bringing Don Buford to the plate. Buford hit a walk-off grand slam, accounting for one-fourth of his season home run total and one-eighth of his season RBI total with that one swing.

Sox 4, Indians 0. As Dan Helpingstine noted in his book, *Chicago White Sox: 1959 and Beyond* (Arcadia, 2004): "In the space of five days, the Sox pitching staff threw an equivalent of five shutouts allowing only 14 hits in 45 innings. They were back in the pennant race."

Indeed they were. The Sox went to Minnesota and swept a three-game series from the Twins. The standings as of September 15, 1967:

Team	W	L	GB
Minnesota	84	64	—
Detroit	85	65	—
White Sox	85	66	½
Boston	84	66	1

With 11 games to go and the best pitching in the league, the White Sox had a legitimate shot to win the AL pennant. As the four teams jockeyed for position heading into the final week of the season, Yaz caught fire and put the Red Sox on his back, but the "other" Sox still had a chance, what with having their final five games against the lowly Kansas City A's and the hapless Washington Senators.

On September 27, 1967, the Sox faced Kansas City in a "twi-night" doubleheader. These days there's a twi-nighter about once every three years, usually because the teams involved have to make up a rainout, but back in the day the twi-night doubleheader was a fairly common thing. You started one game in the late afternoon, and by the time the second game was over, it was pitch-black and everybody was either drunk or asleep or on the way home. (Not the players—the fans. The players usually stuck around for both games. Unless you were Dick Allen.) The A's were 60–95 and in last place after having lost 11 of their last 12 games. With a crowd of about 5,000 scattered about Municipal Stadium (which held only about 30,000 for baseball games) the A's sent their "ace," Chuck Dobson (9–10), to the mound against Gary Peters—and though Peters struck out 10 and allowed only one earned run in 5⅔ innings, he departed with a 3–0 deficit and the Sox lost 5–2, managing just four hits in the game.

Now they really needed Game 2.

Fortunately, the Sox had Joel Horlen (19–6) ready to go against Jim "Catfish" Hunter (12–16), who became a Cy Young–level pitcher for the A's after they moved from Kansas City, but at the time was a fairly green youngster who hadn't been in many high-pressure games. Surely, Horlen's curveball would have the A's pounding grounder after grounder into the dirt, and the Sox would scratch out three or four runs against this kid Hunter.

Or maybe not. A's 4, White Sox 0.

Hunter threw a complete-game, three-hit masterpiece, facing only 30 batters. Horlen was doing fine until the 5th, when he and Wilbur Wood surrendered four runs to the A's—far too large a deficit for Buford, Agee, Ward, and Co. to overcome.

The disheartened Sox returned home to face Washington and were shut out on Friday and Saturday. They managed to score three runs on the final Sunday of the season, but they lost 4–3, not that it mattered anymore. By that last weekend, it was down to a three-team race: the Red Sox, the Twins, and the Tigers. Boston won on the final day of the season, while the White Sox and their fans were left to lament what might have been if only they'd been able to sweep those damn A's on what became known as Black Wednesday. Had the Sox won that twi-nighter, they would have been right in the thick of things, and who knows how they would have fared against the Senators?

"I detest doubleheaders," said Eddie Stanky.

Me, too, Eddie.

The final standings:

Team	W	L	Pct.	GB
Boston	92	70	.568	—
Minnesota	91	71	.562	1
Detroit	91	71	.562	1
White Sox	89	73	.549	3

In 1968, I finally got to put on that Little League uniform. I played shortstop and I took number 11 in honor of Luis Aparicio. Now that I was actually playing in games with an umpire and a scoreboard and bleachers for parents, I was an even bigger fan of the Sox. My team. My dad's team. My family's team. My friends' team.

Alas, the Sox sucked in '68. My most vibrant memory of the 1968 baseball season has nothing to do with the Sox. What I remember best is my fourth-grade teacher, the sports-loving Sister Morrison, wheeling in a black-and-white TV from the A/V room and telling the class we were going to take a break that afternoon and watch the Cardinals and the Tigers in the World Series. As images of Denny McClain, Mickey Lolich, Bob Gibson, Al Kaline, and Lou Brock flickered across the screen during those afternoon games, the idea that the White Sox would someday be playing in the fall classic probably never occurred to me. That seemed about as realistic as my watching movies for a living.

The 1968 season was a disaster for the Sox. They lost their first 10 games, and for all intents and purposes they were dead. The increasingly paranoid Stanky banned the media from the clubhouse, fined his players for minor indiscretions, and fell out of favor with owner John Allyn, who was not so quietly exploring the possibility of moving the Sox to Milwaukee. (The Sox even played 10 "home" games in Milwaukee that year, as Allyn tested the suds, er, waters.) Stanky resigned in July and was replaced by former Sox manager Al Lopez, but not even a wise old wizard could do anything with a ball club that had a team batting average of .228, a team total of 71 homers (fewer than Barry Bonds swatted in his record season), and not a single "slugger" with more than 15 home runs or 50 RBIs. Granted, this was the year when Yaz was the only player in the American League to top .300 and the pitchers dominated so thoroughly that the mound was lowered for the following season, but still—the Sox lineup was filled with guys whose final season statistics wouldn't even have looked that impressive at the All-Star break. Things were so bleak that pitcher Gary Peters batted as high as sixth in the lineup. Poor Joel Horlen had an ERA of 2.37, but he finished just 12–14.

♪   ♪   ♪

If there's ever a time when you understand a fan's switching allegiances, it's when that fan is not yet 10 years old and he's already beginning to get jaded about the failures of the franchise he inherited.

In the summer of 1969, I was nine years old. I was the pitcher/short-stop/clean-up hitter on my Little League team. I got picked first or second in the street-ball games on Maryland Avenue. I was gobbling up issues of *Sports Illustrated, Sport, Baseball Digest,* and the *Sporting News.* I was a walking, talking baseball nut. There were other things going on that summer—like man walking on the moon, college kids marching in the streets to protest the war in Vietnam, and that music festival in the mud—but I was only vaguely aware of these events. What really bothered me in the summer of '69 (and yes, dammit, I can hear that Bryan Adams song in my head right now, too) was that the Sox were once again atrocious, while the Cubbies were in the midst of a seemingly magical season.

We had this one kid on our block who was a Cubs fan. Marco. I think he was a Cubs fan mainly because his parents were Italian immigrants (their German Shepherd obeyed only the Italian commands of Marco's father), and his mother was in love with Ron Santo. Whenever we were outside playing and Santo would hit a home run, you'd hear Jack Brickhouse's "Hey! Hey!" call through the screen door, and Marco's mom would come running out to the porch, yelling, "Marco, Marco, Ronnie Santo hit another a homa-runna-ah!" Really. Homa-runna-ah. I stereotype you not.

There wasn't much cause for dancing on the South Side. The Sox weren't just terrible, they were embarrassingly bad—so bad that Al Lopez resigned as manager just a month into the season, citing stomach pains that were no doubt exacerbated by a rapidly fading pitching corps and a lineup that was improving but still had a long way to go. Lopez was replaced by the legendary Don Gutteridge, one of those utility fielder–turned-coach guys who hangs around the big leagues for his entire life, bothering no one. All of a sudden, at 57, Gutteridge was given a club to run, and he didn't know what the hell to do with it.

Tickets to a Sox Game: Not That Pricey

A look at the price of admission to a White Sox game for selected years, from the time I was six until the 21st century. Note that in some years, there were also bleacher seats, which typically went for about half the price of a grandstand ticket. And in recent years, the Sox, like most major league clubs, have charged more for "premium" games against teams like the Cubs, Yankees, and Red Sox.

Year	Box Seats	Reserved	Grandstand	Bleachers
1966	$3	$2	$1.50	
1972	$4	$3	$1.75	$1
1977	$4.50	$3.50	$2	
1983	$7	$5	$3	
1990*	$9.50	$7.50	$5	

Year	Club Level	Box Seats	Reserved	Bleachers
1991†	$16	$13	$9	$6
1997	$22	$17	$15	$14
2006‡	$46	$32	$28	$27

---

*Last season at Old Comiskey

†First season at New Comiskey

‡The Scout tickets were sold out for the 2006 season, but the cost is $170 per seat, per game.

In the meantime, owner John Allyn and general manager Ed Short had lot of ideas—all of them awful. Management finally acknowledged that the Sox had to find some way to inject some offense into their game, so they came up with a couple of brilliant ideas:

- Genius Idea #1: Astro-Turf
- Genius Idea #2: Bring the Fences In

The problem with Genius Idea #1 was that the Astro-Turf was installed only in the infield. I remember going to a game that year and seeing the pale-green, phony grass infield, and the darker-green, real grass outfield. Had they run out of money halfway through installation?

If that wasn't unsightly enough, the Sox didn't actually move the outfield walls in—they just put up a flimsy looking cyclone fence and slapped on some metal signs with the new dimensions down the line, in the alleys, and in center field. Comiskey Park looked like some kind of temporary softball field that had been installed for a traveling All-Star exhibition series.

The Sox averaged just over 7,000 per game, roughly the same number that attended Sox games at South Side Park in 1904. This was not a franchise on the go—unless you're talking about their going somewhere else. A Milwaukee car dealer named Bud Selig made a serious bid to buy the Sox and bring them to County Stadium, but at the last moment Arthur Allyn sold his controlling share of the Sox to his brother John, which is a little like one Wachowski brother handing the camera to the other brother midway through *The Matrix*, if *The Matrix* really sucked and featured Astro-Turf and cyclone fences.

But that's not how I saw things. I saw a team that finally seemed to be getting some bats with pep in the lineup: guys like Walt "No Neck" Williams, who seriously didn't have a neck; Buddy Bradford, who seemed to have all the tools; and a couple of rookies named Bill Melton and Carlos May. Melton was a strapping Californian who looked like he could be starring as Frankie Avalon's rival for Annette Funicello in one of those "Beach Blanket" movies. Melton walloped 23 homers and knocked in 87 runs in his first full season. The last time someone had hit that many home runs for the Sox, the Beatles were just taking America by storm. (By this time they were growing mustaches and smokin' dope, and no longer playing live together.) Melton was Pete Ward without the dorkiness.

Carlos May had an even bigger upside. The younger brother of Lee May, Carlos wore his hat perched atop his big head as if he were imitating a bobble-head doll. Born May 17, 1948, he was perhaps the only player in baseball history to have his birthday on his jersey:

MAY

17

The 21-year-old May was a powerful, sweet-swinging outfielder, and he tore up the American League in the first half of the season. Carlos made the All-Star team (his brother Lee was on the National League team), and American League manager Ted Williams spoke in glowing terms about the youngster's potential. At the 100-game mark of May's rookie season, he had 18 HRs, 62 RBIs, and a .281 average.

Then he blew off his own thumb. On August 11, 1969, May was a gunner on mortar detail with the Marine Reserve in Camp Pendleton, California. He was cleaning a shell when a mortar misfired, taking off most of the thumb from his right hand. (Weirdly enough, the piece of thumb was retrieved by a marine named Bob Watson, the major league player who replaced Carlos's brother as first baseman of the Astros in the 1970s, scored the one millionth run in baseball history, and is now a top executive for major league baseball.) May endured a series of painful skin grafts and returned to the Sox in 1970, but he was never going to be a 30-homer, 100-RBI guy. A couple of years later, a buddy of mine used to sing a tribute to Carlos whenever we were in the outfield bleachers. Sung to the title track from *Jesus Christ Superstar*, it went something like this: "Every time I look at you I don't understand, how you hit the ball without a thumb on that hand!"

Hey. We were kids.

Even though the Sox finished 68–94 in 1969, some 29 games out of first, and even though the Cubs were having a seemingly magical season, and even though we had the hybrid field and the dopey double-fence, and even though the owner seemed to think Chicago was an on-deck circle for Milwaukee, it never occurred to my nine-year-old self to jump ship. I couldn't stop being a Sox fan any more than I could stop being Irish/German or hazel-eyed or right-handed.

I was in this for life.

Don't Start Believin'

March 31, 2005

The 2004 Chicago White Sox couldn't have been more different from the 1967 squad. With the Sox and the '60s, it was all about pitching and defense and trying to scrape together enough runs to get by. Often they'd hit fewer than 100 homers in a season. The '04 Sox hit 242 home runs—more than the 1927 Yankees, the 1961 Yankees, the 1975 Cincinnati Reds, the 1998 Chicago Cubs, or the 2000 St. Louis Cardinals. Their lineup was loaded with free-swinging power hitters, such as Jose Valentin, Magglio Ordonez, Carlos Lee, Paul Konerko, and, of course, Frank Thomas, who played about a half-season before succumbing to injuries. They were often scoring six, seven, 10 runs a game. Comparing different eras is like comparing apples to really old apples, but if Joel Horlen had enjoyed anything approaching the kind of run production supplied by the 2004 Sox, he might have gone about 24–2 in 1967 instead of "just" 19–7.

Unfortunately, the starting pitching, bullpen, defense, and team chemistry were mediocre to average in 2004, leaving the Sox with an 83–79 record, a full nine games behind the Minnesota Twins in the American League Central. That's what the Sox of the early 21st century had in common with the Sox of the 1960s: They were always finding a way to give fans hope before falling out of the running.

In the winter of 2004–05, Sox management figured it was enough with the Big Sticks and they completely retooled the team. They let Magglio Ordonez and his knee injury hobble off to the Tigers. They said good-bye to Valentin, who had the handsome visage of a rogue sidekick in an Antonio Banderas movie and a propensity for hitting home runs that didn't matter—and don't even get me started about the way he played shortstop like a Gold Glover. (I mean that literally; it was as if the glove was made of gold and the ball would just bounce right out.) They traded Lee to the Milwaukee Brewers for middle reliever Luis "Don't Call Me José" Vizcaino and outfielder Scott "I'm with Lisa Dergen and You're Not" Podsednik.

That last deal seemed like a boneheaded move. Carlos Lee, nicknamed "El Caballo," was just 27, and he was a ferocious hitter who had already put up some impressive numbers. There was talk about Lee being a brooding presence in the clubhouse and occasionally dogging it on the field, but in the last year his outfield play had improved greatly—he was always sliding into the dirt in foul territory as he dove for everything within reach—and he seemed to be on the verge of having a monster year. Who the hell were Luis Vizcaino and Scott Podsednik? Sure, Podsednik had led the National League in stolen bases his rookie year, but he'd had a terrible sophomore season. And though sPod was entering only his third year in the majors, he was actually a few months older than Lee. Obviously, the guy's game had some serious flaws if he was allowed to languish so long in the minors, right?

(Apparently, Lee's fate had been sealed when he failed to slide hard on a double play ball in a 2004 game against the archrival Twins, just one day after Minnesota's Torii Hunter nearly took Jamie Burke's head off in a collision at home plate. At Sox Fest 2005, Guillen told fans, "We had a guy go into second base as if his wife was turning the double play." Ozzie never mentioned Lee by name, but he did say the player in question was no longer with the team. When it comes to holding grudges, Ozzie is the Eddie Stanky of our time.)

Other off-season acquisitions seemed to be the moves of a team with an identity crisis. Having signed Freddy Garcia and Jose Contreras halfway through the 2004 season, the Sox added Orlando Hernandez to the pitching staff—and we would have been excited about that if not for the fact that El Duque was about 117 years old. (The Smoking Gun Web site busted Hernandez, who claimed to be 36 in 2005, by posting divorce papers proving he was born in 1966 and was in fact 40. Of course, everyone from Danny Almonte to Keira Knightley has shaved a few years off the old birthday. I have my doubts about Dakota Fanning. I think she's really a 43-year-old midget.) They signed the oft-injured Jermaine Dye to replace Maggs in right—and even with Maggs's health in question, that didn't seem to be an upgrade. When healthy, Dye was a solid 30-homer, 90-RBI guy, whereas a healthy Maggs could give you 40 homers and 125 RBIs.

The Sox picked up a reliever named Dusty Hermanson and acquired a Japanese second baseman named Tadahito Iguchi, who was supposed to be pretty good. (The Sox hadn't met him in person. They'd only seen him via videotapes, like an Internet bride.)

Nothing against any of these guys, but I guarantee you that during the 2004 season, there wasn't one fan sitting in the stands at the Cell saying, "If only we could get El Duque, Dusty Hermanson, and Tadahito Iguchi, THEN we'd have a ball club!"

And then there was A.J.

For as long as I've been a White Sox fan, management has always had a kind of Oakland Raiders philosophy about acquiring players through trades and free agent signings. From Dick Allen to George Bell to David Wells to Jose Canseco to Carl Everett, they've never shied away from signing free spirits, rebels, freaks, and geeks. I mean, look at their manager. He's great, but he's *nuts.* You think any other team would have put Ozzie in charge?

So it shouldn't have come as a surprise that the Sox would sign catcher A.J. Pierzynski, even though A.J. was regarded as one of the biggest jerkos in the game. After wearing out his welcome in Minnesota, in 2004 Pierzynski moved on to the San Francisco Giants, where he really had trouble making friends. Just one month into the regular season, A.J. had somehow managed to supplant Barry Bonds as the least popular figure in the Giants' clubhouse.

From MSNBC.com, May 1, 2004: "Pierzynski . . . is not only struggling at the plate, he reportedly has developed a poor relationship with his teammates. . . . 'He's the cancer in here,' one Giant, who requested anonymity, told the *Oakland Tribune.* 'The pitchers aren't happy with him. If they can trade him, that would be fine with me. We all know Yorvie [Yorvit Torrealba] can catch this staff.'"

Two of A.J.'s teammates told the *Oakland Tribune* that prior to a game against the Atlanta Braves, pitcher Brett Tomko approached

Pierzynski in the clubhouse and asked him to go over the Atlanta lineup. Pierzynski supposedly ignored Tomko and kept playing cards for 20 minutes. (A.J. claimed he had merely finished one more hand before joining Tomko.)

"'I've never in all my years seen a catcher who didn't watch video before games,' a Giants pitcher told the *Tribune*. 'He doesn't watch hitters—other than the Twins games when they're on TV.'"

Another story had A.J. criticizing Giants teammates to the Padres' Phil Nevin while Nevin was at the plate.

Then there was this cringe-inducing tale from the *San Francisco Chronicle*, published after the Sox had signed Pierzynski.

"One of those now-it-can-be-told stories the White Sox . . . surely haven't heard: During a Giants exhibition game [in the spring of 2004], Pierzynski took a shot to his, shall we say, private parts. Trainer Stan Conte rushed to the scene, placed his hands on Pierzynski's shoulders in a reassuring way, and asked how it felt. 'Like this,' said Pierzynski, viciously delivering a knee to Conte's groin. It was a real test of professionalism for the enraged Conte, who vowed to ignore Pierzynski for the rest of the season until Conte realized how that would look. The incident went unreported because all of the beat writers happened to be doing in-game interviews in the clubhouse, but a half-dozen eyewitnesses who could hardly believe their eyes corroborated it. Said one source, as reliable as they come: 'There is absolutely no doubt it happened.'"

This is the guy the Sox signed to be their everyday catcher—though they did so only after Hawk Harrelson, who has known A.J. since A.J. was a teenager, had extensive conversations with the controversial catcher. (Somehow I don't see Vin Scully getting that involved with the Dodgers' personnel moves.) No doubt Pierzynski was made to understand that you get three strikes in baseball, and as far as his career was concerned, he was standing at the plate with an 0–2 count.

It's not as if fans thought the 2005 White Sox were going to be dreadful. We had young, popular, good-guy players such as Mark Buehrle, who was always good for 16 or 17 wins, Paulie Konerko, who could be maddeningly streaky but was coming off a 41-homer, 117-RBI season, and blue-collar guys like Aaron Rowand and Joe Crede, who would always give you the proverbial 110 percent. We didn't know how the new guys would mesh with the core lineup, but we figured the Sox had enough talent and experience to go at least .500, probably a little better than that.

But nobody was picking the Sox to be a serious World Series contender in 2005. *Nobody.*

In Las Vegas, oddsmakers had the White Sox at about 30–1 to win the World Series. (That's the figure my brother got on a wager he made at Caesars Palace in the spring of '05.) They were ranked far behind the defending champion Red Sox, not to mention the Yankees, the Cardinals, and a host of other teams—including, of course, the Cubs. The Cubs are always extremely popular with bettors in Vegas, which is one of the many reasons why the casinos never lose money.

As usual, the Cubs were Chicago's glamour team heading into the 2005 season. With a starting rotation of Kerry Wood, Mark Prior, Greg Maddux, and Carlos Zambrano, they had four guys capable of winning 18–22 games each if they stayed healthy. (Ahem.) Their starting lineup didn't look any more intimidating than the Sox', but there was enough pop in there to give Cubs fans legitimate hope that their beloved team would hang in there with Houston, Philadelphia, and St. Louis in what was admittedly a stronger division than the AL Central.

Nationwide, though, everybody was focusing on the American League East. In a display of shocking originality, *Sports Illustrated*'s 2005 "Baseball Preview" issue featured Johnny Damon of the Red Sox and Derek Jeter of the Yankees on the cover, because the national media just don't devote enough coverage to that Yankees–Red Sox rivalry.

From the cover:

SHOWDOWN '05:
SI's PREDICTIONS BY DIVISION: YANKEES TOPPLE RED SOX * BRAVES SINK
MARLINS * TWINS HOLD OFF INDIANS * CARDS CLIP CUBS * ANGELS
OUTLAST RANGERS * GIANTS PUT DOWN DODGERS

They found room to mention 12 teams on that cover. Note the absence of the Sox—or, for that matter, the Houston Astros.

Reflecting the consensus of the sports media and of Sox fans, *SI* had Chicago finishing third in the American League Central.

Unless an Iffy Rotation Produces, Small Ball Translates to a Fall in the Standings was the headline.

"The White Sox have one of the most intriguing rotations in baseball . . . because they have five guys capable of winning 15 games each but also because those five guys could just as easily falter," wrote *SI*'s expert.

Sports Illustrated ranked the Sox as the 17th best team in the major leagues. (The Cubs were ninth.)

It was more of the same elsewhere. On MLB.com, the headline on April 1 was Twins Remain Central Team to Beat.

At ESPN.com, 19 analysts listed their predictions for the 2005 season. Sixteen out of 19 had the Twins winning the AL Central. One writer had the Indians, one picked the Tigers—and Rob Neyer was the lone expert who called the Sox' number. None of the other 18 had the Sox getting so much as a wild card berth.

Locally, only Dave Van Dyck of the *Chicago Tribune* and Mike Kiley of the *Chicago Sun-Times* had the Sox winning the division. Nearly a dozen other sportswriters and columnists went with the Twins or the Indians.

Not that I was clearing my October 2005 schedule so I'd have time to watch all those postseason games at the Cell. From 1990 to 2005, there were at least three or four seasons in which I predicted the Sox would win the division and do some serious damage in the playoffs—and there were about a dozen years in which I put my money where my heart was by placing wagers on the Sox to win it all. Every year when I was in Vegas around March or April, I'd check out the odds on the Sox on the big boards at Stardust or Bellagio or Mandalay Bay, and I'd plunk down $500 or $1,000 on my boys to win it all. I'd always get odds like 25–1, 50–1, or 75–1. I'd keep the receipt tucked away for six months—and then, once the Sox were eliminated, I'd tear it up and start thinking about next year.

In April 2005, I put a very small amount on the Sox to win it all. Probably the smallest amount I'd ever placed on them. I play single hands of blackjack for more money. What an idiot.

Truth is, I had no faith that the Sox would do better than about 84–78. What was the point of betting $500 or a grand or more on a dream that had no chance of coming true?

♪   ♪   ♪

That doesn't mean I hesitated when it came time to renew my season tickets in January of 2005. After years as a partial-season ticket holder, I'd made the leap to the 81-game package in the late 1990s. (My buddy Phil was my partner in the deal.)

Oh, that brick of tickets. There's a scene in *Fever Pitch* in which Jimmy Fallon and his pals celebrate Ticket Arrival Day as if they were 10-year-olds and it was Christmas, which is basically how it works with season ticket holders for any team, any sport, any city. (Except Los Angeles. I really don't picture Jack Nicholson racing up and down his driveway with his fresh batch of Lakers' season tickets, clicking his heels, and bellowing, "They're here! They're here!" Wait a minute. Actually, I do picture that.) Each winter, my Sox season tickets arrive in a rectangular box. I always thought it would be cool if the box were shaped like home plate or a base, but that might ratchet up the dork factor to unacceptable levels. The tickets are attached to one another like sheets of money fresh from the mint; you have to carefully separate them at the perforations and match them to the all-important parking pass, which guarantees you a spot no matter what the attendance. (Unlike Wrigley Field, the Cell has major-league–level parking with guys in jackets waving you to the proper lot and charging you a reasonable amount. In Wrigleyville, the Cubs have official parking for about six cars, and after that you have to take your chances with the independent operators. True story: My brother-in-law, a great guy despite the fact that he's a Cubs fan, pulled into a lot near Wrigley Field a couple of years ago. The sign said: *Parking, $20.* When my brother-in-law tried to give the attendant 20 bucks, the guy told him it was $50. "But the sign says $20," said my brother-in-law. The attendant looked at the sign, shrugged and said, "You think you can park *here* for $20? Are you crazy? It's fifty bucks, take it or leave it." Ah, the warmth and camaraderie of Cubbieville. It really is just like Bedford Falls.)

My first season tickets were pretty far down the left field line—about halfway between third base and the outfield wall and a good 25 rows back. Each year at renewal time, I'd ask my sales rep if I could move closer—and each year, somebody with better seats would choose not to buy in for the next season, giving me the opportunity to get closer in leaps and bounds. I went from the left field line to the right field line to about 20 rows behind first base to some beautiful seats directly behind home plate, some 14 rows back. Players' wives, scouts, and visiting celebrities were often seated in my section or just behind me. Jerry Springer, a semiregular presence at the Cell (insert your own joke here about Springeresque fans running onto the field), was about 10 rows behind me.

Heading into the 2005 season, the Sox continued their efforts to spiff up the park, which had been rechristened U.S. Cellular Field in January of 2003 in a 23-year deal that will pay the Sox $68 million over 20 years, which sounds like a lot of money until you do the math and realize it's the equivalent of the yearly salary of a number two starting pitcher on most clubs. They were now in Phase V of a renovation project that had started in 2001—a project that included additional bars and restaurants, upgrades in the video boards and the main scoreboard, the Fan Deck in center field, the Party Deck, and three new rows of seats between the dugouts and foul poles. (Buyer beware: If you're going to a ticket broker for primo seats down the line and he tells you he's got some tix in Row 2, just remember that row 2 is really row 5, because the three new rows are labeled AA, BB, and CC.)

Maybe the best improvement of all: they ripped out the top eight rows of seats from the upper deck, though to this day no one in the White Sox organization will ever admit that those seats *sucked.*

For 2005 the Sox added the FUNdamentals section for kids, and they started ripping out the ugly blue seats and replacing them with more traditional-looking green seats. The most dramatic change was the construction of the Scout Seats directly behind home plate. They looked like the seats you'd see in Hef's private screening room. Each Scout Seat was a padded, oversized, freestanding luxury chair with ample legroom and a beautiful view of the field. The Scout Seat section was to feature premium reserved parking, a private entrance, a self-service island with popcorn, water, soda, ice cream, etc., waitpersons bringing you beer and food, and all sorts of other amenities designed to make you feel as if you were a 10-percent owner of the club.

The construction of the Scout Seats meant that my behind-the-plate tickets no longer existed. I was given the opportunity to move just to the right of the Scout Seats, to a pair of seats that were even a little bit closer to the action—or I could purchase two Scout Seats in the very first row, for a little less than $28,000, which is about the same as I paid for my half-share of the first condo I ever owned.

Now what I'm about to say is probably going to make some White Sox fans very angry, but it's the truth. If I had a been a Cubs fan and I had been in the exact same situation, I probably would have taken a deep breath, pulled the trigger, and bought the damn Scout Seats, even though there's no universe in which you can justify spending that kind of money on baseball tickets. If you had tickets like that for the Cubs, you'd never, ever have any trouble unloading them for the games you wouldn't be attending. In fact, you'd probably make back your investment and then some by selling your tickets for about half the games for double or triple the face value.

I couldn't realistically say that about the Sox. I knew better.

One of the things I learned over the years about being a White Sox season ticket holder: You *will* end up eating some of your tickets every year. (At least that's how it's played out every year until 2006.) If you have season tickets for the Cubs and you can't make it to a particular game, all you have to do is say "Who needs two for the Cubbies game tomorrow?" and you'll hear from friends you never knew you had. If I did that in the *Sun-Times* newsroom, I'd be tackled.

With the Sox—not so much. There were many times, when I would offer two prime location tickets plus a parking pass—not for sale, but for free—and I'd have trouble finding takers. You'd get the feeling that people thought they were doing *you* a favor by taking the tickets off your hands. I'd give someone two tix and the parking pass for a Saturday evening game, which means they'd also get to see the fireworks show. The next time I'd see that person, I'd ask how the game was. About half the time the recipient would shrug and sheepishly admit that he didn't go to the game for some reason or another.

If you're reading this book, you're probably a diehard Sox fan, and I know what you're thinking right now: "Hey, Roeper. Hey *jerko*. You could have given your tickets to *me*. I would have gone to those games."

Maybe so—but for one thing, I don't actually know you. And it's easy for you to say now that you would have gone to those games, but in August 1995 or September 1997 or July 2002 or September 2004, trust me, there were a lot of tickets with no takers.

I couldn't pull the trigger on the Scout Seats, not for a .500 team, not when I knew I wouldn't even be able to give away tickets to some of the games. Instead, I renewed my regular, full-season ticket plan.

And even that seemed like wishful thinking.

Eight Men Out

May 6, 1955

White Sox 1, Tigers 0.

In the spring and summer of 1955, less than a year before my parents were married and four years before I was born, my dad took my mom to a Sox game at Comiskey Park.

And many more games, as a matter of fact.

They had a date at Comiskey on Friday, May 6, and they saw Virgil Trucks outduel Ned Garver in that 1–0 Sox win. (Trucks lives forever in baseball history for having one of the strangest seasons of all-time. In 1952, when he was with the Tigers, Trucks went 5–19, but two of those wins were no-hitters. In another game that season he gave up a leadoff single, induced the next batter to hit into a double play, and wound up retiring 26 hitters in a row for a near-perfect game.)

My parents also attended games on June 1 (White Sox 4, Red Sox 3) and July 3 (Indians 1, White Sox 0). There were other games as well, but I know about those three for sure because I have the original programs at hand, complete with my mom's handwriting on the cover, detailing the date and the final score.

So there it is. Proof that my parents had a life before I was born and that the White Sox existed as well. I was pretty sure of both already, but now I know beyond a shadow of a doubt.

The "Official Score Book" was 10 cents. On the cover it says *Chicago White Sox* in blue-and-red script against a backdrop that's white with blue pinstripes. The year *1955* is etched into a drawing of a baseball.

There's also a cartoon of a little boy wearing an oversized blue Sox hat that covers his eyes. If somebody were to design a deliberately retro-looking piece of art to capture the look of a baseball program of the mid-1950s, it should look just like this.

Fifty-one years ago. Eisenhower was president; Marlon Brando was a movie star; rock 'n' roll was in its infancy. Franchises such as the Angels, the Twins, the Astros, and the Mets had yet to be hatched. My parents have lived in a dozen houses in three states since then, with hundreds of souvenirs and keepsakes eventually finding their way to the trash bin. The basement in the house in Dolton was nearly destroyed by flooding, and everything that had been stored away down there was hopelessly lost.

Yet these programs, as well as a program from a 1954 game, and a yearbook from the 1959 season, and a program from the last game at Old Comiskey Park in 1990, not to mention virtually every edition of *Who's Who in Baseball* from the last 50 years, have survived. They've been boxed up a dozen times, moved from house to house, tucked away in cardboard boxes and later in plastic containers.

Here they are now as I contemplate the history of the Chicago White Sox, dating back to 1901.

♫   ♫   ♫

For in-depth, stats-filled, exhaustive studies of the history of the White Sox franchise, you can check out a dozen other books with that express purpose. (The ultimate resource is Richard C. Lindberg's *White Sox Encyclopedia*.) Here, I simply want to touch on a few highlights, clear up some misconceptions, toss you some peanut bags filled with fun facts, and remind you of some of the reasons why the Chicago White Sox are as star-crossed, cursed, whatever you want to call it, as the far more celebrated Boston Red Sox and Chicago Cubs.

Think about it. There's no other team in the history of organized sports that literally gave away one world championship (1919) and lost the chance at another world championship because of a labor stoppage that was in large part orchestrated by the team's very owner, for crying out loud. And you want to talk to me about billy goats and black cats and Bartman?

In 1901 the very first Chicago White Sox batter in the history of the franchise was one Dummy Hoy. His real name was William Ellsworth Hoy, but everybody called him Dummy because he was deaf and dumb. If that offends you, don't blame me. Get in a time-travel machine, go back there, and tell those people they were insensitive.

Hoy was five-foot-six and about 160 pounds. He was 39 years old at the time and at the end of his career. In his first at-bat for the White Sox he grounded out, but he wound up having a pretty solid year.

The 1901 White Sox were a force in the brand-new American League. They averaged six runs a game, even though this was the Dead Ball Era and nobody on the team had more than five home runs. Playing at the 39th Street Grounds, the Sox outdrew their counterparts on the North Side and they won the American League pennant. The National League refused to have a playoff to determine an overall champion, so you can safely say the Sox were champs, or at least cochamps, in '01.

Other highlights of those early years include the World Series victories of 1906 (against the Cubs) and 1917—the last World Series the Sox would win until 2005. The Sox probably had the best team in baseball in 1919 and they won the pennant, but they somehow lost the World Series, five games to three. (It was a best-of-nine format back in the day.) I don't know, but from what I've read, the Sox might have won that Series if only a few of their key players had tried a little harder. David Straitharn, for one. John Cusack as well. And even though D. B. Sweeney hit .375 for the Sox and had five assists in the outfield, there was something about his play that seemed a little off. It was almost as if he was distracted by something.

I'm not trying to gloss over the disaster of the 1919 Black Sox. It's just that there have been books, movies, and articles devoted to the scandal, and that's not what *this* book is about. There are people working tirelessly to clear the names of Shoeless Joe Jackson and Buck Weaver. God bless 'em. What we do know is that eight White Sox players were accused of conspiring to throw the World Series. They were acquitted of criminal charges, but were banned for life by the commissioner of baseball.

White Sox Ticket Prices and Starting Times in 1955

Box Seats: Adults, $2.50; Children under 12, $1.85
Reserved Grandstand: Adults, $1.75; Children under 12, $1.10
All afternoon games: 1:30 P.M.
Twilight doubleheaders: 6:00 P.M.
Night games: 8:00 P.M.

Jackson confessed to accepting money, but claimed he tried to give it back, twice. To the moment of his death, he maintained that he did nothing but play his hardest. (As for that kid who called out, "Say it ain't so, Joe!," the story is almost certainly pure bull*!@#.)

Weaver knew about the fix but didn't participate. However, he was banned for life because he didn't tell anyone what he knew. Tough call here, and you feel for Weaver's descendants and his supporters—but we're not talking about a player who looked the other way while a teammate corked a bat or ingested an illegal drug. At the very least, Weaver should have been suspended for a full season for keeping quiet while his teammates sullied the integrity of the game and the name of the Chicago White Sox.

Was there ever a "Curse of the Black Sox"? Of course not. Not any more than there was a Curse of the Bambino. But at least with the 1919 Black Sox, we had the ultimate bad-karma story. The whole Bambino thing was so stupid. Why would the Babe curse the Red Sox? Getting sold to the Yankees was the best thing that possibly could have happened to him. Ruth was able to feed his legend (and his belly) on the biggest stage available, and the Yankees won World Series after World Series as he became the most celebrated figure in the entire country. You think he cared about the Red Sox? If anything, those narcissistic Red Sox fans should have been talking about the Curse of Frazee all this time, as it was Boston owner Harry Frazee who sold Ruth to the Yankees. (Popular lore has it that Frazee needed money to finance his girlfriend's Broadway play,

No, No, Nanette. In truth, Frazee had a long track record in the theater, and *No, No, Nanette* was produced a half-decade after the sale of Ruth to the Yankees.) It is true that the Red Sox won five World Series in their first two decades, including three with Ruth, and then went zip for more than eight decades before finally winning in 2004.

You know what that means? It means Red Sox fans went nearly as long as White Sox fans without a World Series title.

Nearly.

In the 1920s, the Sox were just supporting players in the story of Ruth and the Yankees. The ChiSox were very good at finishing fifth, and if not fifth, seventh. In 1924 they finished eighth in an eight-team league. A managerial revolving door of Evers to Walsh to Collins to Evers followed.

The 1930s were even worse. In the years from 1930 to 1935, the Sox were 62–92, 56–97, 49–102, 67–83, and 53–99, respectively. Probably their best year was 1937, when they went 86–68—and they still finished 16 games out.

Luke Appling was the best player on the Sox in their first half-decade—and he was the maybe best hitter in Sox history this side of Joe Jackson all the way up until the 1990s, when Frank Thomas came along. Appling won two batting titles in a Sox uniform, and he was voted into the Hall of Fame in 1964. He was a southern gentleman, a class act, and one of the greatest shortstops the game has ever produced.

But geez, compared to a Lou Gehrig or a Jimmie Foxx or a Mel Ott, Appling wasn't exactly one of the marquee stars of the era. When I was a kid, you know what I always used to hear about Appling? That he had an uncanny knack for fouling off pitch after pitch after pitch until he found one to his liking. Urban legend has it that in at least one game, they ran out of baseballs and had to ask the fans to throw a few back.

So the Yankees had Babe Ruth supposedly calling a home run against the Cubs in the 1932 World Series, and Lou Gehrig playing in 2,130 consecutive games and telling us he's the "luckiest man on the face of the earth," and Joe DiMaggio marrying Marilyn Monroe, and Mickey Mantle dueling Roger Maris for the single-season home run crown—and the

Sox' biggest star of their first 90 years was a guy who was best known for his ability to hit *foul balls*.

How about Appling's nickname? The Yankees had the Iron Horse and the Yankee Clipper; the Red Sox had the Splendid Splinter. These were majestic names, worthy of great talents.

Luke Appling, respected for his tenacity and his ability to play through a variety of injuries, was known as Ol' Aches and Pains.

That sounds like a moniker you'd apply to a three-legged golden retriever in a Civil War movie.

♫　　　♫　　　♫

America was at war in the early 1940s, and rosters were depleted as the likes of Ted Williams went off to fight for their country. Also-rans such as the Detroit Tigers and the St. Louis Browns managed to win pennants in between triumphs by the Yankees. The White Sox? Not so much. They were moseying along in mediocrity, finishing third and sixth and fourth and seventh and sixth again. After the war, the Sox remained remarkably consistent in their irrelevance, finishing in fifth and sixth and eighth and sixth—again. Who can forget the Jack Onslow era? The answer: everybody. (For the record, "Honest Jack" Onslow managed the Sox in 1949 and for the first two months of the 1950 season. His biggest claim to notoriety was his benching of the aging Appling, even though Ol' Aches and Pains was still hitting around .300 and was closing in on Rabbit Maranville's record of 2,153 games played at shortstop. There's another nickname for you. "Rabbit." Even "Rabbit" is better than "Ol' Aches and Pains.")

Finally, the South Side came to life in the 1950s, with the Go-Go Sox electrifying crowds and racking up one first division finish after another—though they were still usually in double figures in games behind the pennant winner come the end of September.

In 1959, the Sox edged Cleveland and clinched their first American League pennant in 40 years. Chicago's air-raid sirens delivered the news, and about half the population celebrated while the other half, having no idea that the Sox had clinched, ran for their basements while babbling "Duck and cover, duck and cover, duck and cover!"

From 1951 to 1967, the Sox had a winning record every single season. That's the third-best such run in Major League Baseball history, behind only the 1968–1985 Orioles and the 1926–1964 Yankees. (What, you thought it was going to be the Senators?) Take a look at Chicago's record during that run:

Season	W	L	GB
1951	81	73	17
1952	81	73	14
1953	89	65	11½
1954	94	60	17
1955	91	63	5
1956	85	69	12
1957	90	64	8
1958	82	72	10
1959	94	60	—
1960	87	67	8
1961	86	76	23
1962	85	77	11
1963	94	68	10½
1964	98	64	1
1965	95	67	7
1966	83	79	15
1967	89	73	3

Yet, during that stretch, the Sox won the pennant just the one time. How frustrating it must have been for the organization, the fans, and the players for the Sox to be good but not great. Not nearly good enough most of the time, as the Sox finished fewer than eight games out only five times in those 17 years. Look at the 1954 team, led by Minnie Minoso, who tore up the league with a .320 average, 19 homers, 116 RBIs, 119 runs scored, 19 stolen bases, and a whopping 18 triples. That Sox squad also featured Phil Caveretta, the longtime Cubs favorite, who had been released by the Cubbies that spring. Cavaretta hit .316 for the Sox in a part-time role.

Cubs fans must have hated that—seeing their 20-year star in a Sox uniform and demonstrating he still had some juice left in his swing. (According to Lindberg's *White Sox Encyclopedia*, the Sox certainly rubbed it in by holding a "Phil Cavaretta Night" that year, as if Cavaretta had spent his entire career on the South Side.) White Sox hurler Virgil "No-Hit" Trucks won 19 games and had an ERA of 2.79. Chico Carrasquel gobbled up everything that came near him at short. Nellie Fox hit a solid .319 and tied for the league lead in hits with 201. Ferris Fain hit .302, and Jungle Jim Rivera had some big games in the field and at the plate.

The Sox finished 94–60—a record that would almost guarantee a postseason berth in the multitiered playoff system of today. In 1954, however, it wasn't even good enough for second place. The Yankees went 103–51 and *they* didn't make the postseason, because the Indians were an otherworldly 111–43. With 94 wins, the Sox finished 17 games out. (All anyone remembers about that 1954 season any more is Willie Mays's over-the-shoulder catch of Vic Wertz's prodigious drive in the World Series. It was about the 37th most spectacular play in Mays' career, but because it happened in the World Series and there's some nice film of the moment, the catch has become The Catch.)

Five years later, a 94–60 record would be good enough for the Sox to win the American League. Unfortunately for Minnie Minoso, he was in Cleveland at the time. Prior to the 1958 season, the Sox traded Minoso to the Indians for Early Wynn and Al Smith (he of the beer cup on the head). They got him back for the 1960 season, just in time for Minnie to play for a couple of middle-of-the-division teams. Talk about missing out. It's like hanging out at the Playboy Mansion for six straight days with not much happening—and then on the day you don't show up, naked triplets are dominating the Jacuzzi. You come back the next day and funnyman Jack Carter and funnyman Chuck McCann are organizing a backgammon tournament near the Woo Grotto. You missed everything!

Remember Oklahoma brand gasoline? Me neither. But apparently it was quite the gas in Chicago in the 1950s. So says the ad on the inside cover of the 1955 White Sox program.

"Watch for us on T.V.!" says the ad, which features a giant, disembodied Jack Brickhouse head and some funky cartoon drawings of a cowboy and an Indian lass. (Because when you think gasoline, you think cowboys and Indians. How do you think they got their horses to keep going all day?) "We'll be bringing you all the daytime home games of the White Sox and Cubs during 1955," read the copy. "JACK BRICKHOUSE will do the play-by-play telecasts on WGN-TV, and our new, all-star TV film cast, OKLAHOMA ETHYL, OKLAHOMA PETE, THE LITTLE INDIAN CHIEF and the OKLAHOMA NEWSBOY will be telling you all about the many advantages of OKLAHOMA 'REFINERY FRESH' GASOLINE AND HEATING OILS."

The program has ads for:

Elliot's Kitchen, ATlantic-5 9755: "Home of the Donut Holes"
Jim Ireland's, 632 N. Clark St: "Shrimp Jambalaya Complete
    Dinner, $2.50"
Camels: "America's First Choice for more pure pleasure!"
Barney's Market Club, Randolph and Halsted: "Yes Sir Senator!
    Famous for the Finest Steaks. Seven course dinners at $2.25"
Sunny Brook Whiskey: "Enjoy the whiskey that's as cheerful as
    its name!"
White Sox souvenir jackets: just $7
Meister Bräu: "You can't serve a finer glass of beer"

And many other restaurants that are long gone, as well as cigarettes, beers, and whiskeys that don't seem to be dominating the market in the 21st century.

The program also has little features such as a profile of "Nelson" Fox, a piece titled "Do You Know How to Score a Ball Game?," and the "Official Ground Rules," with handy tidbits such as "Thrown ball that goes into the dugout: 2 Bases" and "Ball thrown by pitcher from rubber to catch a runner 'napping' at first or third base that enters fence surrounding tarpaulin: 1 Base."

These are things you *had to know* if you were attending a game in 1955.

The program is a neat little piece of White Sox history—but for me the really awesome thing is to carefully flip through the faded, yellowing pages of this half-century's old document, with the knowledge that my mom saved this from the date she had with my dad when they were a young couple in love and eternally optimistic about the future—a future that was sure to include a White Sox World Series sooner or later.

Or much, much later.

Veeck—More of a Maverick than Shrek

For years there's been talk about Bill Murray playing Bill Veeck in the big-screen story of the one-legged maverick who infuriated his fellow owners, delighted fans, and always, always tried to give us our money's worth. Sounds like the blueprint for a helluva movie. Baseball purists howl that some of Veeck's stunts, such as sending a midget to the plate, messed with the integrity of the game. Maybe so—but then again, that midget was only a little shorter than White Sox shortstop Harry Chappas, and Chappas made the cover of *Sports Illustrated*.

From the home office at 35th and Shields, here's my list of Bill Veeck's coolest moves, stunts, and ideas, with or without the White Sox.

1937	Veeck is credited with planting the Ivy on the walls of Wrigley Field and installing the manual scoreboard in center field.
1942	Veeck hatches a plan to sign a group of Negro League stars to the Philadelphia Phillies. Baseball Commissioner Kenesaw Mountain Landis kills the idea. What a great moralist that Judge Landis. He banned the eight Black Sox for life even though they were acquitted on criminal charges—but he wouldn't allow Bill Veeck to integrate the National League. In 1942, black men could go to war and die for their country, but they couldn't play in the big leagues.
1947	Veeck signs Larry Doby to the Indians. Doby becomes the first black player in the American League.
1948	A year later, Satchel Paige is a Veeck signee and becomes the oldest rookie ever, at 42. Had Paige been allowed to

play starting in 1928, he probably would have won 300 games.

1949   After a 26-year-old factory security guard named Joe Earley complains that Veeck is always holding special nights for rich ballplayers who don't need more gifts, Veeck holds "Good Old Joe Earley Night" and presents Earley with a refrigerator, a washing machine, a set of luggage, and a Ford convertible.

1951   Wearing a scaled-down St. Louis Browns uniform with the number $\frac{1}{8}$ and "elf shoes" with curled-up toes, Eddie Gaedel, all three-foot-seven of him, draws a walk on four pitches. For eternity, Gaedel has a spot in the *Baseball Encyclopedia*. His OBP is 1.000.

1951   A few days later, Veeck stages "Grandstand Managers Day." During the course of an actual game, Veeck's public relations guys held up a sign posing questions of strategy, and thousands of fans voted *YES* or *NO* by holding up placards. "Should we walk him?" "YES!" "Should we bring in a pinch-hitter?" "NO!" Like that. The Browns lost 9–3.

1960   A year after becoming head of a group that bought a controlling interest in the Sox, Veeck installs the world's first exploding scoreboard at Comiskey Park. Every time a Sox player hit a home run—and in the 1960s, that was about once every other game—the 130-foot giant rumbled to life, shooting off fireworks, spinning pinwheels, and blaring sound effects that could be heard from miles around, to the sounds of Handel's *Messiah*. (When I was living on the 60th floor of a high-rise on Lake Shore Drive in the early 1990s, I had a clear view to the south, and every time a Sox player hit a home run, I'd race to the window and watch the tiny fireworks exploding over New Comiskey Park. The new exploding scoreboard isn't as cool as the original, but it's just as *bright* and *loud*.)

(Continued on next page)

1975   Thanks to a last-minute infusion of cash, Veeck somehow manages to buy the Sox for a second time. If not for Veeck's heroics, the Sox would have moved to Seattle.

1976   On Opening Day at Comiskey Park, Veeck is the peg-legged fife player leading a bicentennial Spirit of '76 parade.

1976   Veeck installs a microphone just outside the broadcast booth so fans can hear Harry Caray's off-key but enthusiastic rendition of "Take Me Out to the Ball Game."

1980s   After selling the White Sox in 1981, Veeck spends many an afternoon in the bleachers at Wrigley Field.

Front-Runners

May 5, 2005

Let's take a look at the records of some high-profile and major-market clubs as they stood after the first 28 games of the 2005 season:

Team	W	L
Cardinals	18	10
Dodgers	18	10
Angels	17	11
Red Sox	16	12
Giants	14	14
Mets	14	14
Cubs	12	16
Yankees	11	17

The White Sox? Oh, they were muddying along at *21–7*.

The best record in the American League Central, the American League, the major leagues, the world, the galaxy, etc. Yet the national media were just beginning to take note of the Sox with a sprinkle of attention here and there: an ESPN profile of Ozzie, a *New York Times* story, A.J. guesting on Fox's *Best Damn Sports Show*, a nod from *Sports Illustrated*. There was far more national attention focused on the Red Sox' sluggish start and the Yankees' awful first month, with George Steinbrenner bitching in public about his underachieving kazillionaires.

By far the biggest personality on the Sox was Ozzie. The national media loved him because unlike most managers and coaches, Ozzie was filter-free. He said what popped into his head when it popped into his head—and the things popping in his head were something to behold. Within the first month of the season, Guillen ripped Frank Thomas's me-first attitude, mocked Kerry Wood and Mark Prior as he praised Buehrle, and dumped on former catcher Miguel Olivo's pitch-calling. After Magglio Ordonez told the media he didn't have any real interest in talking with Ozzie before the first meeting of the season between the Sox and Maggs's new team, the Tigers, Ozzie reacted as if Ordonez had insulted Guillen's family to the core.

"He's a piece of $!&!@!" roared the Blizzard of Oz. "He's another Venezuelan #@!*&@!."

"$@!& him! He thinks he's got an enemy? No, he's got a big one. He knows I can !$@# him over in a lot of $#*!& ways."

(Interestingly enough, Ozzie actually used those dollar signs, ampersands, and exclamation points when dissing Magglio. OK, not really, but how could we tell for sure? Even Ozzie admitted that it was sometimes impossible to figure out what he was saying. At Sox Fest 2006, he said the reason he turned down Letterman and Leno after the World Series was that nobody would be able to understand him anyway.)

Longtime Sox-watcher Jay Mariotti feared the worst.

"If someone in charge doesn't muzzle Ozzie Guillen with duct tape, inject him with a horse tranquilizer or simply order him to shut the *!@# up—his favorite expression, not mine—the man is going to talk himself out of a job and shame the city and the ball club he represents," wrote Jay in an early season column.

"Sox fans are entertained by the furor more than bothered . . . but those of us who understand the 162-game nature of a six-month marathon know that [Kenny] Williams and chairperson Jerry Reinsdorf must calm him down at once. If not, the Sox . . . will be nationally embarrassed by an Ozzie moment waiting to happen."

Jay had a point. At Ozzie's early season rate, he was on pace for about 150 controversies by September. (And there would be further episodes, such as Guillen pointing out a longtime friend at Yankee Stadium and bellowing, "Hey everybody, this guy's a homosexual! He's a child molester!")

Weirdly, though, none of Guillen's diatribes or sophomoric attempts at humor galvanized any kind of serious protest movement. (Even when he called Alex Rodriguez a "hypocrite" in February 2006, he quickly apologized, A-Rod accepted, and that was that.) Maybe it was because the Sox kept winning. Maybe it was because lifelong Sox fans knew Ozzie from his playing days and realized you just couldn't take him seriously when he went off on one of his rants. And maybe, just maybe, Ozzie got away with things BECAUSE of his infectious personality and his broken English. There was something a little patronizing about the way some in the media treated Ozzie.

Guillen's attention-grabbing theatrics aside, the players weren't getting all that much press.

"These are the days of instant information," noted Brian Hanley in the *Sun-Times*, "but it seems like news of the White Sox' sizzling start is moving across the nation with the speed of the Pony Express."

Imagine the Cubs roaring off to a 21–7 start. They wouldn't just be on the cover of *Sports Illustrated*, they'd probably be on the cover of *Time*, *Newsweek*, *Rolling Stone*, and *Teen People*.

2005 Salaries of White Sox Players

Player	Salary	Worth It?
Paul Konerko	$8.75 mil.	Absolutely
Jose Contreras	$8.5 mil.	After August 1, yes
Mark Buehrle	$6 mil.	And then some
Frank Thomas	$8 mil.	Refund, please
Jon Garland	$3.4 mil.	All-Star bargain
A.J. Pierzynski	$2.25 mil.	Easily
Damaso Marte	$1.25 mil.	Are you kidding? No
Cliff Politte	$1 mil.	Worth twice that
Joe Crede	$400,000	Young and underpaid
Neil Cotts	$300,000	Ditto

Not that Ozzie cared.

"Right now it doesn't matter if you talk about the White Sox," he told the baseball beat writers. "Talk about the White Sox on October 1. That's my goal. People don't believe in us—that surprises me."

The Sox were piling up the one-run victories with stellar pitching, solid fielding, and timely hitting, but the experts weren't buying it. Here's a late-April observation from Baltimore Orioles beat writer Bob Matthews:

"The Chicago White Sox and Baltimore Orioles must be sad that April has to end. They've been the American League's two best teams for the first month of the season, but are they for real?

"I believe the Orioles are a playoff contender and the White Sox are a pretender . . . The White Sox and their fans are dreaming of upstaging the defending champion Red Sox . . . [but the Sox are] 10–1 in one-run games, their pitching staff has overachieved. . . . They figure to return to earth and lose their share of close games . . .

"The hot start might help the White Sox finish above .500, but I'll be surprised if Minnesota isn't the only AL Central team in the playoffs."

Memo to Bob: *Surprise!*

P.S. After a 19–9 start, the Orioles finished 74–88, leaving them just 21 games out of the playoffs.

♩   ♩   ♩

The Sox beat the Indians 1–0 on Opening Day before a crowd of 38,141 at U.S. Cellular Field. It was a game that set the tone for the entire season, in myriad ways:

- We got great starting pitching from Mark Buehrle, who struck out five, allowed two hits, and walked just one batter in eight innings.
- The bullpen came through with a save. (In this case it was Shingo Takatsu, who would be gone before the season was over, with Dustin Hermanson and then Bobby "Captain" Jenks taking over the closer's role.)
- Runs were hard to come by.

• When the Sox finally did put a tally on the board, a little bit of luck was involved. In the bottom of the 7th, Paulie Konerko doubled and moved to third on Jermaine Dye's deep fly to right. Aaron Rowand hit an easy roller to shortstop—but the ball caromed off the heel of Jhonny Peralta's glove for an error, and yes, he spells his name "Jhonny."

Omar Vizquel makes that play in his sleep—but after more than a decade of torturing the Sox with his acrobatic defense, Vizquel is no longer a Cleveland Indian, he's a San Francisco Giant. So Peralta makes the error, the Sox scratch out a run, and Buehrle and Shingo do the rest. The game had a 2:00 P.M. start time—and by 4:00 P.M. the fans were streaming out of the Cell. Buehrle pitches as if he's not sure if he left the oven, the iron, AND the stove on, and he needs to get home as fast as possible.

The players and the fans love it. The South Side beer vendors hate it. When Buehrle's starting, they know they might have less than two hours to make their cash.

♪   ♪   ♪

Even though the Sox are in first place, I'm still having trouble giving away my tickets to early season games against Seattle and Kansas City and Baltimore. As for my own attendance, I've made it to four games, and the Sox have lost three of them. One of the beer vendors, noting that I didn't have much of a record in 2004 either, tells me I should start thinking about staying away from the games for a while.

I think he's kidding. But I tip him an extra buck the next time he brings a round of Millers.

A Sox Fan in Cubbie Nation

May 13, 2005

We sing the songs our fathers sang
When they were growing up
Rebel songs of Erin's Isle in the South Side Irish pubs
And when it comes to baseball
We have two favorite clubs
The Go-Go White Sox and whoever plays the Cubs!

— "The South Side Irish"

Chicagoans might recall that in the late spring of 2005, an oil stain that supposedly looked like an image of the Virgin Mary appeared on the Fullerton Avenue underpass. Hundreds of faithful Christians and dozens of media outlets flocked to the scene, which was soon overflowing with candles, flowers, rosaries, holy cards, photos of deceased loved ones, and handwritten tributes to the dearly departed. It got so ridiculous that the Chicago police had to station a squad car and put up barricades to keep the believers at bay. People were falling to their knees and *weeping*. I kid you not.

I went out to the site to write about it—and I can tell you without hesitation that the oil stain of the Virgin Mary did indeed resemble an oil stain. After I wrote a column about this not-quite-miraculous site, I heard from Butch Brzeski of Chicago—and let's face it, you're not going to find too many names that are more Chicago than Butch Brzeski. You can almost hear the ghost of Harry Caray gargling, "You know Brzeski spelled backwards is Iksezrb! The Iksezrbs, didn't we beat those guys in World War II? Ha, ha, ha, . . ."

Wrote Butch: "I noticed someone scribbled 'Go Cubs' by the image of the Virgin Mary on the Fullerton Avenue underpass. Were they hoping the image would get the Cubs a closer and a left fielder, and heal all the [injured] Cubs players?"

My response, published on May 13:

Now, now, Butch. This is no time to be cynical about things such as wall stains that look nothing like Jesus' mom and nationally beloved teams that are performing far below expectations.

On Sunday the Sox jumped to a first-inning lead against the Blue Jays, marking the 31st straight game they've led. No team in history—not the 1927 Yankees, not the 1929 Philadelphia A's, not the 1955 Brooklyn Dodgers, probably not even your daughter's T-ball team—has ever done that. With that nail-biter of a victory Sunday, the Sox are an insane 24–7. If they stay red hot, they could have a 40-game record of 31–9 or 30–10, which would rank with such teams as the 1998 Yankees, who went 31–9 on their way to a 114–48 mark and a World Series title, and the 1931 Philadelphia A's, who went 30–10 and finished 107–45 and also won the Series. *[Note: The Sox wound up 28–12 after the first quarter of the season.]*

And you know what? Even if the Sox keep up this ungodly pace (which they won't) and the Cubs continue to stumble, the Sox will still be the second-most-popular team in town. The Cubs will outdraw them and garner at least as much media coverage, even if the Sox are 20 games better.

That will never change, and for starters I can give you a half-dozen good reasons:

Sluggers
The Cubby Bear
Hi-Tops
Murphy's Bleachers
Sports Corner
Bernie's Tavern

Among hard-core baseball fans, the Cubs and Sox have an equal number of supporters—but the Cubs have probably 90 percent of the casual fan base . . .

Note how I went on and on about the Cubs even as I advised Butch Brzeski to let it go with the Cubs. That's how we do it in the Southern Hemisphere of Chicagoland.

If Sox fans are going to talk honestly about our obsession with the Cubs and their fans, the first step is to admit we ARE obsessed with the Cubs and their fans. (After a stalker was arrested for trespassing on Jennifer Aniston's property, I wrote that Sox fans were like the stalker and Cubs fans were like Jennifer Aniston, barely aware of the pest intruding on her space. Sox fans got really mad about this. Some of them sent me e-mail after e-mail on the subject. Sort of like stalkers.) When a Sox fan says, "I really don't care about the Cubs as long the Sox are doing great," it ranks up there with all-time bull*!@# comments like "It's an honor just to be nominated" and "You're so beautiful—but really, we don't have to do anything. It's fine with me if we just cuddle all night."

When I was a teenager, there was this series on PBS called *Upstairs, Downstairs*. It was a British soap opera about the rich and their servants. Of course, the servants talked about their employers all the time, and the employers barely paid attention to the personal lives of their servants, unless it was to say something like "Heavens, is that maid pregnant again? How is she going to climb the ladder to reach the upper shelves when she's dusting in the library?" At least that's what I think that show was about; I hardly ever watched the damn thing, but mom liked it.

Anyway, the *Upstairs, Downstairs* model is pretty much how it works with "North Side, South Side." We always pay a lot more attention to them than they do to us. It comes from a lifetime of being the overlooked younger sibling, watching our older brother get more attention, year after year after year after year.

After year.

Why do we resent them so?

Let's get into the clichés, the stereotypes, the myths.

- For every Sox fan in the Chicago area, there are three Cubs fans. *For every Sox fan outside of Chicago, there are 33 Cubs fans.*

- The local media have always favored the Cubs.
  The national media don't just favor the Cubs—they virtually ignore the Sox.
- Cubs fans sip wine and eat brie.
  Sox fans guzzle beer and swallow hot dogs whole.
- Wrigley Field is a cathedral.
  U.S. Cellular Field is a standard-issue ballpark.
- Cubs fans stand up to sing "Take Me Out to the Ball Game."
  Sox fans stand up when they're about to storm the field to tackle an umpire.
- Cubs fans have cute little Cubbie Bear tattoos on their biceps and calves. Not permanent tattoos, of course. These tattoos wash off.
  Sox fans have tattoos depicting skulls, Harleys, and the names of girlfriends who swore they'd remain faithful even if parole was a long time coming.
- The women at Cubs games are gorgeous babes with beautiful bodies and glowing tans. They wear shorts and tank tops.
  The women at Sox games are stout gals with broad shoulders and deep voices. They wear jeans and Blackhawks jerseys.
- Cubs fans want their team to win—but they're just happy to be attending a game at beautiful Wrigley Field. A good time is guaranteed, no matter what the outcome.
  Sox fans want their team to win—why else would they go to a game? If the Sox lose, their fans bitch and curse all the way out to the parking lot.
- Wrigley Field is known as "The Friendly Confines."
  Comiskey Park was known as "The World's Largest Outdoor Tavern."
- Every Cubs game is sold out, regardless of where the Cubs are in the standings.
  The Sox never sell to capacity. No matter how well the Sox are doing, you can walk up to the ticket window five minutes before game time and buy four box-seat tickets.
- A trip to Wrigley Field is a Disney-like experience, filled with sunshine and balloons and cheerful exchanges with your fellow fans.
  A trip to the Cell is a bleak excursion to the South Side, with a real potential for danger, especially at night.

- Cubs fans are forever loyal and optimistic, always looking on the bright side even when their team is down and out.
  Sox fans are brooding pessimists who will find any excuse to jump ship.

And so it goes.

Some of these stereotypes have at least a foundation of truth; others are simply ridiculous. For example, there's at least much drinking going on at Wrigley Field as there is at the Cell—and there's much more partying before and after games in Wrigleyville than there is in Bridgeport.

Females? I've seen gorgeous women at Sox games and at Cubs games. The difference is that the female fans of the Sox know the game. I've never talked to a woman who was at a Sox game the night before and can't even tell you who won, but that happens all the time with female Cubs fans. (On TV, it always appears as if Wrigley Field is stocked with women who have just walked out of a *Stuff* magazine photo shoot. That's because for the last few decades, their telecasts have led the big leagues in gratuitous cheesecake shots of scantily clad women bouncing down the aisles and sunning themselves in the grandstand. Not that there's anything wrong with that.)

These days, you're probably more likely to get into a fight outside Wrigley Field than at the Cell, mainly because the area is so crowded and crazy with young drunks, who weren't even at the game. Nobody goes to the South Side to tailgate in the parking lot unless they've got a ticket to the game. Thousands of fans that don't have tickets flood the bars around Wrigley Field on game days. True, Sox fans can pull some bonehead stunts, like the infamous father-son tag team, the Ligues, the guy who tackled the umpire, and the fan who reportedly slapped Craig Biggio's wife on the back of the head at a World Series game.

Those people are idiots. Morons. Jerks. Not real Sox fans.

But if a fight, a real fight, breaks out at the Cell these days, yellow-jacketed security guards will be there in a heartbeat. The Cubbies have a security detail as well—but their first line of defense consists of all those ushers who are slightly older than Jimmy Carter. Whenever I go to a Cubs game and I need help finding my seat—and I always need help finding my seat, because I pride myself on *not* knowing the layout of the park—I always feel bad about getting assistance from one of those ushers. It's like getting escorted down the aisle by Helen Hayes in her later years.

Double-Dippers

When Bobby Howry was traded from the Indians to the Cubs prior to the 2006 season, the one-time Sox reliever was asked about playing on the North Side of town.

"You mean the popular side?" cracked Howry on WGN-TV. "I'm happy for [the Sox] that they won it all. But it's still a Cubs town. I saw the celebration they had and the people who showed up. I can hardly imagine what would happen if the Cubs won it. I would love to be a part of that."

I agree with Howry on one thing. I, too, can hardly imagine what would happen if the Cubs won the World Series. Nobody can imagine it. Stephen Hawking and Steven Spielberg can't imagine it.

Howry is a much-traveled veteran, and it isn't that startling to see him in a Cubs uniform. For some Chicago players, however, it was just weird to see them wearing the uni of the "other" team.

Former Cubs Players Who Didn't Look Right in Sox Uniforms:
Ron Santo
Don Kessinger
Phil Cavaretta

Former Sox Players Who Didn't Look Right in Cubs Uniforms:
Jason Bere
Rich Gossage
Donn Pall
Hoyt Wilhelm
Wayne Nordhagen

Announcers Who Played for the Sox and the Cubs:
Steve Stone
Darrin Jackson

The idea that Cubs fans are benign masochists who never complain about their team—are you kidding me? Ask Corey Patterson about that one. If anything, Cubs fans in recent years have become surlier than Sox fans. Maybe it's because they still have the bitter taste of 2003 on their tongues, but a lot of Cubs fans start practicing their heckling around mid-February every year. If their guys go 3–5 to start the season, let the booing begin.

As for the attendance figures: It's true that over the last several years, the Cubs and Wrigley Field have been much bigger draws than the Sox and Comiskey Park II/U.S. Cellular Field. Game after game, season after season, the Cubbies draw crowds of 30,000-plus.

Let's take a look at Wrigley Field attendance since 1998, when Sammy had his monster season and the Cubs gained a wild-card berth by beating the Giants in a one-game playoff.

Year	Total Attendance	Avg. Per Game
1998	2,623,194	32,186
1999	2,813,854	34,739
2000	2,789,511	34,438
2001	2,780,465	35,196
2002	2,693,071	33,248
2003	2,962,630	37,032
2004	3,170,184	39,138
2005	3,100,262	38,753

Contrast that with the Sox and their numbers at the Cell:

Year	Total Attendance	Avg. Per Game
1998	1,391,146	17,175
1999	1,349,151	16,656
2000	1,947,799	24,027
2001	1,766,172	22,077
2002	1,676,804	20,701
2003	1,939,524	23,944
2004	1,930,537	24,437
2005	2,342,834	28,932

In that eight-year span the Cubs averaged 79 wins and 81 losses. They made the playoffs twice, in 1998 and 2003.

In that same span the Sox averaged 85 wins and 77 losses. They made the playoffs twice, in 2000 and 2005.

So on average, the Cubs were about six games per year worse than the Sox. They had a couple of great regular seasons. So did we.

For approximately 640 home games from 1998 through 2005, the Cubs have averaged 35,591 fans per game—and the Sox have averaged 22,243 fans per game.

Ouch.

Even as the Sox made their magical run in 2005 while the Cubs floundered on their way to a sub-.500 season, the Cubs outdrew the Sox by nearly 800,000. Any Sox fan that tells you his team is just as popular as the Cubs is living in a state of denial.

In the January 30, 2006, edition of the *Chicago Tribune*, Rick Morrissey addressed the eternal Cubs–Sox question in a column titled WINNING HEARTS: THE WORLD CHAMPION SOX ARE HOT, BUT IT WILL TAKE MORE TO DISLODGE THE CUBS AS CHICAGO'S TEAM.

Morrissey's lead: "A fan asked me at Sox Fest whether Chicago is becoming a White Sox town. I asked him how much longer the morphine drip would be attached to his arm."

Angry Sox fans filled Morrissey's e-box with insults and counterarguments—but that just sort of proved the point. Even with the World Series trophy in hand, we were still pissed off about being in second place in the race to become Chicago's team.

When business travelers are in Chicago for a couple of days in the summer, they ask the concierge to help them secure tickets to a Cubs game. If you're a casual fan of the game and you go to only one or two games a year, you're heading to the North Side. If you're of a certain age and you don't give a *!@# about baseball and you just want to hang out, drink beer, and maybe get lucky—you go to Cubs games.

I have never, ever ever ever ever ever ever *ever* considered becoming a Cubs fan—but I can understand the mentality of the 23-year-old college graduate from out of town who lands a job in Chicago. Where's he going to live? Which team is he going to adopt? (And yes, we could say "she" instead of "he" and the equation would be same.) Is he going to try to find an apartment in Printer's Row and take the L train to 35th for White Sox games? Or is he going to room with a couple of guys in Lakeview and hit the Wrigleyville bars twice a week? Where's he going to find more people his age, more nightlife, more opportunities to meet the opposite sex?

Cubbie-town, of course.

⎗ ⎗ ⎗

I'm a Sox fan in a Cubs town, a Cub nation, *a Cub world.*

It hasn't always been this way. From 1951 to 1967, the Sox outdrew the Cubs every year except 1958. The Sox were also the more popular attraction a couple of times in the 1970s, at the outset of the 1980s, and again in the early 1990s. Longtime Cubs fans can tell you that the Wrigleyville area wasn't always crawling with sports bars, and the bleachers were often empty by mid-August. There were few places as cold and desolate as the upper deck in Wrigley Field circa the mid-1970s.

But in my 40 years of Sox fandom, the Cubs have dominated the market at least 80 percent of the time. Most of the time it hasn't even been close. In 2000, when the Sox went 99–63 and won the American League Central and the Cubs were a horrendous 65–97, the Cubs outdrew the Sox, 2.8 million to 1.95 million. That's like *The Fantastic Four* making more money than *Crash* and *Brokeback Mountain* combined (which is exactly what happened. It's wrong, but it's reality.).

It's not just about the per-game attendance. It's the perception that the media favor the Cubbies, especially since Tribune Co. bought the team in the early 1980s. There may be some truth in this, but it's kind of a chicken-and-egg thing. The media devote more attention to the Cubs because the Cubs have far more fans. The Cubs have many more fans in part because they receive so much media attention.

Not that Sox fans are rational on this topic. The *Tribune* could publish a 10-page special section on the Sox for every game, and Sox fans would say, "Why not 12 pages?" The program director at WGN Radio could announce that the station's official slogan had become "Cubs Suck," and Sox fans would say, "Of course they're going to mention the Cubs in their slogan! Those biased bastards."

Most of our resentment is reserved not for the media, but for Cubs fans. They're just so . . . *Cub-like* about the whole thing. So proud, so sentimental, so in-your-face. (I know: this is coming from a guy who's writing a book about being a Sox fan. But when I finish with my 75,000 words, I'll shut up about it for a day or two. Cubs fans never, ever stop talking about being a Cubs fan and bleeding Cubbie blue and all that *!@#. It's nauseating.) I'm sure that in the first half of the 20th century, Sox fans had to hear Cubs fans whining about the 1906 loss to the White Sox, and Ruth's called shot against Charlie Root in 1932, and the World Series defeat at the hands of the Tigers in 1945, and God knows what else. But we never talked about that stuff when I was a kid. When we got into Cubs–Sox arguments during recess at St. Jude's or between pick-up games at Drexel Park, no Sox fan ever said, "We beat your butts in 1906, and we'd do it again today!" That was ancient history.

My Cubbie resentment starts in 1969 and always harkens back to those beloved flopsters. For most Americans, 1969 is remembered as the year when man walked on the moon. For Cubs fans 1969 is remembered as the year when the Cubs broke their hearts.

Bull*!@#.

For one thing, the 1969 Cubs weren't some lovable collection of scruffy underdogs who almost pulled off a miracle run at the pennant. They had three Hall-of-Famers in Ernie Banks, Billy Williams, and Ferguson Jenkins—not to mention Ron Santo, who by all rights *should* be in the Hall. This was a veteran team with the best starting lineup in the National League, quality starting pitching, a good-enough bullpen, and some decent sticks on the bench. They raced off to a 12–1 start, and by the second week of August, they had an 8½ game lead in the National League East over the New York Mets.

Here's where the myths kick in. According to Cubbie lore, there are myriad reasons why the Cubs blew that sizable lead:

- The wear and tear of day games caught up with the veteran team.
- Manager Leo Durocher didn't rest his starters enough.
- The bullpen was weak.

- During a game against the Mets in Shea Stadium in September, a black cat scurried past Santo as he was in the on-deck circle. A couple of days later, the Cubs were out of first place for good.
- The curse of the Billy Goat was in effect.
- When Neil Armstrong took that one small step for [a] man and one giant leap for mankind, he kicked up some moon dust, and a month later it got in Don Young's eye and he lost a fly ball at a crucial moment.
- Whatever.

You want the truth, Cubs fans? You want answers? *You can't handle the truth!*

But I'll tell ya anyway.

The 1969 Cubbies faded in the stretch because they weren't as good as the Mets, who sucked in the early 1960s but were rich with talent by the end of the decade. History dubs them "The Amazin' Mets," but that team won 100 games and cruised into the playoffs against the Braves. (That's another thing Cubs fans conveniently forget: that 1969 was the first year of the two-division set-up. Even if the Cubs had outlasted the Mets, they wouldn't have been in the World Series. They would have been in the semifinals.) The Mets swept the Braves in three games to get into the World Series, and then whipped the powerhouse Orioles four games to one. This was no fluke team that got lucky and squeaked past the Cubs. The Mets deserved to win it all.

Besides, the race wasn't all that close. When the Cubs beat the Mets on the final day of the season at Wrigley Field, that "narrowed" the gap between the teams to *eight friggin' games.* The third-place Pirates and the fourth-place Cardinals finished a lot closer to the Cubs than the Cubs did to the Mets, but you don't hear anyone talking about the 1969 Pirates, do you?

Check it out. The 1967 White Sox finished much closer to first place than the 1969 Cubs.

As did the 1972 White Sox.

And the 1981 White Sox, in both halves of the strike-affected season.

Not to mention the 1982 White Sox.

And the 1985 Sox.

Heck, the 1987 team was 77–85, yet they finished eight games out—just like the 1969 Cubs. Same goes for the 1991 edition of the Sox, as well as the 2001 team.

The 1997 Sox finished closer to first than the '69 Cubs.

So did the 2003 team.

In other words, over the last four decades, White Sox teams have finished closer to first place than the 1969 Cubs on 10 occasions—a full 25 percent of the time. (Not to mention the division winners in 1983, 1993, and 2000, and of course the champs of '05.) Granted, these teams didn't have a huge lead in mid-August—but please, Cubs fans, let's try to remember that once the '69 Cubbies faded, they disappeared more quickly than George Lazenby's career as a leading man. Phillies fans have the right to moan about the final-week collapse of 1964, mainly because it happened in *the final week*. When Cubs fans sing songs and write poems and cry in their Corona Lights about the tragic collapse of 1969—and they've been doing so for more than 35 years—their heartbreak isn't really grounded in factual baseball history. The Cubs had a star-studded veteran team that couldn't beat the Mets in a 162-game marathon. Fans on the North Side had a hell of a summer—just as fans on the South Side did in '67, '72, '77.

But here's the thing. We haven't turned those disappointing summers into folklore—and we don't see story after story about those teams in the media, as we do with the 1969 Cubs. At this point there's probably been more written about the team that *didn't* win the National League East in 1969 than the team that won the division, the pennant, and the World Series. For once, the Chicago team seems to get more attention than their New York rivals.

Too bad all that attention isn't justified.

"I can't tell you how many fans come up to me and say, 'No matter what you do, beat the Cubs.' I ask them, 'Wouldn't you rather have us win the division?' You'd be surprised how many say no."

—Sox manager Tony LaRussa in 1986,
as quoted in *The White Sox Fan's
Little Book of Wisdom*

In the 1980s, my two favorite players in the National League were Steve Garvey and Will Clark. Not for what they did for their teams. For what they did *to* the Cubs in the postseason.

Normally a robotic, Ken doll–type like Garvey would be one of my least favorite players, but that all changed when Garvey and the Padres took on the Cubs in the 1984 playoffs. Remember, it was a two-division world in those days (and just a five-game format), so if the Cubs had beaten the Padres they would have moved on to the World Series—and it would have been a rematch of the 1945 Series against the Tigers, and what Sox fan in his right mind would want to deal with *that* *!@#? Oh, no—we needed the Padres to beat the Cubs.

The Cubs won the first two games at Wrigley, including a 13–0 shellacking in Game 1. North Siders (and South Side Cubs fans) were euphoric. After four long decades their beloved Cubbies were about to make it to the World Series!

Even after the Padres won Game 3 at Jack Murphy Stadium in San Diego, the Cubs were still just one victory away.

For Game 4 a buddy of mine held a Padres Party at his apartment in south suburban Riverdale. There were about eight Sox fans—and a couple of my friends who insisted on being Cubs fans even though they were from the south suburbs and should have known better. We drank Pabst Blue Ribbon, ate White Castles, and razzed each other as the teams battled back and forth. With the scored knotted at 5 in the 9th, the Cubbies loaded the bases, but former Dodger Ron Cey couldn't deliver the clutch two-out hit.

What a shame.

In the bottom of the 9th, another former Dodger became an instant South Side hero. With one out and one on, Steve Garvey squared off against Lee "Big Slick" Smith, the Cubs closer who always had this pained expression on his face, as if he'd stepped on a rusty nail.

With one quick, short, mighty swing, Garvey launched a walk-off home run off Smith, sending the San Diego fans into what passes for a wild orgy of enthusiasm in San Diego, and turning my friend's apartment in Riverdale upside down. As the two Cubs fans among us shook their heads and paid off their bets, the Sox fans danced and hollered while singing the "Na Na Hey Hey" song. It was a great moment in Sox fan history, even if the Sox weren't playing.

The Uncivil Wars

From 1903 to 1942, the Sox and Cubs played a total of 25 Windy City Series—exhibitions for Chicago bragging rights. The Sox won 18, the Cubs won six, and there was one tie. The teams faced off in other exhibition games throughout the years, but the fans always cared a lot more about these contests than the teams. You'd often see minor league prospects on the mound, and most of the stars would bat just once before taking a seat. Probably the most memorable of these pretend games was on April 7, 1994, when nearly 38,000 fans jammed Wrigley Field to see a prospect named Michael Jordan play right field for the Sox against the Cubs. To the astonishment of everyone and the delight of Sox fans in the crowd, Jordan went two for four and smacked an RBI double. Even though it was a practice game, it was probably Jordan's finest moment in a baseball uniform.

In 1997 the teams started playing for real. The purists worried that interleague play would somehow dilute such rivalries and cheapen the game. Nonsense. We should be more excited about Cubs–Brewers or Sox–Devil Rays than Sox–Cubs? Please! And what's more fun—arguing about which team is better or seeing them face off in games that count? Every year, Wrigley Field and the Cell are electric with excitement for the six games between the teams, regardless of where they're at in the standings.

From a Sox fan's point of view, the best games in the rivalry:

- **June 18, 1997: Sox 3, Cubs 0.** Wilson Alvarez pitches a four-hitter and the Sox win the rubber game in the first for-real series between these teams in 91 years. With the exception of post-season games, I don't know if I've ever heard New Comiskey Park as loud as it was in the 9th inning of this game. We really, really wanted this one.
- **June 13, 1999: Sox 6, Cubs 4.** Light-hitting shortstop Mike Caruso hits his first home run of the season in the 8th inning to propel the Sox to victory in the deciding game of the series.
- **June 9, 2000: Sox 6, Cubs 5 (14 innings).** Sammy Sosa whiffs in each of his first four at-bats, much to the delight of the Sox

fans at Comiskey—but the substantial number of Cubbie backers in the crowd have their moment of glory when Sosa wallops a game-tying, two-out, two-run homer off Keith Foulke in the bottom of the 9th. *Two hours later, Ray Durham of the Sox ends it with an RBI single. That's a shame, Cubs fans.*

- **June 10, 2000: Sox 4, Cubs 3.** This might be my personal favorite. The Cubs had runners on first and third in the 8th when Sox reliever Sean Lowe tried the oldest trick in the book—the old fake-to-third, throw-to-first pickoff play. Mark Grace, the reigning pretty boy of Wrigleyville, fell for it. He was dead to rights and he knew it. For Sox fans, it was the equivalent of watching the prettiest girl in the bar dump a pitcher of beer on the stud muffin before going home with the Chris Farley lookalike.

- **June 8, 2001: Sox 7, Cubs 3 (10 innings).** Carlos Lee wins it with a walk-off grand slam. I was in the stands for that one. We stopped cheering, hugging, and high-fiving about 18 minutes after the ball left Lee's bat.

- **July 13, 2001: Sox 7, Cubs 2.** Jose Valentin celebrates a home run in Wrigley Field by imitating Sammy Sosa's self-aggrandizing, contrived, phony tap-tap, kiss-kiss deal. Hilarious.

- **June 28, 2002: Sox 13, Cubs 9.** The Cubs fans in the crowd at Comiskey are rubbing it in our faces when their guys go up 8–0, but the Sox storm back, capturing the lead in a six-run 6th high-lighted by a Paulie Konerko homer. With the tying run at third in the 9th, Sosa steps in against the immortal Antonio Osuna. See ya. There is no joy in Cubville; mighty Sosa has struck out.

- **June 24, 2005: Sox 12, Cubs 2.** The Sox hit three homers and Freddy Garcia dominates in the biggest blowout in the series to date. With the victory, the Sox upped their record to 50–26 while the Cubs fell to 36–36. At that point it was pretty obvious that for the Cubs, it was time to start thinking about next year while the Sox, like Al Pacino in the courtroom finale in *Scent of a Woman*, were just gettin' warmed up.

The Cubs had their ace, Rick Sutcliffe, on the mound for the deciding game, and they jumped out to a 3–0 lead, but the Padres rallied for two in the 6th and four in the 7th—the latter rally fueled by Leon Durham's misfortunes at first base. San Diego completed the three-game home sweep and won the series 3–2. Who cares that they lost to Detroit in the World Series? The point is that the Cubs weren't there.

(Contrary to popular Cub lore, the Cubs didn't get shortchanged out of hosting the deciding game because they didn't yet have lights. The format at the time was two home games for one team, followed by up to three home games at the other team's venue.)

In 1989 the Cubs again won their division, and this time they were to face the Giants in a best of seven format. In the opener Giants first baseman Will Clark went four for four, with four runs scored, a double and two home runs, including a grand slam off Greg Maddux. The Giants went on to defeat the Cubbies 4 games to 1, with Clark hitting .650, scoring eight runs, and registering a slugging percentage of 1.200. He was like one of those six-foot, 175-pound 12-year-olds who dominates the Little League World Series.

Will Clark. My hero.

In one of my admittedly less gracious moments, I decorated my work station at the *Sun-Times* with a giant, glossy, black-and-white photo of Clark crossing home plate after hitting that grand slam in Game 1. Some Cub fan tore it down one night—but he didn't realize that a friend on the *Sun-Times's* photo desk had given the picture to me, and I had a supply of backup copies. The day after the vandalism I just put up another copy of the same photo.

But hey, I'm not one to rub it in. By Opening Day 1990, I was more than happy to take down the reminder of yet another Cubbie heartbreak.

The 2003 Cubbies were five outs from making the World Series, and I have to admit I had mixed emotions as I watched some of those playoff games at Wrigley Field. You get to a certain point in your life where you have friendships and even a romance or two with lifelong Cubs fans, and you almost begin to see these people as human. You hear about the 87-

year-old grandfather who just wants to see the Cubs in the Series before he dies, or the nun who prays for the Cubs every morning before she goes out and does about 14 hours' worth of good deeds, and you think, "Ah, maybe it wouldn't be so bad if the Cubs won something for the sake of these fine people."

Complicating matters even more was the fact that I have made the acquaintance of some members of the Cubs organization over the years, including players past and present. I participated in Kerry Wood's charity bowling tournament in 2004, and I had a great time heckling the likes of LaTroy Hawkins, Mark Grace, Ryne Sandberg, and Jim Hendry as I kicked their tails on the lanes. (Hey. I'm from the south suburbs, remember? You think I can't bowl?) Every Christmas for the last couple of years, I've received a beautiful card from Wood and his wife, Sarah. (Judging by the calligraphy, I'd say Sarah's the one sending the cards.) They're nice people. I genuinely hope that Kerry stays healthy for about 10 straight years so we can really see him reach the potential that Cubs fans have been talking about since that 20-strikeout game.

However. I can't say I was actually rooting for the Cubs against the Marlins in that 2003 playoff series. I felt like a villain in a Batman comic who takes some good-citizen pills and tries to behave but cannot help but revert to his true nature. Even as I was surrounded by Cubs fans in a Cubs suite, the best I could do was say something like "He really got all of that!" after a Cubbie homer, or "That has to hurt," when the Marlins rallied. There was a bandwagon, and it was parked right inside that suite at Wrigley, but there was no way I could jump on the thing.

As for the Bartman game, here's a little of what I wrote in the *Sun-Times* in December of 2003, as my friends at Harry Caray's Restaurant were preparing to blow up the infamous baseball:

> Like Babe Ruth's called shot in the 1932 World Series—as well as the Billy Goat curse and the collapse of the 1969 Cubs—the Bartman ball has become the stuff of Cubbie legend. But that's the thing about legends—the truth gets lost as the story grows. . . .
>
> The Cubs did not miss the World Series because Moises Alou wasn't allowed to make that catch. In fact, that wasn't even the most pivotal play in the 8th inning of Game 6. If there's one moment the Cubs and their fans could have back, it's got to be the double play grounder that shortstop Alex Gonzalez muffed.

Let's recap the inning. The Cubs were up 3–0, and Mike Mordecai opened with a fly out. Juan Pierre doubled to left. The next batter was Luis Castillo. He lifted a foul fly, and Alou *probably* would have made the play if not for Bartman. Probably. In any case, Mark Prior still could have retired Castillo—but he walked him.

After a wild pitch, Ivan Rodriguez singled to left, scoring Pierre. Now down 3–1, the Marlins had runners on first and second with one out. The next batter, Miguel Cabrera, hit a ground ball to the hole in short—and if Gonzalez had fielded the ball cleanly, he would have gotten one out for sure, and might have turned a double play to end the inning. But he booted it. Derrek Lee tied the game with a two-run double, and the Marlins were off to the races, scoring a total of eight times before the inning mercifully ended with none other than Luis Castillo popping out.

According to the legend, the Red Sox lost the '86 Series because of [Bill] Buckner, and the Cubs didn't make the '03 Series because of Bartman.

And that's not fair ball.

♫   ♫   ♫

[The White Sox] have to win for people to show up. [The Cubs] have to show up for people to show up.

—Eddie Einhorn

In my lifetime, the Sox have never been as popular as they were in the winter of 2005–06.

During the off-season, I hosted a viewing party for the White Sox championship DVD, with appearances by Bobby Jenks and Neal Cotts, who came onstage with the World Series Trophy. Nearly 3,000 people turned out to watch the DVD on a big screen, and they cheered the highlights as if they were seeing the games for the first time and the outcome was in doubt.

For the first time in history, Sox Fest was completely sold out in 2006, with fans waiting in line for hours for the chance to cheer for heroes, such as Paul Konerko, and welcome new faces like Jim Thome.

The Sox sold out their self-imposed limit of 20,000 full-season ticket packages—and they'll probably average more than 30,000 per game this year. There's much talk in the media about whether Chicago is becoming a Sox town.

It isn't. I know that's a tough thing for Sox fans to handle, especially as we're still basking in the euphoria of the 2005 season, but the truth is that in the long run, the Cubs will remain the darlings of the city and of the nation.

At the Cubs' convention, catcher Michael Barrett gave an interview to WGN-TV and talked about watching the Sox "parading down OUR streets." It sounds more arrogant in print than Barrett's actual tone. The reality is that if the Cubs ever did win the World Series, there would be twice as many fans lining the downtown streets, twice as much national coverage, twice the number of books and tribute DVDs.

It all goes back to television. In the late 1960s you could catch the Cubs and the Sox on Channel 9, and the two teams took turns dominating the market, mainly based on how the respective clubs were performing on the field. But then the Sox signed with a UHF station, WFLD-TV—and all of a sudden my dad and the dads in thousands of other Sox households were up on the roof, adjusting the antenna and adding boosters and doing whatever they could to improve the damn signal so that it didn't look like it was snowing in Comiskey Park in the middle of July.

Later, the Sox would try things like pay-per-view while the Cubs and WGN-TV were going the superstation route. Of course, it didn't help that the Sox let Harry Caray escape to the North Side at just about the time when Harry was making the transition from popular but controversial announcer to full-blown pop culture legend.

For the 2006 season the Cubs are adding extra bleachers and building an entertainment complex adjacent to Wrigley Field. If they could figure out a way to add a third deck, they'd do it. The rooftops, which were once populated by diehard fans sitting on lawn chairs and drinking beer from cans, have now become outdoor suites, with the landlords forking over about 17 percent of their profits to the Cubs. (Remember when the Cubbies erected those friendly screens a few years ago to block the views of fans on the roofs?) It's silly to say the Tribune Co. doesn't want the team to win. A World Series for the Cubbies would mean increased ticket revenue, more souvenir sales, improved circulation for the newspaper, better ratings for WGN-TV and WGN Radio, and the chance for Trib-Co executives to show off that Tiffany trophy in the corporate boardroom.

They want to win—but they're not going to exceed their budget to buy a championship, and they're not going to be heartbroken if the fans keep streaming to the ballpark to watch a .500 team.

We are Sox fans living in Cub Nation. We'll always resent that a little bit, but we wouldn't change colors for all the beer in Wrigleyville.

North Side Obsession

Over the last 15 years I've written at least 100 full columns about the White Sox, and I've mentioned them in at least a hundred other pieces. When talk turns to the Sox, it often turns to the Cubs as well. Just a few examples:

October 5, 1993: The Sox were facing the Blue Jays in the playoffs—so I headed to Wrigleyville to see how Cubs fans were doing.

I talked to a couple dozen Wrigleyites and didn't encounter any who were gnashing their teeth about the Good Guys in Black.

Did they actually care about the Sox? Well, no. But were they actively hoping for a South Side heartbreak? Not at all. And therein lies the key to Chicago's decades long rivalry: South Siders actively dislike North Siders, whereas North Siders have, at worst, mild disdain for life south of McCormick Place. Mostly, they're not interested.

Dina Sloan, 24, magenta hair and black wardrobe, was walking near shuttered Wrigley Field on Monday when she was asked her feelings about the Sox.

"Of course I'm a Cubs fan. I live here and everything," she said. "But I don't like hate the White Sox or their fans. Why would you want to wish doom on people just because they live on the other side of town?"

I dropped in on Chicago Engine Company 78, just across the street from left field at Wrigley, figuring that maybe these tough fire guys would have some hearty, healthy hatred for the Sox.

"Everybody here is a Cubs fan," said Mark Aguilera, a paramedic and lifelong North Sider. "Hey, I didn't even know the Sox existed when I was a kid. To tell you the truth, I like the Yankees in the American League."

Even the souvenir stores across the street from Wrigley Field are saluting, if not hopping on, the Sox bandwagon. At Sports World on Clark, three racks of White Sox merchandise were prominently showcased in the center of the shop.

"The Sox stuff is moving pretty well," said Carlos Rodriguez, who nevertheless was wearing a Cubs sweatshirt on Monday.

"Our attitude up here is all Chicago teams should win," said Rodriguez. "Sure we favor the Cubs, but we don't hate the Sox. The South Side has an attitude, but we don't."

North Siders are so nice. I hate that about them.

♩   ♩   ♩

May 31, 1995: I wrote about National Public Radio asking me to come on and talk about how well the Cubs were doing, and how poorly the Sox were faring.

The Cubbies were supposed to be taking up their usual space in the cellar while the White Sox were one of the preseason favorites to go all the way, but so far it's been just the opposite. The irony is so thick it's ridiculous.

I guess NPR wanted me to do a little junior Ken Burns riff on the two teams, and that would have been easy enough. I could have talked about the Black Sox scandal and the Cubbies' heartbreak of 1969 and maybe recite a little of "Tinkers to Evers to Chance" and talk about Luke "Ol' Aches and Pains" Appling and all that jazz, but the problem is, I don't want to get all poetic about the Cubs and the White Sox. All I want to say is "I hope the Cubs win because it will make a lot of 80-year-old lifelong heartbroken fans happy, and I'm sick of the White Sox because they stink, and I hope they lose every game. They stink stink stink stink stink!"

They don't let you say stuff like that on NPR. It would cause their listeners to spill their lattes in shock at hearing such crudities, so I think I'll take a pass on the interview.

♩   ♩   ♩

October 16, 2003. After the Cubs came within five outs of clinching the National League pennant, only to lose the last two games of the NLCS to the Marlins, I moaned about how this would affect Cubs fans.

This is horrible. This is the worst thing that possibly could have happened, and it's going to haunt me for a long, long time.

Seriously. I'm not acting like a heartbroken, bandwagon-hopping newbie Cub fan, nor am I being sarcastic. I'm saying that for myself and for White Sox fans everywhere, it would have been much better if the Cubs had made it to the World Series.

No matter how the Cubs would have fared in the World Series, a pennant would have meant the end of a 58-year drought—and more important, it would have at least slowed the incessant whining and crying and complaining and bitching and moaning and singing about the lovable losers and the Curse of the Billy Goat and the greatest fans in the history of the universe having their hearts broken one more time.

But this—oh my. This ugly, horrible, breathtaking collapse—this is epic. This is the stuff of Greek tragedy, and I'm not just talking about the Curse of the Billy Goat.

This is something Cubs fans, and their children, and their grandchildren, and their yet-to-be-born great-grandchildren, are going to talk about for the rest of their lives.

God help us.

Winning Lucky

June 4, 2005

In one respect, the heavens were not smiling on the White Sox in the first few months of the 2005 season.

More often, they were raining.

Seemed like every time the Cubs were in town, the sun was shining and the breezes were soft and friendly. As soon as the Sox rolled into Chicago for a home stand, it turned chilly, wet, and gray. (Chilly, Wet, and Gray—one of the lesser-known double play combinations for the Sox in the early 1950s.) Not to sound like a paranoid Sox fan—ah screw it, I know this sounds like I'm a paranoid Sox fan, but it *happens to be the truth*, and if you don't believe me you can ask Tom Skilling.

On June 4, the first-place Sox were set to host the Cleveland Indians for a Saturday afternoon game. The start was delayed by rain, but Mark Buehrle and bullpen coach Man Soo Lee (he's the "Babe Ruth of Korea," in case you haven't heard) entertained fans with a belly-flop competition on the infield tarp.

Now, I love Buehrle. If I were to compile a list of my all-time favorite players from the last 40 years—and now that I've thought of it, I'm going to do just that at the end of this chapter—Buehrle would be in my starting rotation. I love the way he pitches. I love his sense of humor. I love his enthusiasm for the game. I love his respect for the White Sox, their fans, and the city. (Even if he might end up closer to home one day, playing for the Cardinals.) I've always liked the characters of the game, from Jimmy

Piersall to Dick Allen to Mark "The Bird" Fidrych. Who wants a sport filled with robo-players?

That said, Buehrle is killing me with the tarp sliding in the rain. One of these days he's going to twist a knee or land wrong on his shoulder, and we're all going to wonder why the Sox never told Buerhle that when it rains, he shouldn't turn the infield into his personal Slip 'n' Slide.

Despite the steady rain, you knew there would be baseball that night at the Cell. In this age of 162-game schedules and murderous travel routines and TV-dictated matchups and start times, Major League Baseball will do just about anything to avoid a rainout. After about a 15-minute delay, the tarp was removed, the infield was packed with sand—and we were good to go.

Jon Garland (8–2) looked shaky in the first, prompting a few grumbles in the stands. Garland had started the season 8–0, but he had lost a couple of games in a row, and a lot of us had viewed that streak with skepticism. Year after year, there'd been talk about Garland's potential, with Hawk Harrelson telling fans that Garland's "stuff" was as good as anyone's—and year after year, Garland would win 12 games and lose around the same number, with an ERA somewhere between 4.50 and 5.00. He was still a kid in his mid-20s, but he was starting to look like a guy who was going to wind up 145–151 for his career. Nearly every time Garland picked up a win, I'd talk with my dad on the phone, and we'd have the same thought: it was nice to see the tall right-hander piling up the victories, but it wouldn't be a surprise if he finished 16–13 or 15–17.

Garland surrendered three singles and a sacrifice fly in the first but escaped with only a 1–0 deficit. ("Sure could have been worse!" Harry Caray would have said back in the day.) By the time Garland exited in the 7th, he had given up four runs and nine hits—but the Sox had the lead, thanks to homers from Konerko and Joe Crede, and a big, two-out, two-run double from Aaron Rowand.

With two out in the 9th and Dustin Hermanson on the mound, Grady Sizemore lofted a catchable fly ball to left—but NOW the damn sun was out, and Podsednik lost the ball in the high sky. Sizemore ended up on third. (In late September, Sizemore would have a sunny misadventure of his own. More on that later.) Coco Crisp hit a grounder to first—

and it took a funky bounce and went over Konerko's head. Sizemore scored, and the lead was down to one. Hermanson induced the dangerous Travis Hafner to ground out, and the Sox escaped with yet another one-run victory.

"Good teams find a way to win close games," wrote veteran baseball scribe Dave van Dyck in the *Tribune.*

"The White Sox, therefore, qualify as a good team, raising their record in one- and two-run games to 26–10 with a second straight last-minute escape in Saturday's 6–5 victory over Cleveland."

After the game, Ozzie Guillen told the press, "We find a way to win by one run all the time."

The victory meant the Sox were guaranteed to win their 14th series in 18 for the season. It was also notable because Frank Thomas had his first hit since returning to active duty in late May. Thomas even scored all the way from first on Rowland's double—but it was painful to watch him lumber around the bases. Frank had worked his tail off to get back in the lineup, but it was obvious to longtime fans that he was never going to be the same. The truth is that Thomas, always a big man, had allowed himself to balloon up over the years—and that had to have contributed to his foot problems. Whether it's Shaquille O'Neal in basketball or Frank Thomas in baseball, when you're that gargantuan, your feet and ankles just can't take the constant pounding.

The best hitter in White Sox history was destined to be a supporting player in the best season in White Sox history.

In late May, I made my first visit of the year to Wrigley Field—to see the Sox, of course. As usual, the air was electric in the neighborhood, with the bars overflowing and Clark Street jam-packed with fired-up fans showing their colors and heckling one another. You see all the Cubs–Sox couples holding hands, posing for pictures in front of the Harry Caray statue. The vendors selling unsanctioned T-shirts with messages like *SOX SUCK* and *CUBS SUCK.*

The problem for Cubs fans was that their ball club was under .500, while the Sox were nearly 20 games over. Even at this early juncture, Cubs fans were desperate to see their team win at least two out of three from the Sox, so there would be *something* to take away from the 2005 season.

Game 1 went to the Sox, courtesy of a stellar outing by Freddy Garcia, who always seems to be sweating profusely before he even throws his first pitch. Freddy is what they like to call a "horse." Like Bartolo Colon or the Cubs' Carlos Zambrano, he's a big (six-foot-four, at least 235 pounds), heavy-legged stud who just keeps firing away until the manager tells him it's time to hit the showers. You love to have a horse, an innings-eater, in your rotation.

The Sox also won the second game, but the Cubs avoided a sweep in Game 3 by defeating rookie Brandon McCarthy, who was making his first major league start.

A month later, after the Sox hammered the Cubs 12–2 at the Cell on June 24, their record was an insane 50–22. They were getting to the point where a .500 record the rest of the way would ensure a postseason berth. The Sox bats fell silent in the next two games, with the Cubs winning 6–2 and 2–0, so the teams wound up splitting the six-game season series—and ya know what? Sox fans really didn't care. Of course, we would have been in hell had the Cubs won five or six of the games, but a split—that was fine. We wouldn't have to put up with Cubs fans lording a season series victory over us, and we could move on to more important things, like establishing an insurmountable lead in the American League Central while Cubs fans booed Dusty and heckled Corey Patterson and wailed about the fragile bodies of Mark Prior and Kerry Wood.

As interleague play continued, the national media slobbered all over the Cubs–Red Sox series, working the whole "cursed" angle to death. One team had finally lifted the curse, the other team was still trying, and let's make sure we run some footage of fans at the Billy Goat Tavern, blah, blah, blah. There was far less attention focused on the Sox playing their old 1959 rivals, the Dodgers—but it was pretty sweet when the Sox swept all three. The Sox lost two out of three to the Diamondbacks, but they won series against the Padres and the Rockies, scoring a season-high 15 runs in one game in the hitter-friendly atmosphere of Coors Field.

The Sox were playing solid baseball—but they were also the luckiest Sox team I'd ever seen. When you're winning that many games by one run, it's not always because of clutch hitting, great defense, and a lights-out closer. You have to be the beneficiary of lucky bounces, generous calls from the umps, fluke hits, unlikely heroics from banjo-hitting bench players—and the Sox were getting all of that and more.

It's not that I didn't believe in this Sox team. They were finding all kinds of ways to win, and what's not to like about that?

I just wasn't sure they were World Series material.

Neither were the national media. In mid-June the *Wall Street Journal* had a front-page article on the Sox, but it was titled SOX ARE HOT, SO WHY ARE FANS IN CHICAGO SO BLASÉ? On *Baseball Tonight*, the Red Sox, Yankees, Cardinals, Cubs, Phillies, Braves, Astros, et al. were still getting at least as much airtime as the team with the best record in baseball. It was a catch-22. ESPN couldn't lead with the Sox because the Sox don't have a national fan base, and one of the reasons the Sox don't have a national fan base is they never get the star treatment from the national media.

In a column for the *Sun-Times*, I made the argument that the Sox had one of the most colorful teams in baseball:

- Carl Everett, known as "Crazy Eights" because he wears No. 8 and he's, well, crazy, is the wackiest player in the game today. Everett told *Maxim* magazine he doesn't believe dinosaurs existed and that paleontologists just make "bones in the lab." Asked why people would make up something like dinosaurs, Everett said, "Why would they say a lot of things that aren't real? That's the thing—no one thinks for themselves. If everybody would think logically, then they would come to their own conclusions. That's what I do."

  If you were on the train and the guy next to you said all that, you'd move to another seat.
- A.J. Pierzynski was essentially kicked off two other teams because he didn't get along with his teammates. . . . What a sweetheart.
- They've got two guys who defected from Cuba.
- They've got one guy (Scott Podsednik) who's engaged to former Playboy Playmate and Fox broadcaster Lisa Dergan.
- They've got another guy (Jon Garland) who's dating Olympic gold medal softball babe Lovie Jung.
- They've got a second baseman from Japan and a bullpen catcher who's known as the "Babe Ruth of Korea."

- Their center fielder nearly got himself killed when he rode his dirt bike off a cliff in the desert a few years ago. Now he just runs into outfield walls.
- The manager's son is the team interpreter. The manager's wife's niece is married to one of the starting pitchers (Freddy Garcia).

These guys have personality—and in the immortal words of Jules from *Pulp Fiction*, personality goes a long way. Yet nobody knows who they are. They're just that team that keeps winning, even though they're not supposed to be any good.

In June I received an e-mail from a pissed-off Sox fan who had just discovered a blog entry from earlier in the year, written by Mark Bechtel of *Sports Illustrated*. Bechtel listed the "Top Five Worst Teams to Root For" in all of sports:

5. Los Angeles Clippers
4. Atlanta Hawks
3. Tampa Bay Devil Rays
2. Cleveland Browns
1. Chicago White Sox

"Though they haven't won the World Series since 1917—a drought almost as long as the Cubs—the Sox can't win for losing," wrote Bechtel. "The Cubs have Wrigley, the Sox have a character-less barn. The Cubs had Harry Caray, the Sox have Ken Harrelson. . . .

"And I don't buy this year's fast start. Their lineup just doesn't seem that good, and Ozzie Guillen looks like he needs to take a deep breath. . . ."

My e-mailer was livid. "Who is this idiot?" he wrote. "Rich, you've got to take this guy to task for this."

I could come up with at least 20 sports franchises that are less fun to support than the Sox, from the Florida Panthers to the Washington Nationals to the New York Jets to the Kansas City Royals—and I've always said the Cell looks more like a Neiman Marcus store than a barn. (The old Chicago Stadium—*that* was a barn.) But I couldn't get too worked up about Bechtel's blog. Even as the Sox cruised through June, I had to admit that deep down, I was a bit worried about Ozzie's manic intensity, and like Bechtel, I wondered if the Sox lineup really was that good.

My Favorite Players, 1966–2006

I'm not saying these are the best 25 players from the last 40 years—but they are my personal favorites, for the way they played the game, the memories they created, and the entertainment they provided.

Dick Allen	Paul Konerko
Luis Aparicio	Carlos May
Ken Berry	Jack McDowell
Jermaine Dye	Bill Melton
Carlton Fisk	Magglio Ordonez
Terry Forster	Gary Peters
Rich Gossage	A.J. Pierzynski
Ozzie Guillen	Scott Podsednik
Joel Horlen	Aaron Rowand
Tadahito Iguchi	Frank Thomas
Bobby Jenks	Robin Ventura
Lamar Johnson	Wilbur Wood
Ron Kittle	

That '70s Show

August 23, 1972

On a Wednesday afternoon in late August of my 13th year, I was sitting with a couple of my buddies in the center field bleachers at Comiskey Park, approximately 500 feet from home plate. As usual, my buddy's father had given us a ride to the park in his van, taking us up the Dan Ryan, and parking within walking distance of the entrance gate. (Pay for parking? Never!) We had arrived a good two hours before game time. In those days, regardless of what your tickets said, you could camp out in the left field grandstand and try to shag batting practice home runs. With five bucks of spending money in my pocket, I was set for the afternoon.

We had general admission tickets, and we opted for center field seats because we wanted to be as close as possible to the great Harry Caray, who was doing a series of daytime broadcasts from the center field bleachers that summer. His oversized fishing net leaning against a long, wooden table crowded with scorecards, research materials, a microphone, and endless cups of beer sent by the fans, Harry would take off his shirt and soak up the sun as he delivered play-by-play, like some wacky fan living out a fantasy.

For the first time since the heartbreak of '67, the Sox were in the thick of things fairly late in the season. They had actually taken possession of first place for a brief glimmer of time the previous Sunday, beating the Red Sox 9–7 on a three-run homer from Pat Kelly in the bottom of the 9th. The White Sox lost the second game of the doubleheader and had to settle with a first-place tie for Oakland—and by midweek they were back in second place, but only a half-game behind.

We had a chance. A real chance.

On the mound that day for the Sox was Wilbur Wood, the portly knuckleballer who was in the middle of one of the most astounding five-year stretches in modern baseball history. After a decade in the big leagues as a reliever for a variety of teams, Wood became a full-time starter for the Sox in 1971 at the age of 29—and he started racking up numbers that would give today's typical All-Star pitcher a sore arm if he just THOUGHT about working so much. If you averaged Wood's stats from 1971 to 1975, the line would look like this:

W	L	Games	Complete Games	Innings Pitched	ERA
22	18	45	20	336	3.11

I don't care if you're throwing a knuckleball, a Wiffle Ball, a Nerf ball, or a tennis ball—to average 20 complete games and 336 innings pitched over a five-year period is a jaw-dropping accomplishment. With the number of games he pitched, Wood was like a whole college team unto himself. In 1973, he won 24 games—and lost 20. In 1972, Wood pitched 376 innings. On that August afternoon in 1972, there was still more than a month left of baseball to play, but Wood was already a 21-game winner (and an 11-game loser). His opponent that day was the reliable Mel Stottlemyre. Looking at the box score more than three decades later, I see that Stottlemyre yielded three runs in six innings, and Wood went the distance and give up two runs (one earned) on seven hits. Thurman Munson committed two errors for the Yankees, and Pat Kelly hit a double for the White Sox.

Honestly, I don't remember any of those details. All I remember is one at-bat. One swing.

Only three players had ever reached the center field bleachers at Comiskey: Jimmie Foxx, Hank Greenberg, and Alex Johnson. It took a

400-foot drive to clear the center field fence in 1972—but to reach even the first row of the bleachers, we're talking about a 450-foot shot.

To call those center field stands "bleachers" is to give them an upgrade. The bleachers in Wrigley Field are La-Z-Boys compared to the worn, narrow, rickety wooden benches at Comiskey Park in the early 1970s. Not only that, you were at least 500 feet from home plate. At least.

We didn't care. We were 12. Besides, even though we were about two football fields away from home plate, we were only about 10 yards from Harry Caray, with the silver hair and the giant glasses, the summertime tan, and the plastic beer cups stacking up next to his microphone. He didn't seem like a traditional play-by-play announcer; he was like a slightly crazy but wildly entertaining uncle.

The Sox were nursing a 3–2 lead in the bottom of the 7th. Lindy McDaniel was on the mound in relief of Stottlemyre, and there was one runner aboard when Dick Allen stepped to the plate.

Dick Allen was Fonzie before anyone ever heard of Fonzie. He was that cool, mysterious, slightly dangerous loner who had a unique style without ever once appearing as if he were trying to affect a style. In the early 1970s, Allen and Walt "Clyde" Frazier of the New York Knicks were the coolest athletes in all of sports. There wasn't anybody in third place. (I remember Frazier's paperback book, *Rockin' Steady: A Guide to Basketball and Cool* (Prentice-Hall, 1974). It had a diagram in which Clyde demonstrated how to catch a fly in midair. I wasn't quite quick enough to catch flies using Frazier's backhanded method, but I was an ace at capturing lightning bugs.)

In their long history, the Sox didn't always have the best teams—but they usually had some pretty cool duds. From the classic uniforms of 1906 and 1917 to the green warm-up jackets of the mid-1930s to the black-and-white striped socks of 1959 to the deep blue hats of 1967, the Sox had style.

Not so much that year. In 1972, the Sox had the most garish uniforms in their history to that point. (It would get worse in the 1980s.) Red! They were friggin' red and white, like the Cincinnati Reds or the damn Phillies or something. Who in the world thought it would be a good idea for the Chicago White Sox to go Santa Claus red?

Their home uniforms were white, with red pinstripes. The famous scripted *SOX* logo on the left chest was red, as was the player's number, just below the right chest. Also red were the hats, the sweatshirts you wore underneath your jersey, and even the red leather belt. *Not even Cher was wearing a red leather belt in 1972, for crying out loud.*

Yet Dick Allen looked like a god in his red White Sox uniform. He never wore a standard baseball cap—even on the field, he wore a batting helmet with no earflaps. This was a trademark that harkened back to his days with Philadelphia, when the fans were so brutal that Allen felt the need to protect himself from flying objects.

Although Allen was just five-foot-eleven, he weighed about 190, and there wasn't an ounce of fat on him. His upper torso was a V, and he had tremendous strength in his biceps and forearms, but he always wore a long-sleeved sweatshirt under his uniform, even on a hot summer day in August. He also sported long, muttonchop sideburns, a mustache, and tinted aviator glasses. It was like having Superfly at first base.

When Allen was with the Phillies, he would use his cleats to scribble messages in the dirt. On Mother's Day he wrote *MOM*. When he felt as if he might hit a prodigious home run, he'd write *COKE*, for the Coca-Cola sign on the left field roof at the old Connie Mack Stadium in Philly.

When the fans got on his case, he'd write *BOO*.

After Allen came to the Sox, I gave up Aparicio's number 11 for my Little League uniform and wore number 15, just like Dick Allen. I wrote messages in the infield dirt around shortstop, much to the confusion of the kids from other teams who would go out there and see *MOM* or *GO SOX* scribbled near second base. I had tinted, prescription, aviator-style glasses. And just like Allen, who wielded a ridiculously heavy 42-ounce bat, I used the heaviest stick available. I even imitated his vicious, all-or-nothing swing. Dick Allen might be the only player in Sox history who would receive ovations from the fans *even after striking out.* His swings were so mighty and so ferocious that even a whiff would give you a thrill.

Two months before that August game, Dick Allen was on the cover of *Sports Illustrated.* I still have that cover. It's in a frame and it's on my desk as I write this.

SEASON OF SURPRISES, reads the headline. CHICAGO'S DICK ALLEN JUGGLES HIS IMAGE.

The cover photo is an all-time *SI* classic. Allen is in the dugout at Comiskey Park. In the background, a catcher—I think it's Tom Egan—is buckling up his shin guards. Allen is wearing his trademark batting helmet, and he's focusing on the task at hand: juggling three baseballs.

And he's got a lit cigarette dangling from his mouth.

Can you imagine the furor if *Sports Illustrated* published a cover photo in 2006 featuring a superstar smoking while in uniform? Fuggedaboutit. The magazine would be issuing apologies, the league would be issuing a fine, and talk show hosts would be screaming about the athlete as a poor model.

You know what I thought about that cover in 1972, when I was 12? I thought it was the coolest thing in the world. I didn't take up smoking; I took up juggling. To this day, I've never had a cigarette—*but I can juggle, baby.*

So there I was in the bleachers at Comiskey Park on that August afternoon, with Dick Allen at the plate and Harry Caray at the microphone. The call from Harry, courtesy of the audio playback available on the Flying Sock's White Sox Interactive fan site:

"Two balls, no strikes, now the pitch, here it is, *there's a long drive to deep center,* way back, it might be, it could be, hey, almost into the net, Holy Cow! Richie Allen hit one into the up—into the center field stands. I almost got it with my net! It hit a fan's hands, right in front of me. Never has a ball been hit any farther. Holy Cow! A home run, with a man on, the White Sox now lead, 5–2. It almost came into the net here in center field!"

I have never seen a ball hit so hard and so deep. Yankees center fielder Bobby Murcer took a couple of steps back and then just turned and admired the rocket shot as it cleared the 400-foot fence and reached the unreachable bleacher section, a good 500 feet from home plate. As the fans in the background hollered, "Harry! Harry!," Caray tried to keep us updated on the next batter as he reveled in the amazing.

HARRY: Here's the pitch now to Carlos May. Wait a minute now, let me talk to you a minute. The man who caught the ball, here's the pitch, strike call, just to let you now I'm not exaggerating. How close was that to my net?

THE FAN: About five feet or so, well five yards, five yards or so or so.

HARRY: It almost bounced off your hands into my net! What's your name?

THE FAN: Jim [unintelligible].

HARRY: Hey Jim, I know you'll be proud of that baseball.

When that ball reached the center field bleachers, maybe 30 feet from where we were sitting, I danced—literally danced. Got up and jumped around and bounced around and did a little dance of joy. It may have been the only time I actually danced at a Sox game.

Other than Elvis Night, of course.

♫   ♫   ♫

God, to be 12 years old and to be a baseball fan, a baseball player, a baseball nut. I can still smell the leather of the Rich Reichardt glove as I held it just to my face during pick-up games at Drexel Park in Dolton. Twelve is the last year when you're still just a kid, and you're not expected to do much more than be a good kid. You turn 13 and the world turns upside down. Girls, junior high school, weird things happening to your voice and your body.

At 12, though, you're still collecting baseball cards and dreaming of becoming a big league ball player. You're still spending your summer days playing baseball and going to as many White Sox games as you can.

That was Richie at 12. (Not Richie Allen. Richie Roeper.) I was never a more passionate fan of any team at any time in my life than I was in 1972 of the White Sox. I knew every player's number by heart, and at any given point in the season I could have recited the batting averages, home runs, and RBI figures for just about everybody in the starting lineup.

I played the game in one form or another nearly every waking minute. Every afternoon after school, we played "fast-pitch" in parking lots. It was the simplest of games, pitting teams of two against each other. You spray-painted a strike zone on the brick wall. You had one pitcher and one fielder. The pitcher was on the honor system and would have to call whether a pitch was inside the strike zone—though the on-deck guy for the other team would also monitor each pitch. There were lots and lots of walks and strikeouts, punctuated by the occasional ball in play. You hit a grounder or a pop fly into the "infield," you were out. You hit a liner in front of the one fielder, it was a single. Chalk lines in the parking lot marked the minimum distance for doubles, triples, home runs.

In the summer, there were daily pick-up games at Drexel Park. You didn't make phone calls or send text messages or arrange play dates. You just rode your banana seat Stingray bicycle to the park, and there would be 10 or 15 or 20 other kids there, and you'd choose up sides. If you didn't have enough players for two complete teams, you'd have "right field out" or "right field foul," meaning that if you hit the ball to the empty pastures in right, it was a strike or an automatic out. (If a lefty came to the plate, it would be "left field out.") Another problem was the Little Calumet River, just beyond the fence down the right field line. If you sliced a foul or hit one over the backstop, sometimes the ball would land in the thicket of weeds sloping down to the Little Cal—and sometimes it would thunk in the muddy river, and we'd hopelessly watch it drift away. If you lost your entire supply of baseballs, well, you went home.

There was organized ball from May until early August. You'd have one or two Little League games during the week, plus a Saturday or Sunday afternoon game. When it rained heavily in the afternoon, the skies turning green and dark and the heavens opening for hours, and you knew they were going to cancel the game, it was worse than someone calling off Christmas. (Later, we'd get tarps for the three fields, labeled A, B, and C. Field A was the best and the biggest; it even had lights. Field B was OK. Field C was the worst of the bunch, but it did have a short porch in left field. As I recall, the tarps were donated by Lou Boudreau, the Hall of Famer player and Cubs broadcaster who lived a few blocks away from us in Dolton.)

For about five years, I was good. I made the Little League and Babe Ruth All-Star teams, and I was the Game 1 pitcher on squads trying to make it to the Little League World Series in Williamsport. I threw hard, I could play a little shortstop, and I had some power and speed. But I was never the best kid in the league, and the best kid in the league was never as good as the best kid in some other league, who was never as good as the best guy in the area, who was only good enough to be drafted in the 17th round and never played in the big leagues. (This is why I crack up when some fat guy in the stands who "used to play the game" is heckling Pedro Guerrero, telling him he sucks. Dude, you have no idea.)

When I was 12, I took the mound in an All-Star game against Dixmoor. We were up something like 14–0 and I was cruising along with a no-hitter until our right fielder jinxed everything by telling me I had a no-hitter, thus breaking the oldest superstition in baseball.

I started walking guys right then and there. Then I hit two batters in a row, creating a near riot in the stands, with one mom threatening to kill me because I had hit her baby. (My control wasn't good enough to plunk somebody on purpose.) We ended up winning 17–2. I struck out 14, walked six, hit two, and gave up one hit. I was like a mini–Nolan Ryan.

I was also about as good as I was ever going to get. Even though I played organized ball well into my 20s, it was mostly "semipro" stuff, which means that we could get a few dollars for expenses and the sponsor could buy us beer after a victory. There were about 50,000 guys between me and a major league spot. Maybe 100,000.

Not that I cared. I knew by the time I was 13 that I didn't have the ability to make a living playing baseball. (And that's when I thought, I'll be a pirate!) That doesn't diminish the thrill you feel when you make contact with the sweet part of the bat, or you range far to your left to scoop up a grounder and you make a perfect throw to first. Doesn't matter if you're doing it in a fast-pitch game at the age of 12 or in a senior softball league at the age of 72. The game is the game.

Not that the Sox were giving me much to work with at the outset of the 1970s.

Of all the bad White Sox teams I've seen over the years, the 1970 team had to be the worst. They were "led" by the immortal Don Gutteridge, another one of those nice-guy baseball lifers who seemed to be over his head as a manager. Put him in third-base coach's box, he was fine. Put him in charge of a ball club populated by aging veterans, mediocre journeymen, and a few young guys with potential, and it spelled disaster.

According to the *White Sox Encyclopedia*, Gutteridge didn't even know how to conduct a decent spring training camp: "During spring training, Gutteridge neglected the fundamentals—teaching run-down plays, the cutoff. Instead, he emphasized batting practice—hours and hours of batting practice." Then again, Gutteridge could have emphasized years and years of batting practice, and it wouldn't have made a hitter out of John "Pineapple" Matias, who hit .188 in 117 at-bats for the Sox in 1970. Or Rich Morales, who hit .161 and had exactly one home run and two RBIs in 112 at-bats. I swear I could do better than that. Or how about Rich McKinney, who hit .168 in 199 at-bats.

Folks, these aren't pitchers we're talking about. These guys were part-time position players.

By 1970, Joel Horlen, my favorite pitcher from the 1960s, was done—but that didn't stop the Sox from trotting him out there every fourth game. Horlen finished a brutal 6–16 with a 4.87 ERA, which is the equivalent of about a 6.87 ERA in today's game. The leader in wins on the staff was Tommy John, who had 12 victories—and 17 defeats.

It's so funny the things you remember. I swear to God in heaven that even before going to the research materials, I knew that in the 20th game of the 1970 season, the White Sox beat the Tigers at home to raise their record to 8–12. I also knew that Bill Melton was thrown out of that game for getting into a tussle with Tigers' second baseman Dick McAuliffe, who was also thrown out of the game. (McAuliffe had one of the funkiest batting stances in baseball history. Standing at the plate, he looked like some guy from New Zealand who had never heard of baseball and had just been handed a bat for the first time in his life.)

I remember those details because I was at that game with my dad, and for some damn reason it resonates with me more strongly than some of the games I saw during the championship run of 2005. (One factor: I probably wasn't drinking as much beer at the games in 1970, being 10 and all.) As was the case with the first game I ever saw back in 1966, this was another Friday night contest. A sparse crowd of 7,265 was scattered about the park to see my old friend Joel Horlen against a young hurler for the Tigers named Les Cain.

The 33-year-old Horlen yielded two runs in the top of the first, but the Sox rallied in the bottom half of the inning. Actually, the Sox' lineup that year didn't seem too bad through the first four hitters. We had Walt "No Neck" Williams leading off, followed by Luis Aparicio, who was long past his prime in the field but ended up having a career year at the plate in 1970, with a .313 average. Batting third was Carlos May and his one and a half thumbs. The cleanup hitter was Beltin' Bill Melton, who had swatted 23 homers in his rookie season and had instantly become a favorite in the Roeper household. A third baseman with power! What a concept.

As I remember it, Melton knocked in a run in the bottom of the 1st with a single, but he was out at second trying to stretch it into a double. Melton and McAuliffe started jawing at each other; maybe McAuliffe felt that Melton had come in with his spikes high, or Melton didn't like the way McAuliffe had applied the tag. What I know for sure is that my dad hollered, "Hit him, Bill!"

I think it's the only time in my life I ever heard my dad exhort anyone to hit anyone else, and I'm sure he was only half serious at the time. To my amazement, however, that's just what Melton did—he took a swing at McAuliffe, and the benches emptied. When the dust had settled, Melton and McAuliffe had been thrown out of the game, which pretty much sucked for me because I had come to the game hoping to see Beltin' Bill Melton hit a home run. Instead, he tried to literally belt someone, and he was tossed. Without Melton in the lineup, the Sox' biggest threats were Ed Herrmann, who couldn't beat a statue in a footrace, and Carlos May, who somehow managed to swat a dozen home runs in 1970 despite the absence of that thumb.

Horlen and the Sox fell behind 4–2, but in the bottom of the 6th the Sox put up a whopping eight-spot, highlighted by a three-run home run from Bobby Knoop (pronounced "Ka-NOPP"), who later that year would make an appearance at the A&P Grocery in the Almar Plaza, just down the block from my house. My black-and-white glossy from Bobby Knoop occupied a place of honor on the "sports wall" in my bedroom for the remainder of the year.

Final score: White Sox 13, Tigers 6.

On the drive home from Comiskey in my dad's Ford Torino, I curled up in the back seat and watched the streetlights and the signs marking the way south. When we reached the "Magikist" sign with those gigantic, neon lips, I knew we were soon to be leaving the South Side and entering Dolton.

The next morning as we gobbled up our Saturday donuts from Bartel's Bakery, I studied the American League West standings in the *Chicago Daily News*. Okay, so even with the victory the Sox were only 8–12, but that was a lot better than the 6–12 record they'd been sporting earlier in the week. They were only 4½ games out! It was the beginning of May, and there was a whole season to be played. I had hope.

A few days later, the Sox would raise their record to 11–13, but that's as close as they would get to .500 for the rest of the season. They'd lose nine out of 10, win a few, then lose eight in a row. They'd lose four straight, win two—and then lose three in a row. Before the season was over, general manager Ed Short and manager Don Gutteridge were gone. In September, the new GM, Stu Holcomb, hired a 42-year-old unknown named Chuck Tanner to take over the team. Unlike the kindly Gutteridge, Tanner was a fiery, intimidating presence, said to be physically stronger than any of his players.

A personal note from the 1970 season. I wanted to go to Helmet Day on June 28 more than I wanted to see Christmas morning. For months all I could talk about was the Helmet Day doubleheader against the Twins. I didn't care about the Twins—though I always did love doubleheaders as a kid. Two games for the price of one? Awesome. But what I really cared about was getting that cool batting helmet.

A few days before Helmet Day, I was on the mound for my Little League team, S&H Standard, in a key game against Rose Suburban Auto Parts. It was pretty rare for a 10-year-old to be a starting pitcher in a league open to 10- 11- and 12-year-olds, but I was pretty tall for my age and I had good stuff. Well, OK, I didn't have good "stuff"—I could throw hard. The game was tied at 2—in fact, the line was exactly the same for both teams, with two runs, five hits, and no errors—and I believe it was the 5th or 6th inning when my dad collapsed in the bleachers. He ended up being fine, but he had to be hospitalized for tests.

A day or two later, my dad was still in the hospital. He called home, and my mom put me on the line.

I hope I asked my dad how he was doing. I don't know that I did. At 10, I was good for about six words a day. I never talked; I just thought and thought and thought about things. What I do remember is my dad's telling me that he was sorry but we weren't going to be able to get to that Sox game against the Twins.

You don't understand how great your parents are until many years later. At 10 you don't consider things from the other side. Here's my dad, he's 40 years old and he has four children between the ages of 8 and 13. He's just suffered some sort of seizure. He's worried about his future, his health, how he's going to provide for his kids. And what's he doing? He's telling me he's sorry that we won't be able to go to a Sox game.

The Sox finished the 1970 season with a record of 56–106, setting the all-time franchise mark for most losses in a single campaign. Nice. They drew fewer than a half-million fans for the season and averaged just over 6,000 fans per game. One of the few bright spots of the season occurred on September 21 in a game against the Kansas City Royals, when Beltin' Bill Melton became the first White Sox player ever to hit 30 home runs in a season. EVER. (In the field, Melton was still a work in progress. During a game against Baltimore, he lost a pop foul in the lights, and it hit him squarely in the nose.) In classic Sox fashion for the time, Melton reached this milestone in a home day game after school was back in session.

Announced attendance for the game: 672.

No, that's not a misprint.

In 1971, the Sox came alive. A 79–83 record isn't that impressive on its own, but when you consider they had won just 56 games the year before, the Sox were probably the most improved team in baseball. There were more than a dozen new faces in the dugout, and for the first time in years the Sox had a little pop in the lineup, with five guys reaching double figures in home runs. In spring training Tanner converted Wilbur Wood to a starter, and Wood started that remarkable five-season run—and there were some good young arms in the rotation, most notably Bart Johnson and Tom Bradley.

Salaries

The reported salaries of selected White Sox players in 1970:*

Lee Stange: $39,000   Ken Berry: $27,000
Luis Aparicio: $38,000   Gail Hopkins: $15,000
Bobby Knoop: $35,000

Source: Baseball Almanac.

And check this out: Not only did Bill Melton top the 30 mark in home runs, finishing with 33 for the second year in a row—he actually *won the home run title.* On the last day of the season, Melton was tied with Norm Cash and Reggie Jackson at 32 dingers. Tanner put Melton in the lead-off slot in a move to get him maybe one extra at-bat. It had to be the one and only time in Melton's career that he led off a game.

In the third inning, Melton reached the left field seats—a blow that proved to be the winning margin in a 2–1 victory. Neither Cash nor Jackson went deep that day, so Melton finished the season alone atop the home run chart.

Attendance for the game: 2,814.

Of all the changes for the White Sox in 1971, perhaps the most historic move of all occurred in the broadcast booth.

After the brutal season of 1970, the Sox were such an unattractive commodity that WMAQ-AM dropped them from its lineup. They were reduced to signing with two suburban radio stations: WEAW in Evanston and WTAQ in LaGrange. As for television, the sleep-inducing Jack Drees was the lead guy on WFLD-TV, which back then was a lowly UHF outlet. Nobody, and I mean nobody, had a crystal-clear picture on Channel 32. Sometimes the snow was so bad and the signal was so weak that you'd just give up and watch *Mary Tyler Moore* or *Bewitched*—or the Cubs. Who knows how many Chicago-area fans switched allegiances in the late 1960s and early 1970s simply because it was too damn frustrating to catch the Sox games on radio or TV?

From the Great Depression through World War II through the Eisenhower 1950s and the Kennedy/Johnson/Nixon 1960s, the great Bob Elson was the primary play-by-play voice for the Sox. (He announced Cubs games as well back in the day.) He was on WGN, WBBM, WIND, WJJD, and he was partnered with a variety of cohosts, from the familiar (Jack Brickhouse, Milo Hamilton) to the forgotten (Grayle Howlett, Don Wells, Bob Finegan). Elson parted ways with the Sox after the 1970 season—it was their idea, not his—and spent one season doing Oakland A's games before retiring.

Enter Harry Caray, who had just a spent a single season of his own doing the A's games after a long and sometimes controversial career calling games for the St. Louis Cardinals.

Decades before Harry Caray became immortalized as a statue outside of Wrigley Field, had an Italian steakhouse named after him in Chicago, inspired a Will Ferrell *Saturday Night Live* character, and became known as the eternal mascot for sunshine, baseball, and good times at Cubs games, he was an accomplished play-by-play man with a keen understanding of the game, a monumental ego, and a willingness to rip into players and management when things were going bad. More than a few players who heard Caray's commentary while they were in the clubhouse or were told about Caray's remarks by friends expressed the desire to visit him in the booth and set him straight.

The fans always loved Harry. With players, owners, and Harry's broadcast partners, however, it was more complicated. Eight years after Caray's death, veteran broadcaster Milo Hamilton devoted an entire chapter of his memoir, *Making Airwaves* (Sports, 2006), to ripping Caray: "I see [the statue of Harry] every time the Astros visit Wrigley Field," wrote Hamilton. "When I get off the bus, I say to myself, 'I gotta go get some peanuts and feed the pigeons so they'll fly over the statue all day long. . . . He rode managers. He rode players. It didn't matter. He treated everyone the same way. In short, he was a miserable human being."

That might say a lot more about the bitterness eating away at a nearly 80-year-old man who needs to learn to let go—but it's a reminder that

Harry was a much more complicated person than the caricature of a good-time fan favorite who never met a Bud he didn't like and had a lot of fun pronouncing players' names backwards. (More on Caray in the "Sox Culture" chapter later in the book.)

In 1971, though, we didn't know that much about Harry. For my father's generation, he was known as the voice of the Cardinals. As far as the local media were concerned, the hiring of Caray was a nonstory. After all, the Sox themselves were pretty much a nonstory at the outset of the decade. That's why they were on those two suburban radio stations and the puny little UHF-TV outlet.

Not that Harry was even doing TV in his first couple of years with the Sox. He was just a voice on the radio, moaning, "Paaaaaaaaaahhhhhped it up! Boy, oh boy!" Sharing the booth with Harry were the likes of Ralph Faucher, Gene Osborn, and Bill Mercer.

It was during that 1972 season—that's when we saw that Harry might become a folk hero in Chicago. Sitting in the bleachers, quaffing beers during games (though his preferred drink in private was something stronger), bantering with fans during commercial breaks, taking off his shirt to work on his tan, waving that ridiculous net around—he was like nothing Chicago broadcasting had ever seen. Let's put it this way: Bob Elson wasn't going to sit in the bleachers with his shirt off, drinking beers, any more than he was going to wear a tutu and a clown's nose.

As a 12-year-old, I loved Harry. He kinda reminded me of my dad's older brother, my uncle George, who also had silver hair, big glasses, a big personality, and a fondness for libations. Compared to Jack Brickhouse (who would later become a friend of mine) and his cheerleading style for the Cubbies, all that "Hey, Hey!" stuff, Harry just seemed like such a perfect fit for Sox fans, who always had a more cynical, edgier worldview.

He was from St. Louis, but he seemed like one of us.

The 1972 White Sox had an entirely different personality than the teams I had known in my first six or seven years as a fan. For one thing they were the youngest team in baseball. And they had some legitimate stars, led by MVP Dick Allen and 25-game-winner Wilbur Wood.

Allen's numbers—37 HRs, 113 RBIs, .308 average, 19 stolen bases— were gaudy enough on their own, but it was his flair for drama that makes his '72 season perhaps even more impressive than Frank Thomas's monster MVP years for the Sox in the mid-1990s. Thomas hit some prodigious home runs and he didn't exactly disappear in the clutch, but he never had Allen's gift for creating moments that almost defied description. I remember seeing Allen break from first on a wild pitch—and never breaking stride until he reached third base, much to the shock of the catcher who had casually trotted to the backstop to retrieve the errant pitch. (Twenty years later, when I joined Allen at the Pump Room for Bloody Marys and I brought up that play, he knew exactly what I was talking about.)

The Sounds of the Game

The best Web site dedicated to the White Sox is WSI's Flying Sock ("Chicago White Sox Coverage With Totally Biased Attitude!") (www.flyingsock.com or www.whitesoxinteractive.com). I urge you to visit once a day. The Flying Sock has interviews with former players, tons of photos, updates on the current team, fan debates, and some hilariously cranky essays from Sox loyalists who see bias in every article and love to rail about the newspaper they call the "Cubune."

There's also a tremendous audio archive, dating all the way back to the 1950s. You can hear Bob Elson delivering the call on May 16, 1953, when White Sox pitcher Tommy Byrne hit a pinch-hit, grand slam against the Yankees; Jack Brickhouse whooping it up as Luis Aparicio turns the double play that clinches the 1959 pennant; Vin Scully calling the All-Star game at Comiskey Park in 1983; and much more.

On Sunday, June 4, 1972, the Sox hosted a doubleheader against the Yankees. Dick Allen had played in every inning up to that point in the season, but he had this thing where he rarely played second games of twin bills—not even against the Yankees, not even on Bat Day in front of a packed house of nearly 52,000 fans. So Allen was on the bench—actually, probably in the clubhouse—as the Sox were trailing the Yankees 4–2 in the

9th inning of the second game. With two men on base and two out, the Yankees' manager called on his ace, Sparky Lyle—and Sox' manager Chuck Tanner countered by bringing in Allen to pinch hit.

Mike Andrews, a friend of Lyle's from the days when they were both on the Red Sox, was on first base for the Sox. As legend has it, Andrews waited until Lyle reached the infield and then called out, "Sparky, you're in deep *!@# now!

Courtesy of WSI's audio archives, here's the transcript of the call from Yankees announcer Phil Rizzuto (whose voice was later immortalized on the "lost key chain" episode of *Seinfeld*).

"I'll tell you, there have been some tight, tense, dramatic moments in ball games, but this is a big one. Lyle against Richie Allen, what a battle. The two top men facing each other. The pitch—oh, he creamed one, and the ball game is over! Holy Cow I don't believe it! I don't believe it. Richie Allen pinch-hits a three-run homer, and the White Sox beat the Yankees. Ohh-hhhhhhhhhh! Unbelievable. I know it happened because I can hear that scoreboard going off. . . ."

As I wrote in the *Sun-Times*, hearing this audio for the first time in more than three decades was better than hearing a lost recording by Brewer & Shipley.

On July 31, 1972, against the Twins, Allen hit two homers.

Two inside-the-park homers.

The inside-the-park home run is perhaps the most rare play in baseball. It takes a confluence of events involving a long drive to the farthest reaches of the ballpark, a speedy runner, maybe a crazy bounce, or an outfielder who slips and falls. You can go your entire career and never hit an inside-the-parker. The odds against doing it twice in one game are beyond calculation.

That was Dick Allen.

Even though the 1972 Sox didn't have the firepower down the stretch to keep up with an Oakland A's club that was on its way to the first of three consecutive world championships, what the club had accomplished in just two years was remarkable. The record improved from 56–106 to 87–67, attendance more than doubled, they had their first MVP since Nellie Fox, and they even had a rising star in the broadcast booth.

I thought my teen years as a White Sox fan would include at least a couple of World Series appearances.

I was wrong.

The Sox in the 1970s were like the Oakland Raiders, only without the winning, and many of the fans reflected that personality.

There was always controversy, in the clubhouse, in the locker room, in the corporate boardroom. Just a few of the highlights and lowlights:

- 1973   Some of Allen's teammates begin to express resentment over the preferential treatment accorded the superstar.
- 1973   After complaining about their salaries, Mike Andrews and Rick Reichardt are released.
- 1973   Hitting .316, Dick Allen fractures his kneecap on June 28 and is out for the season.
- 1973   General Manager Stu Holcomb loses a power struggle and is fired.
- 1974   The Sox acquire heel-clicking Ron Santo, one of the South Side's least favorite Cubs players. Unfortunately, Ronnie's just about done, and it doesn't help that the Sox make him DH and play second base.
- 1974   Leading the American League with 32 home runs, Dick Allen abruptly "retires" on September 14. He changes his mind over the winter, but never plays again in a Sox uniform.
- 1974   In a season-ending interview, Bob Waller grows tired of Chuck Tanner's eternal-optimist act and asks some tough questions about the underperforming Sox. Tanner gets pissed and walks off in midinterview, leaving Waller to deliver a monologue about the Sox. Waller is not invited back for the 1975 season.

- 1975　On the verge of bankruptcy, unable to meet payroll, owner John Allyn makes no secret of his desire to unload the Sox on any sucker willing to fork over $6 million for Comiskey Park and $14 million for the team.
- 1975　On Allyn's orders to keep expenses to a minimum, the exploding scoreboard barely fizzles when the Sox hit a homer. On some occasions, it doesn't go off at all.
- 1975　Allyn is about to sell the team to a group that would have moved them to Seattle, when Bill Veeck swoops in at the last-minute and puts together a deal to keep the team in Chicago.
- 1976　The Sox are literally kneecapped once again when Ron LeFlore hits a line drive that shatters Wilbur Wood's knee and effectively ends his career.
- 1976　Veeck outfits his players in short pants for the first game of a doubleheader. They refused to wear the ridiculous getup for the second game. Doesn't matter, as the short-pants Sox will be mentioned forever on every list of the worst sports uniforms of all time.
- 1978　With Bill Veeck as the owner and Bob Lemon and then Larry Doby as the managers, the Sox management team looks like a reunion banquet from the 1950s.
- 1978　The Sox wear those ridiculous old-school uniforms with the collars and *CHICAGO* in early 19th-century script across the chest. They look like extras in a bad movie about the nascent days of the game.
- 1978　A desperate Veeck trades for aging, injury-plagued name players such as Bobby Bonds and Ron Bloomberg, who contribute nothing to the cause.
- 1979　The Sox had a long tradition of great shortstops. Harry Chappas was not one of them. Nevertheless, in March of 1979, Chappas makes the cover of *Sports Illustrated*, primarily because he is five-foot-three, 150 pounds, and he looks a little like the midget Bill Veeck once sent to the plate. Chappas bats .288 in 26 games, but he's a butcher in the field and the Sox send him to the minors.

- 1979   Hard-throwing left-hander Bobby Douglass gets a tryout with the White Sox. But if Douglass couldn't hit a receiver as a Bears quarterback, why do the Sox think he can hit a catcher's mitt from 60½ feet? He can't.
- 1979   Disco Demolition—the most memorable stunt gone wrong in sports history. More on this event in the "Sox Culture" chapter.

The Sox finish the decade with a .469 percentage and only two winning seasons, in 1972 and 1977.

They never reached the postseason.

I didn't mention the 1977 season in that timeline because to this day that's still one of my favorite Sox years of all time—maybe second only to the 2005 team.

Part of this has to do with the nature of the team: the South Side Hit Men, who were more like a bunch of homer-happy 16-inch softball players than a typical White Sox team. More important is the fact that I was a teenager with an Ashton Kutcher *That 70s Show* haircut, a few bucks in my pocket, and the free time to go to about 30 Sox games that year.

The 12-year-old kid in striped T-shirts and Levi's had given way to a gangly teenager with long hair, bell-bottoms, sketchy sideburns, and a thing for the music of Black Sabbath and Boston. At 17, I was still two years away from the legal drinking age in Illinois at the time—but check this out, back in the day they had paper driver's licenses with no photos. That made it obscenely easy to get a fake ID that was reasonably believable. For a couple of years there, I was Larry and my birthday was September 21.

Not that we needed to sneak into bars to enjoy a beer. All we had to do was go to a Sox game.

You could bring beer into the park in those days. Not by the can or by the bottle—but if you filled a dispenser with beer, they just didn't care. I remember entering the park in 1977, and a security guard asked me to unscrew the lid of the gallon jug I was carrying. I opened it up, he saw the beer inside—and he waved me in.

The 1977 Sox were a ragtag collection of rent-a-sluggers, such as Richie Zisk and Oscar Gamble, wacky veterans like Ralph Garr, and brash young players, such as Brian Downing. Their pitching was average at best. They had virtually no speed on the base paths. Their defense was sometimes frightening. But, oh, could they swing the bats. The Sox had nine players in double figures in home runs and set a franchise mark with 192 homers. They were the South Side Hit Men, one of the best nicknames ever given to a sports franchise. (The origins of the name are unclear. I do remember my South Side Hit Men T-shirt, featuring a cartoon drawing of unshaven Sox players holding violin cases.) Harry Caray's most famous plea that year: "Oh, for a long one right about here." More often than not, Gamble or Zisk or Wayne Nordhagen or Eric Soderholm responded.

It wasn't just that the Sox contended for most of the season—it was the manner in which they won games. They'd just sort of keep clubbing you, like Joe Don Baker in *Walking Tall*. Five-run rallies in the bottom of the 7th, come-from-behind wins by scores of 12–10 and 9–8, that kind of thing.

In July of 1977, the Sox went 22–6. In all my years of going to games, I've never heard crowds that loud—and yes, I'm including the 2005 World Series. If you could stretch a decibel meter across the decades, it's entirely possible that the 2005 crowds were louder—but the 1977 fan base was more *intense*.

I didn't realize it at the time, but we probably were the most obnoxious franchise—players as well as fans—in all of baseball that year.

The first weekend in July was all about the Sox, who were hosting the Minnesota Twins in the biggest series at Comiskey Park in at least five years. On Friday, Richie Zisk hit two homers and knocked in all five runs as the Sox defeated the Twins 5–2 before a raucous crowd of more than 35,000 fans. I wasn't at that game, but I was there the next day to see Jim Spencer hit a grand slam in the 4th inning and a three-run shot in the 8th to propel the Sox to a 13–8 win. When the Sox recorded the final out, Spencer stood near the mound and flung the ball deep into the stands, like a rock star hurling a drumstick to the adoring masses.

Sunday was a doubleheader, with Wilbur Wood hurling a complete game, three-hit shutout in Game 1. The second game was more typical of the season, with the Sox building an 8–2 lead after four and hanging on for a 10–8 victory and a sweep of the four-game set.

That was also the game when the infamous curtain call was born.

You can't blame the players for this one. It was our fault. We were just nuts in the stands. I don't know if it was the frustration of all those lousy years, the lingering hangover from the disappointments of the early 1970s, or the fact that I have never seen a higher percentage of fans in their late teens and 20s—but we treated those games more like rock concerts than baseball games. When the Sox took the field in the first, we'd stand and roar as if they were Fleetwood Mac taking the stage. When an opposing pitcher was taken out of the game, we'd stand and sing, "Na na na na, na na na na, *hey heeeeeeeeeeeeeey,* good-bye!"

And when Jim Spencer hit a home run in the first inning of that second game against the Twins, we just wouldn't shut up. We stood on our chairs and cheered, and we kept on cheering, and Ralphie Garr had to step out of the box because he couldn't concentrate, and this obscure pitcher for the Twins named Jeff Holly stood on the mound in bewilderment—so Spencer stood on the top step of the dugout and tipped his cap to the fans, and then we *really* went wild.

That started the craze. Nearly every time a Sox hitter knocked one out of the park, we stood and cheered and *demanded* that he come out for a curtain call. If the other teams disliked us for that "Na Na Hey Hey" stuff and for singing "Take Me Out to the Ball Game" with Harry Caray in the 7th, they despised the curtain call.

Especially the Royals. Oh, how the Royals hated us!

At the end of July, Kansas City rolled into town for a series that was even bigger than the Twins series at the beginning of the month.

The standings among the contenders in the American League West on July 28:

Team	W	L	GB
White Sox	59	37	—
Kansas City	55	40	3½
Minnesota	56	45	4
Texas	52	44	7

There was a huge crowd—more than 45,000—for the first game of the series. The Royals jumped out to a 3–0 lead in the 1st inning, temporarily silencing the fans, but Chet Lemon smacked a three-run shot as the Sox put up a big six-spot in the 3rd, and they held on for an 11–8 win.

I remember being in the left field stands for Saturday's game. The Sox and Francisco Barrios fell behind 3–0 to Sox-killer Paul Splitorff—but we never gave up that year. Sox fans never went home early in the summer of 1977. Soderholm's two-three shot in the 7th put the Sox ahead, and Orta's solo homer in the 8th sealed it. After each home run, there was a standing ovation and a curtain call. When the Sox recorded the final out in the 6–4 victory, we stood and sang the "Na Na" song as the Sox players celebrated on the field, and several members of the Royals lingered in the dugout, watching their season possibly slip away. They were now 5½ games back, and the Sox seemed to be on the roll of a lifetime.

July 31, 1977: a doubleheader against the Royals. We were sitting way, way, way back in the upper deck for this one. All of a sudden, Sox tickets were a tough "get."

Announced attendance for the game: 50,412.

That's more than 10 percent of the Sox' total attendance for 1970.

In Game 1, Marty Pattin and Steve Stone locked up in a classic duel, and the game was tied at 2 after nine. The gritty Stoney took the mound for the 10th inning, but he was touched for two runs before Lerrin Lagrow put out the fire. Down 4–2, the Sox weren't about to give up. Chet Lemon tied it with a two-run blast, Ralph Garr singled in the winning run—and 50,000-plus fans nearly crumbled Comiskey Park with the weight of their celebration. The lead over the Royals was now 6½. If the Sox could complete the sweep, Kansas City would stumble out of town, never knowing what hit them.

It wasn't to be. Dennis Leonard kept the Sox hitters in check, and when Hal McRae popped a homer in the top of the 7th to put the Royals up 5–2, the Sox and the fans seemed wiped out. We just didn't have anything left after all the rallies and parties of the first three games.

After his homer, McRae circled the bases in what seemed to be slow motion. He tipped his cap to the crowd as he rounded third, and he pretended to take a curtain call once he was in the dugout.

The Royals had had it with our *!@#. They won the game 8–4. They left town feeling good about their chances, and they proceeded to get red-hot and leave us in the dust. As much as I hate to admit this, the 1977 Sox are similar to the 1969 Cubs. We had a memorable summer, and there were moments when it seemed as if we were going to win it all—but the truth is, we didn't come that close. The Sox finished 92–70, in third place in the AL West, some 12½ games behind the Royals.

But, as Danny Zuko would say, *oh, those summer nights . . .*

Hey Now, They're All-Stars

July 12, 2005

By the All-Star break, it was clear that this White Sox team was special in ways that transcended their blazing start on the field. General manager Kenny Williams and manager Ozzie Guillen had assembled a perfect blend of veterans and emerging stars who genuinely seemed to like each other. Somehow, moody clubhouse presences, such as A.J. Pierzynski, Carl Everett, and Frank Thomas, were coexisting with upbeat team guys like Mark Buehrle, Aaron Rowand, and Scott Podsednik.

In one of those 21st-century gimmicks designed to stimulate fan interest, the selection of the final All-Star roster spot for each league was to be determined by an online election. Buehrle, Garland, and Konerko had been selected to the team already—and Podsednik was on the ballot for the final spot, along with one fellow underdog, Carl Crawford of the Tampa Bay Devil Rays, and three established stars: Derek Jeter, Hideki Matsui, and Torii Hunter. Scott was a long shot, but the Sox mounted an aggressive campaign. White Sox employees wore *Vote For Scott* T-shirts and pins. A voting booth was set up at the Cell. The Sox had a laptop computer set up in the dugout so Podsednik's teammates could vote for him. Prior to a couple of home games, Buehrle took a microphone and urged fans to vote for his buddy. How cool and retro is that? The guy who would become the starting and winning pitcher in the All-Star game acts like he's on the Durham Bulls and he's trying to help his teammate win a free steak dinner by getting named Player of the Week.

It worked. When the votes were tallied, Podsednik had scored the upset win and had snared the 32nd spot on the All-Star squad.

You gotta love the Yankee-centric headline on the Associated Press story about the voting: PODSEDNIK PICKED OVER YANKEES CAPTAIN JETER.

Guess that's one way to look at it.

After becoming the first White Sox pitcher in 70 years to win his first eight starts, Garland had settled back to earth, but at the break he was still a robust 13–4 with a 3.38 ERA, plenty good enough to make the All-Star team.

Buehrle was named the American League's starter. He pitched two scoreless innings, fanned three, and picked up the victory. Podsednik and Konerko both got in the game, but sPod never got to the plate and Konerko fanned in his only at-bat.

No matter. The American League won the game, thus securing home field advantage in the World Series—and this year, that might actually mean something to Sox fans.

Not that I agree with this stupid idea. Here's a thought: How about giving home field advantage in the World Series to *the team with the best regular season record*? Why not reward the club that performs better over a 162-game stretch? Hey, I was thrilled that the Sox were going to have the chance to host four home games in the World Series—but was it really Houston's fault that Baltimore's Miguel Tejada homered off the Braves' John Smoltz in the All-Star game? To be sure, the Sox deserved the home-field advantage—but only because their regular season mark was superior to that of the Astros.

Even with four players on the All-Star roster and the best record in the game, the Sox remained one of the least popular teams in baseball. A poll conducted later in the summer will find that only 1 percent of fans consider the Sox to be their favorite team. For the 1 percent, though, the first half of the season had been glorious. The standings at the All-Star break among the top three teams in the American League Central:

Team	W	L	GB
White Sox	57	29	—
Minnesota	48	38	9
Cleveland	47	41	11

The Chicago media were cautiously optimistic—but the media in Minnesota and Cleveland were all but handing the AL Central to the Sox.

TWINS EMBRACE WILD-CARD HOPES: DIVISION RACE BECOMES MORE OF A LONG SHOT was the All-Star break headline in the *Saint Paul Pioneer Press*.

WITH MILD SLATE ON TRIBE'S PLATE, A WILD-CARD DATE? asked the *Cleveland Plain Dealer*.

Still, we had our worries. Joe Crede's back. Frank Thomas's foot. Dustin Hermanson's back. Orlando Hernandez's stamina. Damaso Marte's everything.

I figured the Sox might come out of the break with a mild case of complacency. They had the big lead; they were basking in the glow of the All-Star triumph. It was only natural that they'd suffer a bit of a letdown.

Not with Ozzie at the helm. He's got the killer instinct of Jason Voorhees on Friday the 13th.

The Sox won five straight out of the break, with a four-game sweep (including two shutouts) at Jacobs Field that seemed to be the foot on Cleveland's throat. These guys were done, the Twins were fading, and we might as well start blocking out dates in the first week of October.

Here's how the AL Central looked on August 1:

Team	W	L	GB
White Sox	69	35	—
Minnesota	54	50	15
Cleveland	55	51	15

If the Sox lost 10 in a row and either Cleveland or Minnesota won 10 straight, the Sox would *still* have a comfortable five-game lead. There were two months left to go. Barring an utter and complete breakdown, the Sox were looking at the first postseason appearance in five years.

All-Stars

White Sox All-Stars, 1966–2005

1967	Tommie Agee, Ken Berry, Joel Horlen, Gary Peters
1968	Tommy John, Duane Josephson
1969	Carlos May
1970	Luis Aparicio
1971	Bill Melton
1972	Dick Allen, Carlos May, Wilbur Wood
1973	Dick Allen, Pat Kelly
1974	Dick Allen, Wilbur Wood, Ed Herrmann
1975	Bucky Dent, Rich Gossage, Jim Kaat, Jorge Orta
1976	Rich Gossage
1977	Richie Zisk
1978	Chet Lemon
1979	Chet Lemon
1980	Ed Farmer
1981	Carlton Fisk, Britt Burns
1982	Carlton Fisk
1983	Ron Kittle
1984	Richard Dotson
1985	Carlton Fisk, Harold Baines
1986	Harold Baines
1987	Harold Baines
1988	Ozzie Guillen
1989	Harold Baines
1990	Ozzie Guillen, Bobby Thigpen
1991	Carlton Fisk, Ozzie Guillen, Jack McDowell
1992	Jack McDowell, Robin Ventura
1993	Jack McDowell, Frank Thomas
1994	Frank Thomas, Jason Bere, Wilson Alvarez
1995	Frank Thomas
1996	Roberto Hernandez, Frank Thomas
1997	Frank Thomas, Albert Belle
1998	Ray Durham
1999	Magglio Ordonez
2000	James Baldwin, Ray Durham, Magglio Ordonez
2001	Magglio Ordonez
2002	Mark Buehrle, Paul Konerko
2003	Esteban Loaiza, Magglio Ordonez, Carl Everett
2004	Esteban Loaiza
2005	Mark Buehrle, Paul Konerko, Scott Podsednik, Jon Garland

10

Sox Culture
October 22, 2005

Less than one hour before the first World Series game on the South Side in 46 years, I made my way through the media entrance, took the walkway inside the bowels of U.S. Cellular Field, walked through the photographers' bin next to the Sox dugout, and stepped onto the field. I couldn't help but think of another Sox game in 1979, when my brother Bob, armed with a professional-looking camera and a lot of moxie, quietly hopped the infield fence before a game and snapped photos of Yankees veterans Reggie Jackson and Tommy John, among others. Nobody kicked my brother off the field. He snapped up a few batting practice baseballs, dropped them into his photography bag, hopped back over the fence, and said, "Think I got some pretty good shots out there."

Thirty years later, my brother is in the stands with my father, and I'm on the field with my media credentials prominently displayed around my neck—and I'm probably more worried about getting kicked off the field than my brother was in 1979. You're not supposed to be inside the Field of Dreams—you're supposed to be watching it on TV, or if you're lucky, from your seat in the stands.

But, of course, I'm there for legitimate reasons. I'm snapping a few pictures because it has occurred to me only this week that it might be fun to write a book about the Sox—and more immediately, I'm on the field to meet with a producer from ESPN who wants to interview me about being a "celebrity" White Sox fan.

Celebrity Sox Fans

Never mind the bandwagon-jumpers. Here's a list of some *real* fans who frequented the Cell and/or Comiskey well before the 2005 season.

Richard J. Daley

Richard M. Daley

William Daley

The whole darn Daley family

Steve Dahl

James Denton

Bernie Mac

Jerry Springer

Jean Shepherd, author of *A Christmas Story*

George Wendt

Dennis DeYoung

And, um . . . well, I think that's about it.

Celebrity, as in I'm the cohost of a nationally syndicated television show about the movies. Celebrity, as in "Let's face it, there are dozens of famous Cubs fans, but who do the Sox have? George Wendt? Dennis DeYoung from Styx? Oh, and that guy from the movie show. The other guy. He's a Sox fan, right?"

I get it. I'm fine with it. I understand that if I loved the Cubs as much as I love the Sox and the Cubs were the team in the World Series, the media wouldn't exactly be beating down my door. Why would they need to talk to me when they could interview everyone from Bill Murray to Billy Corgan to William S. Petersen, and that's just a partial list of the Williams who are famous Cubs fans.

This is the way it goes with Sox Culture. We have our traditions, our movies, our books, our folklore—but it's not nearly as well known or as widespread as the popular culture surrounding the Cubbies, the Red Sox, or the Yankees. Nevertheless, we celebrate it.

As the fans file into the ballpark and the players keep loose by playing catch, stretching, and doing half-speed runs around the warning track, the local and national crews from Fox have prime spots down the base lines, while other reporters do stand-ups near the on-deck circles and home plate. Sox officials try to keep us from trampling on the sod, which gleams emerald green but has been soaked by the rain.

Here's a tidbit you might not know about all those recorded interviews you see with all those talking heads on all those programs on E!, ESPN, MSNBC, and the Fox News Channel: Most of the time, the anchor or reporter who's fronting the story is nowhere near the scene during the actual question-and-answer period. Oh, sure, Lesley Stahl will sit down with Dick Cheney, and Barbara Walters will go one-on-one with Tom Hanks—but to feed the insatiable appetite of the thousand-channel cable monster, to churn out interview after interview after interview, you need so many sound bites that it would be impossible for the on-air talent to be there at every turn. So you get a producer and a camera operator and maybe a sound and lighting person, and they do all the legwork. The producer stands off-camera and asks the questions, and you look at the producer and give your answers, and then they cut and paste it together. (This is different from the live, or the live-to-tape, interviews on shows such as *The O'Reilly Factor*, when you're in a little room in Chicago, and the host is in New York or L.A., and you answer the questions while staring directly into the camera. If you focus your gaze elsewhere for even a moment, you look like a lying, shifty eyed criminal.)

So it was with the ESPN interview. The producer asked me a series of questions about the White Sox, including my picks for Hollywood actors who could play key members of the team in a movie. (I thought Benicio Del Toro would make a good Ozzie.) As the interview progressed, other reporters lingered nearby—and as soon as I was done with ESPN, at least four other media outlets tried to grab me. Not because I'm me and I'm so great, but because there wasn't a single other nonsports, semi-recognizable personality in sight. Within a minute of completing the ESPN interview, I had a microphone in my face and I was hooked up to an earpiece, and I was on the air . . . somewhere with Larry Bowa. I believe it was a satellite radio interview. After that, I talked to a couple of radio reporters and a print guy with a tape recorder—and then I was hustled down the third base line, where I joined Corey McPherrin of the Fox affiliate in Chicago, along with former Sox pitcher "Blackjack" McDowell. We were perched on canvas-backed director's chairs, encircled in a blinding light.

Asked for a prediction, I said I had a sneaking suspicion that Roger Clemens was a bit more banged up than he or the Astros were letting on, and that he could be making an early exit from the game. McDowell just shook his head, and when we were off the air he muttered something about Clemens "only being one of the greatest pitchers ever." Maybe he thought I was disrespecting the Rocket, but I was just going on a hunch, based on the way Clemens seemed to be laboring in his last start against the Cardinals. Besides, I wasn't about to say, "I figure Houston wins this one on a shutout from Clemens." Where's the fun in that?

♩   ♩   ♩

In a later chapter I'll have a bit more about my on-the-field adventures before Game 1—but I wanted to share my interview story with you in the "Sox Culture" section as evidence that the Sox don't have much celebrity juice.

NO CELEBS? NO PROBLEM was the headline in an October 12, 2005, story in the *Sun-Times*.

"The Boston Red Sox have actors Ben Affleck and Jennifer Garner as fans," wrote Dave Newbart and Mark J. Konkol. "The Cubs count Bill Murray and Billy Corgan in their ranks. But at Sox Park, there are virtually no celebrities around, except for Mayor Daley and former Sox minor leaguer [and Bulls great] Michael Jordan.

"'We don't need celebrities here,' Sox chairman Jerry Reinsdorf said. "We have real fans."

Damn straight.

From the time I was seven until I was 27, I attended literally hundreds of Sox games—and I can't think of a single incident in which there was a bona fide celebrity sighting. Of course, in those days I was sitting in the outfield stands or in the far reaches of the upper deck—so if Alan Alda or Farrah Fawcett or Eddy "Electric Avenue" Grant or some other pop icon of a particular era *had* been at a Sox game, I might not have seen Alan/Farrah/Eddy. But I'm reasonably certain Comiskey Park wasn't teeming with celebs back in the day. There would be a minor flurry of excitement if we had a Chet Coppock sighting, for crying out loud. Kids would be excited if they got Bill Frink's autograph.

In later years, you'd occasionally see a local jock from the Bears or the Bulls or maybe Dennis DeYoung from Styx—and of course, the mayor. Say what you will about the Daleys as a political dynasty, you can't fault their loyalty to their neighborhood team. Richard J. Daley, Richard M. Daley, Bill Daley, the whole lot of them, have always been White Sox fans and have never tried to sugarcoat that reality. It's not that Richie Daley rooted for the Marlins against the Cubs in 2003—but he certainly didn't try to pretend it was HIS team in the playoffs. His team is on the South Side.

Unlike Illinois Governor Rod Blagojevich, a diehard Cubs fan who tried to sprinkle himself with some of the Sox' glory dust in '05, or Hillary Clinton, a Park Ridge native and Cubs fan who pandered to Yankees fans in a quest for votes, the Daleys are legitimate sports fans—and the voters respect that. We're not idiots. We don't see Governor Blago in a White Sox jacket or Senator Clinton in a Yankees hat and actually *fall for that crap.*

Besides, who the hell votes for a candidate based on that person's favorite baseball team? I don't care if my chosen candidate is a Cubs fan— as long as he's consistent with it and he doesn't straddle the fence or switch allegiances in mid–pennant race. I'm not going to vote for you because you're a Sox fan or against you because you're a Cubs fan—but I might vote against you if you're a flip-flopping cynic. That tells me something about your character, or lack thereof.

That's why I had such a problem with John Cusack's seemingly sudden interest in the Sox in autumn of 2005.

I don't know John Cusack, but I'm a fan of his work. He's a natural talent who puts a quirky, smart, everyman spin on his roles, in terrific films ranging from *Say Anything* to *The Grifters* to *High Fidelity.* (Not to mention *Eight Men Out,* with Cusack as Black Sox third baseman Buck Weaver.) If anything, Cusack is underrated as an actor because he's not as flashy as some of his peers. By now, the guy should have a couple of Oscar nominations on his resume, just like his sister, Joan, who is widely known as the "nicer Cusack."

What pissed me off was Cusack's attempt to pass himself off as a Bi-Soxual—equal parts Sox fan and Cubs fan—after the Sox were in the playoffs in 2005. I don't know, maybe I missed it, but in all my years of going to Comiskey and the Cell, I never saw Cusack in the stands, and I never heard about him going to any games. (Nor did a Nexis search turn up a single item about Cusack attending a Sox game from 1985, the year of his first starring role in *The Sure Thing*, to 2005. You'd think that in two decades of being a movie star, a Cusack sighting at a Sox game would have been recorded at some point by the media. I'm not saying he never ventured to the South Side. I'm just saying he spent a lot more time on the North Side.) I'm not doubting Cusack when he says he's a fan of both teams—but don't try to tell us it's a 50/50 thing. The guy lived at Wrigley Field in 2003 when the Cubs were making their playoff push. And there's this: When Oprah asked him to describe a perfect day, Cusack said: "I had one the other day! I woke up, and I had breakfast with [friends], and then we went on their boat. I came back and went to a Cubs game. In the evening, I went and had dinner with my sister, two nephews and mom and dad. Perfect! A beautiful June day, and the Cubs won!"

There's nothing wrong with that—though something tells me a truly perfect day for the "lad" might also involve a starlet or two—but you'll notice there wasn't any mention of the Sox in that "perfect day" scenario. Nothing about both teams winning, or the Sox and Cubs meeting in some fantasy World Series scenario.

Let's put it this way: if the Cubs and Sox *did* meet in the World Series, who do you think John Cusack would be rooting for?

Exactly.

But the Cubs were dead and the Sox were hot in 2005, so there was Cusack calling Jerry Reinsdorf's office trying to get tickets for Game 1 of the American League Championship Series against the Angels—and there was Reinsdorf turning him down. Cusack then reportedly called Reinsdorf and said he was a Sox fan as well as a Cubs fan, and it must have worked, because there was Cusack at Game 2, in a suite, wearing a White Sox cap.

"I made sure I cleared that up with Mr. Reinsdorf," Cusack told MLB.com. "I'm a fan of both teams. I grew up loving the Cubs and the Sox. I'm not sorry. I won't apologize for it. I'm just a fan of Chicago baseball."

Well I think that's friggin' *weak*—and real Cubs fans and real Sox fans would agree with me. One more thing. Cusack makes millions per film—and yet he's calling the Sox chairman for tickets? Geez. When I wanted to

Before Game 1 of the 2005 World Series, members of the 1959 team pose with Southpaw, the annoying mascot. PHOTO COURTESY OF RICHARD ROEPER

Note to Cubs fans: Long before he moved to the North Side, Harry Caray was a South Side legend.

PHOTO COURTESY OF THE *CHICAGO SUN-TIMES*

Bill Veeck was like a cool dad who actually encouraged you to turn up the volume on your stereo. Check out the speakers he installed in center field in the 1960s. PHOTO COURTESY OF THE *CHICAGO SUN-TIMES*

A rare sight in 1967: the Sox actually scoring a run.

PHOTO COURTESY OF THE *CHICAGO SUN-TIMES*

From my collection of Sox memorabilia. Note the *Sports Illustrated* cover of Dick Allen with cigarette. PHOTO COURTESY OF RICHARD ROEPER

The Sox-O-Gram, aka the First Blackberry. PHOTO COURTESY OF THE *CHICAGO SUN-TIMES*

My brother snapped Reggie Jackson in the days before Sox fans were running onto the field to tackle coaches and frighten umpires.
PHOTO COURTESY OF BOB ROEPER

That's not the 1968 Democratic Convention, it's Disco Demolition. Many records were harmed in the making of this promo. PHOTO COURTESY OF THE *CHICAGO SUN-TIMES*

1983: Jose Cruz scores the winning run and the Sox are AL West Champs.

PHOTO COURTESY OF THE *CHICAGO SUN-TIMES*

Comiskey Park II as it looked shortly after its birth in the early 1990s.

PHOTO COURTESY OF THE *CHICAGO SUN-TIMES*

PLAYER PROFILE

Q & A WITH OZZIE GUILLEN

Shortstop Ozzie Guillen has been among the league's top hitters so far this season.

Ozzie has developed into one of the best defensive shortstops in all of baseball.

A Chicago legacy was born on December 6, 1984, when then-General Manager Roland Hemond traded Sox pitchers LaMarr Hoyt, Todd Simmons and Kevin Kristan to San Diego for pitchers Tim Lollar, Bill Long, infielder Luiz Salazar and a little-known Venezuelan shortstop prospect named Ozzie Guillen.

This fun-loving shortstop has given Sox fans many reasons to cheer. The affable Guillen has blossomed into one of the premier shortsops in the game, making the trade one of the best in Sox history.

Guillen continues the legacy of Venezuelan shortstops, following in the footsteps of Luis Aparicio and Chico Carrasquel. Guillen, who made his major league debut April 9, 1985, took the league by storm, easily winning the Baseball Writers of America balloting for American League Rookie of the Year.

Ozzie's consistent play has continued over the years, with each season showing a marked improvement. In 1988 he was named to the A.L. All-Star team but did not play, due to an injury. Now, in 1990, Ozzie has been on a tear. Always outstanding defensively, Ozzie has become an offensive threat, leading all Sox players through mid-season in batting average and was among the A.L. leaders, as well.

What makes this vivacious Venezuelan tick? Read on to find out!

What do you think about the 1990 White Sox and how does this year differ from other years here at the White Sox?

"A winning attitude. That is the difference this year. Everyone is thinking positive. We are winning, and winning is contagious. Our pitching staff is different from years before. This year everyone has been pitching well consistently all year long. Everybody in the clubhouse has the 'winning attitude,' we're all having a lot of fun."

What were your feelings when you found out you were named co-captain with Carlton Fisk?

"I felt honored to be named co-captain with Carlton. I mean, to be 26-years-old and to be named a co-captain which really is a leader of the team, is a lot of responsibility. I am proud to have this job. This is the first time in 60 years the White Sox have had captains. I think it was a good thing to bring back. Having co-captains is a good thing for the team. It has been a positive all the way around."

What has been the most memorable moment of your career so far?

"The most memorable moment of my career would have to be in 1985, when I was voted Rookie of the Year. That was a big thrill. I knew I could play well, but to be recognized around the league was really special.

Another great moment was when I made the All-Star team in 1988. Just being around all the best in baseball was exciting, even though I couldn't play. I also remember when Tom Seaver won his 300th career game in 1985 at Yankee Stadium. I had the game-winning hit, it was very exciting."

This being the last year of Comiskey Park, what are your memories of this place and are you looking forward to playing in the new park next year?

"Yes, I am looking forward to getting out of here. We needed a new ballpark and now we are getting it. The new park will have better conditions for the players and everybody else involved. Not that Comiskey Park was such a bad ballpark. It was great in its day, but it is not in good condition now like it was in the old days. I will miss it. There have been a lot of great ballplayers here. The history and tradition of the park will be missed, but we will start a new history and tradition across the street."

If there was something you wanted Chicago fans to know about Ozzie Guillen, what would that be?

"Ozzie Guillen is kind of wild and crazy in his house as well as at the ballpark. Ozzie Guillen always has fun on and off the field. But most of all, I love my family more than anything else in the world. They are the most important thing to me."

51

From the 1990 Sox program: a profile of a young shortstop. Wonder what happened to that guy. PHOTO COURTESY OF RICHARD ROEPER

An autograph-seeking fan reminds Michael Jordan that he's better off with a bigger ball. PHOTO COURTESY OF THE *CHICAGO SUN-TIMES*

This was not Photoshopped, honest! Here I am, on the field before Game 1 of the World Series. PHOTO COURTESY OF THE *CHICAGO SUN-TIMES*

Sox players just minutes before Game 1 against Houston. I kept waiting for someone to tell me to get off the field. PHOTO COURTESY OF RICHARD ROEPER

April 2, 2006: Mark Buehrle unleashes the first pitch of the 2006 season. PHOTO COURTESY OF RICHARD ROEPER

get some extra tickets for playoff games, I paid a broker. I didn't suck up to the team owner.

Also catching flak for sending mixed signals was James Denton, the *Desperate Housewives* star who once was a bartender at Harry Caray's. Denton was on record as saying he preferred the Sox during his time in Chicago—but photos surfaced of him in a Cubs jersey at Wrigley Field. I'll give Denton a pass on this. He's a guy on a TV show featuring a bunch of hot women who are more ruthless in seeking media heat than guided missiles. He's gotta do what he's gotta do during his short window of opportunity to make a name for himself.

Bernie Mac also took a lot of heat from Sox fans. The south suburban resident had long proclaimed his loyalties to the Sox, especially when he was promoting the baseball movie *Mr. 3000.* On *Good Morning America* in 2004, Charles Gibson asked Mac, "[Were you a] White Sox kid or a Cubs kid?"

Mac answered, "White Sox. You know, South Side, black kid. You know, Cubs, rich folks . . ."

But Sox fans didn't dig it when Mac showed up at Wrigley Field and sang "Take Me Out to the Ball Game" in Game 6 of the NLCS against the Marlins—that's right, the Bartman game. As the Sox made their run in '05 and Mac began showing up for games, Chicago radio personality Steve Dahl repeatedly played a clip of Mac saying he was "done with the White Sox." Mac was taking so much heat for his apparent flip-flop that he had to make a public declaration. The headline in an October 24, 2005 story in the *Sun-Times* read: MAC ATTACK: "I AIN'T NEVER BEEN NO CUBS FAN."

Beers Through the Years

Featured Beers at Sox Park

1966	Hamm's	1982	Budweiser
1968	Meister Bräu	1984	Old Style and Budweiser
1972	Falstaff	2000	Miller
1980	Stroh's		

The Voices of the Sox

From the mid-1960s to present day, the voices of the Sox from selected years:

RADIO

Year	Station	Announcers
1966	WCFL	Bob Elson, Bob Finnegan
1971	WTAQ/WEAW	Harry Caray, Ralph Faucher
1974	WMAQ	Harry Caray, Lorn Brown
1977	WMAQ	Harry Caray, Jimmy Piersall*
1981	WBBM	Harry Caray, Jimmy Piersall†
1982	WMAQ	Joe McConnell, Early Wynn
1992	WMAQ	John Rooney, Ed Farmer
2006	WSCR	Ed Farmer, Chris Singleton

TV

Year	Station	Announcers
1966	WGN	Jack Brickhouse, Lloyd Pettit
1972	WFLD	Jack Drees, Bud Kelly
1974	WSNS	Haray Caray, Lorn Brown
1980	WSNS	Haray Caray, Jimmy Piersall
1984	WFLD‡	Don Drysdale, Hawk Harrelson
1993	WGN/Sportschannel	Drysdale, Tom Paciorek
2005	Multiple stations	Hawk, Darrin Jackson

*Along with Lorn Brown and Mary Shane
†Also, Rich King and Joe McConnell. This was Harry's last year with the Sox. I'm not sure what he did after that.
‡The Sox were also on Sportsvision—not that anyone was actually watching Sportsvision.

"The Cubs asked me would I [sing 'Take Me Out to the Ball Game' in 2003]," said Mac. "I said yeah. I'm from Chicago, and we've finally got a winner, and I didn't want to not support them.

"I ain't never been no Cubs fan. They hate us, and we hate them."

Maybe so, but we don't usually show our hatred by donning Cubs gear and singing, "Root, root, root for the champions!" at Wrigley Field during a playoff game.

I've seen Jerry Springer at White Sox games. To paraphrase Bernie Mac, I ain't never seen no Oprah Winfrey at a White Sox game. I don't recall hearing about Oprah ever attending ANY sporting event in Chicago, not even during the reign of Michael Jordan and the Bulls in the 1990s. She's not a sports fan, she doesn't pretend to be a sports fan—and that's fine. Oprah Winfrey will quaff a beer on the South Side around the same time I load up on candles and soaps featured on oprah.com.

That didn't stop Oprah from welcoming the Sox to her show just after the World Series. But what the heck, the players seemed to get a kick out of it, and Oprah didn't even pretend that she knew a thing about baseball. It was just a quick chat, with nobody on the team getting anywhere near Tom Cruise's jumping sofa.

We know Oprah's not a Sox fan. We know Denton and Mac are Sox fans that cheated a little bit on the North Side. That we can forgive.

We believe Cusack when he says he's a fan of both teams. But if the Cubs ever make it to the World Series, it'll be interesting to see how Cusack spins the whole Bi-Soxual thing.

Where is the Sox' place in popular culture? They're not the Yankees or the Red Sox or the Cubs or the Dodgers. The Sox don't have as many celebrity fans, they're not the subject of nearly as many books and documentaries, and they don't have the lore. As the Sox were storming through the postseason in 2005, it seemed as if half the national stories out there were about how the Sox weren't nearly as popular as the Cubs.

From the October 10 edition of *USA Today*:

> When the Boston Red Sox won the World Series last year, every conscious soul in North America knew it ended the Curse of the Bambino, triggering an avalanche of celebratory products ranging from $130 DVD boxed sets to love tomes from best-selling horror authors. Exorcism!
>
> When the Chicago Cubs came close two years ago, the nation embraced the Loveable-Losers-turned-winners, until fate struck in the outstretched hand of an overeager fan (not to mention the bumbling hands of the shortstop). Curses!

On the South Side, the White Sox and their fans have been without a
championship for almost as long. But they suffer in silence. As the second
team in the Second City, they get no respect, not even for historic droughts . . .

[I]t's a mystery why the White Sox's streak of empty Octobers pales so in
comparison to Boston and the Cubs, who last won the World Series in 1908.
In the nation's consciousness, it's *The Jerry Springer Show* compared to *Oprah*.

Gee, thanks.

In that same piece, Paul Konerko pointed out that Boston has just one
team while Chicago has two, "and there's only so much misery that people can project out there. It's split over two teams."

So true. Even with all those Celtics championships (and just recently,
the triumphs of the Patriots), Bostonians have managed to convince
themselves that they're the most noble, most long-suffering fans in all
the land. A lot of this has to do with so many of them being Irish, and I
can say that because I'm Irish. Also, the Red Sox actually came close to
winning a World Series, most notably in 1975 and 1986, so they had more
dramatic disappointments. The Cubs and the Sox have had their heartbreaks—but most years, our teams were just bad. There's no romance in
just being bad. As Guillen put it last year, it's not about curses, it's about
having "horse*!@# teams."

This is not to say there isn't a rich and varied Sox Culture. The Sox
might not have the cachet of the Yankees or Red Sox, but they've made
a bigger impact on the popular culture than other senior franchises,
including the Cardinals, the Giants, the Indians, the Orioles, the Pirates,
and the Tigers. The Sox have made their presence known throughout the
pop landscape, from hip-hop artists who dig the silver-and-black look to
the "Na Na Hey Hey" tradition at sports arenas to movies such as *Eight
Men Out*.

Granted, it's not always been a positive thing. In the movie *Angels in
the Outfield*, the White Sox are the villains. In *Only the Lonely*, John
Candy's lovable-loser cop is such a White Sox fan that he arranges a private picnic at Comiskey Park. It's a nice gesture and all, but the Candy
character is such a mope compared to, say, Cubs fan Ferris Bueller, who
goes to a game at Wrigley Field and catches a foul ball. (Legend has it
that writer/director John Hughes wanted Ferris to be a Sox fan, but how

> ## *Burn Your Own Sox CD*
>
> "Thunderstruck" —AC/DC
> "He's a Pirate" —Klaus Badelt
> "Don't Stop Believin'" —Journey
> "Na Na Hey Hey Kiss Him Goodbye" —Steam
> "Let's Go Go Go White Sox" —Captain Stubby and the Buccaneers
> "South Side" —Moby
> "South Side Irish" —*neighborhood anthem*

many games do the Sox play on school days? It's *Ferris Bueller's Day Off*, not *Ferris Bueller Takes Cameron and Sloane to a Night Game on the South Side*.) And, of course, *Eight Men Out*, while a helluva film, is about the only team that threw a World Series.

Shoeless Joe Jackson is a key character in another great baseball movie: *Field of Dreams*, which is based on W. P. Kinsella's novel *Shoeless Joe*. In one of the stranger bits of casting in cinema history, Ray Liotta, the pale-skinned, dark-eyed actor who specializes in playing tough guys, mobsters, and cops, was cast as the ghost of Shoeless Joe. When Liotta emerged from that cornfield, I wondered if he was going to try to murder Kevin Costner and his whole family. Liotta's a fine actor, and he seemed a lot more comfortable playing catch than, for example, the chicken-armed Rob Lowe in *About Last Night . . .*, but there was a bit of a problem with Liotta's portrayal of Jackson: He hits right-handed, and Shoeless Joe was a lefty. They couldn't find one guy in Hollywood who could hit from the left side of the plate? Was Robert Redford in *The Natural* the last natural left-handed hitter/actor?

When the outside world does think of the Sox and their fans in a larger-than-baseball kind of way, how do they regard us? Do they note that some of the biggest stars in hip-hop have sported White Sox hats and jerseys? Do they talk about how cool it is that Nike gods Michael Jordan and Bo Jackson tried to spread their wings as members of the White Sox? Do they talk about the Carlton Fisk statue? Are they impressed that Comiskey Park II was the backdrop for the Julia Roberts/Cammie Diaz vehicle *My Best Friend's Wedding*? Do they credit the Sox for the exploding scoreboard, the crazy stunts of Bill Veeck, the shower in center field, the launch point for the Harry Caray version of "Take Me Out to the Ball Game," and the "Na Na Hey Hey" raspberry to the opposition?

No. Sorry, Sox fans, but, No.

If the outside world thinks of the South Side, the team, and the fans at all, they hear the theme from *Cops* more than they hear Moby's "South Side."

Steam

In 1969, pop musician Gary De Carlo met with fellow popsters Paul Leka* and Dan Frashuer in a studio at Mercury Records in New York. De Carlo needed a B-side, throwaway single and he needed it fast, so they dusted off an old, nearly forgotten number from 1961, with a wacky chorus that went, "Na na na na na, na na na na na, hey hey, goodbye."

The narrator of the song wasn't saying good-bye to an old lover—he was exhorting a girl to say good-bye to HER lover, because, after all, "He'll never love you, the way that I love you, cause if he did, no, no, he wouldn't make you cry . . ."

They gave the song an unwieldy title: "Na Na Hey Hey Kiss Him Goodbye." Mercury wanted to release it as a single—but there wasn't a group they could attach to it. It was Leka who came up with the name of Steam. "Na Na Hey Hey" became a number one hit, with lead vocals credited to one Garrett Scott—aka Gary De Carlo, according to the pop legend.

With "Na Na Hey Hey" a surprise hit, Leka put together a touring version of Steam that didn't include De Carlo, who wanted nothing to do with the bubblegum trappings of the song. Steam issued a second single, but it didn't even crack the Top 40, and the "band" was given instant admittance to the One-Hit Wonder Lounge.

Enter Nancy Faust, the energetic organist for the White Sox, who seems to know every song in the history of popular music. In the mid-1970s, Faust started playing "Na Na Hey Hey Kiss Him Goodbye" as the walk-off taunt for opposing pitchers—and for any visiting player or manager who got tossed by the ump. Most of the fans didn't know the real title or meaning of the song, and we sure as hell didn't know Steam—we just liked to bellow, "Hey HEY, Goodbye!"

I remember going to a Friday night game in the late 1970s featuring a miniconcert by Steam. It's entirely possible that nobody on that stage had anything to do with the original recording, but they gamely belted out a couple of cover songs before launching into a spirited rendition of their one and only hit.

Thirty years later, "Na Na Hey Hey" is a staple at dozens of sports arenas, and Faust continues to play it whenever a pitcher hits the showers.

Enough.

I wouldn't mind if we kept singing it on those rare occasions when a player gets tossed—but to do it EVERY TIME a pitcher comes out of the game in this day and age is ridiculous. If Johan Santana shuts down the Sox on three hits over eight innings but the Twins decide to pull him in the 9th because he's up 7–0, should we really be taunting him—or giving him some old-school respect for a job well done? It's also silly to "sing off" a situational reliever who's been brought in to face only one batter. The guy comes in and gets a key strikeout, the manager hustles out and gives him a pat for a job well done—and we're singing "Hey hey, goodbye"?

It's time to say good-bye to the good-bye song.

---

*Leka was also the cowriter for "Green Tambourine" by the Lemon Pipers, the only hit ever written about a street musician who threatens to play any song you want on his tambourine. The funniest thing about "Green Tambourine" is that you don't really hear the tambourine until the very end of the song, and the deejays would usually talk over that fade-out. The second-funniest thing about "Green Tambourine" is that it was featured in the closing credits for the animated children's film *Recess: School's Out.* On lead vocals: Robert Goulet.

They think of the Black Sox.

The Second Team in the Second City.

Disco Demolition.

Streakers.

Smokers.

"The World's Largest Outdoor Tavern."

Brawlers.

The "bad neighborhood."

Fans running onto the field to go after a coach or an umpire.

For years, the Sox have had the dubious distinction of being among the most popular teams among gang-bangers who like the silver-and-black color scheme. I guess the yellow-and-green of the A's just doesn't strike fear in the hearts of your enemies on the mean streets of the city. (Say what you will about those ugly uni's worn by the Sox division champs of 1983—at least the bad guys wouldn't be caught dead in 'em.)

Sox fans know that there's as much drinking (if not more) at Wrigley Field than at the Cell. They know the park has become family friendly to the extreme in recent years. They know that a few idiots running onto the field has nothing to do with 99.9 percent of the fan base. They know that the so-called dangerous neighborhood is mostly friendly, and it hardly comes into play when you're going from your car to the game to your car (or to one of the neighborhood bars).

We know there's a lot more to Sox Culture than the easy stereotypes—and you know what, we don't even mind the easy stereotypes all that much. I went to a lot of games in 1979, and I can assure you that Disco Demolition was far more entertaining than anything else that took place on the field that year.

The Yankees are Frank Sinatra.

The Red Sox are the Standells and Neil Diamond.

The Cubbies are Jimmy Buffett.

The White Sox aren't Journey. They're AC/DC.

And we're proud of it.

"Take Me Out to the Ball Game"

Sox fans loved Harry Caray in the early and mid-1970s. We knew he had a long history with the Cardinals and he had even done a one-year stint in the booth with the Oakland A's, but circa 1974 we felt that he was *ours*. Caray was as much of a homer as Hawk Harrelson—but he was never an apologist. If Tadahito Iguchi loses a pop-up in the sun and it falls behind him in short right field, Harrelson will launch into an extended explanation for the miscue: "Well, that's gonna happen right there. You can't do anything about it, so you just cinch it up and hunker down. Tadahito's as good as anyone I've ever seen on the pop-up to short right, so if he loses the ball in the sun, dadgummit, you KNOW the sun is gonna be tough on their guys, too." Or if Hawk's in a sour mood, he'll simply say . . . nothing. The ball falls behind Tadahito, the guy gets a cheap double, the crowd is making noise—and Hawk won't say a word. He'll just funk it out until the next batter steps in.

When Jorge Orta lost a ball in a game in the mid-1970s, Harry bellowed, "Aw, how could he lose the ball in the sun, he's from Mexico!"

That was Harry Caray. He was a bitchy, funny, acerbic, egotistical, enormously entertaining presence in the broadcast booth, and he lived and died with the White Sox. If Wayne Nordhagen killed a rally with a sky-high pop-up, Harry would bellyache, "Paaaaaaaaahhhhpped it up. That wouldn't be a home run in a phone booth. Boy, oh, boy, he got a fastball right down the middle and he hit it straight up in the air."

But if the Sox came through—nobody was happier than Harry. I can still hear him after the Sox beat Texas with a 9th-inning rally and inched closer to first place in the mid-1970s. My dad recorded the radio call, with Harry literally singing with glee: "The White Sox are coming, tra la la la! The White Sox are coming, tra la la la!"

Harry will never be forgotten, not with all those *Saturday Night Live* skits featuring Will Ferrell, the statue outside Wrigley Field, and the "Take Me Out to the Ball Game" gimmick, and the restaurant—but what sometimes gets lost is the fact that he was a great play-by-play announcer who really knew the game. In 1971 and 1972 Harry's gig with the Sox was strictly radio. (That's one of the reasons it was so much fun to join Caray in the center field bleachers—you didn't get to see the stunt on TV.)

Harry's style was markedly different from Bob Elson's or Vin Scully's, but he was their equal in bringing the action alive for fans who had only his voice to guide them through the action.

In 1973 Harry's profile exploded. The Sox upgraded their radio home from a couple of suburban stations to WMAQ-AM, giving Harry a much bigger audience, and they put him in the TV booth as well, alongside the immortal Bob Waller, who would be succeeded by the immortal J. C. Martin, followed by the immortal Lorn Brown, and finally the occasionally insane Jimmy Piersall, who once said, "I'm crazy, and I've got the papers to prove it!" The Sox were on WSNS, channel 44, a UHF station that never delivered a picture anywhere near as clear as the image on WGN-TV, home of the Chicago Cubs. But among hardcore Sox fans, Harry was a superstar. Whether the Sox were contending for a division crown or fading fast in the stretch, we could count on Harry to reflect the mood of the average fan, whether it was cautious optimism, foolish confidence, or utter disgust.

After the excitement of the short-lived Dick Allen era, the Sox fell into a funk in the mid-1970s, finishing 22½ games out of first in 1975 and 25½ games behind in 1976. In 1976, the Sox were an uninspired club in ugly uniforms. They went 64–97. Nobody in the lineup hit more than 14 home runs, and nobody on the pitching staff won more than 10 games. The Sox' combined attendance for 1975 and 1976 was just a little more than half of what they drew in 1991.

So Harry was probably a little fed up, a little bored, and just maybe a little bit juiced when he started singing "Take Me Out to the Ball Game" for the benefit of the long-haired, beer-drinking fans who liked to sit near the broadcast booth behind home plate and yell "Harry!" and "Hey Harry!" and also "Har-REEEE!" all game long.

Always one to recognize a promotional gimmick, Sox owner Bill Veeck installed a public address microphone in the booth so Harry could share his off-key warbling with the entire park—and so it was in the summer of 1976 that "Take Me Out to the Ball Game" was transformed from a hoary cliché that was ignored by half the fans in the park to a cult phenomenon that still thrives some three decades later at Wrigley Field—long after Harry himself has left this world.

It's funny: I remember Cubs fans making fun of Harry for his corny cries of "Let me hear ya!" and "All right, we need some runs!" They mocked us for our enthusiastic sing-alongs with Caray, in which we sounded about as clear as the Kingsmen doing "Louie Louie." They thought it was really funny when Harry went into a studio in Fort Wayne, Indiana, in the spring of 1978 and recorded a disco version of "Take Me Out to the Ball Game." (The B-side was an even more ridiculous cover of "Na, Na, Hey, Hey, Kiss Him Goodbye.")

Then Harry went North, and they fell in love with him.

We didn't care what Cubs fans thought of Harry. We figured they never liked him anyway, what with him being the longtime voice of their archrivals, the Cardinals. And even though Harry worked on the South Side, he was already the Mayor of Rush Street on the Near North Side in the late 1970s. He lived in a hotel suite on the Gold Coast and he worked the bars in the Division Street area like nobody's business. From a 1978 profile in *Sports Illustrated*:

"It was the shank of a summer evening in Chicago—and Harry Caray, the inimitable White Sox broadcaster, was sauntering up State Street sipping a banana daiquiri."

How great is that! The guy was like a walking one-man Mardi Gras.

Also from *Sports Illustrated*: "Harry's wee-hour constitutionals, particularly those undertaken in the drinking quarter where State and Rush streets converge, have become the occasion for impromptu civic celebrations. Hordes of revelers trail him along the streets, shouting, 'Hey Harry' . . . Cab drivers stall traffic to hail him. Barflies pressed against dusty windows seeking a glimpse of him . . ."

Memo to Cubs fans: Harry became a national sensation courtesy of the superstation exposure on WGN-TV, but he was a local legend well before he came to the North Side.

Not that Caray was universally loved back in the day. Sox players and their wives often pleaded with management to muzzle Caray's criticisms. After Caray encouraged fans to boo an underperforming Richie Zisk, one of Zisk's former teammates said Harry should have his lights punched out. That just made it worse on Zisk. The poor guy didn't know what hit him.

He eventually issued a mea culpa, defending Harry's right to "say anything he wants."

If Caray was Dean Martin, Jimmy Piersall was Jerry Lewis—a mercurial talent given to fits of self-aggrandizement and self-destruction. Caray and Piersall were brilliant together—the veteran broadcaster with a taste for wine, women, and off-key song, and the baseball lifer who as a player was known for his fine defense, his keen knowledge of the game, and stunts like running the bases backward after his 100th career homer and climbing the backstop. (When Piersall was with Cleveland, he once tried to take out the Comiskey Park scoreboard by hurling a baseball at it. This was about as effective as firing a BB gun at King Kong.)

Piersall once tried to throttle Rob Gallas, a local beat reporter who would go on to become the Sox' vice-president of public relations. He got into big trouble as a guest on a TV show hosted by the late columnist Mike Royko when he said players' wives were "a bunch of horny broads," and referred to Bill Veeck's wife, Mary Frances, as a "colossal bore."

In 1982, Piersall was hosting a postgame show, and he said that whoever was coaching the outfielders was doing a lousy job. Sox manager Tony LaRussa and coaches Charley Lau and Jim Leyland drove to the studios and confronted Piersall, with LaRussa accusing Piersall of trying to get Leyland fired. But it was Piersall who was fired from his TV gig after the 1982 season.

By then, Harry was gone, too—to the North Side. If you think the Sox gave up on Sammy Sosa too soon, that was nothing compared to letting Harry go.

Here's how it happened. Heading into the 1982 season, the Sox were set to try a bold new experiment that was the brainchild of co-owner Eddie Einhorn. It was called Sportsvision, and it was a pay-channel with a steady diet of Chicago sports, including the White Sox, the Bulls, the Blackhawks, and the Sting. You'd pay $50 to sign up, and there'd be a monthly subscription fee.

Problem was we weren't used to paying for TV in the early 1980s. Only a few homes had fledgling cable channels such as HBO and ESPN—but on ESPN you could see all kinds of wacky sports from all over the country, and on HBO you could see naked breasts and hear people cursing. Why would we pay to watch the Sox when we'd been getting more than 100 games free our entire lives?

The Sox had a goal of 50,000 subscribers. The Cubs were on powerful WGN-TV, about to become one of the nation's first superstations. A potential viewer base in the tens of thousands, or the tens of millions? That was the "choice" facing Harry. He considered the numbers, factored in the uneasy relationship he had with Reinsdorf and Einhorn—and he bolted for Wrigleyville. It's probably safe to say that Reinsdorf and Einhorn didn't exactly try to tackle Harry and drag him back to the South Side so they could offer him bags filled with money and try to talk him out of it.

The 50,000 figure was wildly optimistic. At best, some 30,000 viewers signed up for Sportsvision. I couldn't afford to subscribe, but from time to time I tried to watch the squiggly, unscrambled Sportsvision signal. It was hopeless. In the meantime, North Siders welcomed Harry with open arms and endless supplies of Budweiser. He was a Cubs fan, a Bud man, and a cult icon in the making.

These days nobody says a bad word about Harry. (Nobody except Milo Hamilton, that is.) But when the Sox clinched the West Division in September of 1983, WGN received permission from Sportsvision to broadcast the final inning and the celebration so that people in Chicago could actually see the damn thing. Reinsdorf was still so bitter that he said, "Wherever you're at, Harry and Jimmy, eat your hearts out. I hope people realize what scum you are."

Geez.

Harry took the "Take Me Out to the Ball Game" shtick to the North Side, and the fans loved it. By the time Caray passed away in 1998, he was so identified with the Cubs that the players actually wore patches on their uniforms with a little cartoon caricature of the announcer. (Ironic, given Harry's career-long tendency to get under players' skins with his blunt critiques.) The Cubs, always an organization willing to exploit a tradition and ride it for every bit of marketing goodwill it could bring, decided to continue the tradition with guest singers. At first they tried to get celebrities or local notables who were actual Cubs fans, but over time it became an "in thing" for just about any visiting celebrity. When you've got Ozzy

Osborne in the booth and he has no idea what he's singing, why he's there, or even who he is, your gimmick has jumped the shark.

These days, "Take Me Out to the Ball Game" is an integral part of the whole Cubbie Experience. As a giant cartoon caricature of Harry looks down on Wrigley Field from a nearby building, the 7th inning stretch is all about the song. The guest singer, wearing his brand-new Cubs jersey or jacket, exhorts the crowd to join him in the unofficial Cubbie National Anthem. Little kids, hot babes, guys with Cubbie tattoos, older fans who still keep score—they all love it. They sing "Take Me Out to the Ball Game" with more pride and emotion than they can muster for the "Star-Spangled Banner." They get tears in their eyes when they think of ol' Harry, and they throw their arms around one another as they do their Harry Caray impersonations, punctuating the song with cries of "Let's get some runs!" and "Ah, you can't beat fun at the old ball park."

I guess you can't hold this against the Cubs and their fans. The Sox are the ones who let Harry get away, and it was classic Caray to take a job on the North Side and stick it to Sox ownership for more than 15 years. Reinsdorf told Harry and Jimmy to eat their hearts out in 1983, but for the next decade and a half, it was Jerry who should have been eating his heart out. Who knows how many fans the Sox lost by going to Sportsvision and cavalierly showing Harry the door in '82?

Disco Demolition

> "CHICAGO—disco is getting rocked and socked in this town, with the battles inspired by a pudgy 24-year-old disc jockey named Steve Dahl and his 'Insane Coho Lips Antidisco Army.'"

> —the Associated Press, August 1979

Like every other Sox fan between the ages of 40 and 60, I make the claim that I was at the infamous "Disco Demolition" game in 1979.

But I really was there. Honest.

Chicago has always been a strong radio town. When I was a little kid, my mom listened to Howard Miller and Wally Phillips in the morning. In the late 1960s and 1970s, I was a huge fan of WLS and WCFL, and jocks such as Bob Sirott, Larry Lujack, and John "Records" Landecker. They wouldn't just read the time and temp and "hit the post" as they talked over the intro to a song—they'd do comedy between songs. (At night, a 50,000-watt AM station could reach 38 states. David Letterman, who could catch the Chicago stations from his home in Indiana back in the day, has said he was influenced by Sirott's show.)

From time to time, Lujack would make a crack about management. He'd gripe nearly every morning about his job. He'd pause and there'd be nothing to hear but dead air and the muffled sounds of Tommy Edwards trying to suppress his laughter. Compared to the canned corniness of the Dick Biondi's of the world, this was groundbreaking radio.

But nothing prepared us for Steve Dahl's arrival in 1978.

These days it's nothing special to hear a morning radio personality make fun of a competitor by name. We're used to the hosts trotting out producers and interns and executives for comic fodder. Listener contests, remote broadcasts, hosts interrupting the newscast for irreverent mono-logues, management suspending the host for insubordination—all that stuff is commonplace now, but when Dahl came to Chicago from Detroit and shattered taboo after taboo while breaking new ground nearly every day, it was like being at the birth of an entertainment revolution. Guys in their teens and twenties didn't just listen to Dahl here and there—we tuned in as soon as woke up, and we stayed locked to that dial until sign off. Other radio personalities had become celebrities in Chicago, but Steve Dahl was the first one to become a rock star.

I woke up one morning in December of 1978, clicked on the clock radio to Steve Dahl's station, WDAI, 94.7 FM—and heard a disco record.

It had to be a joke. Dahl was spinning disco records to mess with our heads. Any second now, he'd come on the air, make fun of the music, and get on with the show.

But it wasn't a joke. Literally overnight, WDAI-FM had gone disco, and Dahl was out of a job. A few months later, Dahl and partner Garry Meier were scooped up by rival station WLUP-FM, where Dahl launched a war on the music that had cost him a job. His parody song, "Do Ya Think I'm Disco?," became a bona fide hit, earning a gold record and gaining Dahl national attention. He and Meier "blew up" disco records on the air and constantly poked fun at the lame music craze sweeping the nation. Dahl formed "The Insane Coho Lips Anti-Disco Army"—and thousands applied for membership cards.

It was all in the name of comedy and ratings, but Dahl had tapped into a culture war that was taking place between two very different groups: the beer-guzzling, shot-drinking, rock 'n' rollers in their jeans and denim vests, and the coke-sniffing, polyester-clad disco crowd. If you were 19 in 1979, you could go to a bar, drink 16-ounce mugs of Old Style for a buck a pop and listen to a Bob Seger cover band—or you could go to a disco, drink Rob Roys, and dance to the sounds of "Funkytown." In my hometown of Dolton, the Ramada Inn gave way to the Nimbus Disco, the largest dance club in the Midwest. A disco in Dolton! Unbelievable. (Eventually the Nimbus gave way to a retirement home.) We stayed away.

Dahl didn't turn the war on disco into a racial thing—but race WAS a factor in some of the fights that broke out in Chicago and in the suburbs. Bars were turned into discos, and discos attracted a racially mixed crowd—and all of a sudden you'd have rock 'n' rollers in the same joints as guys in flowered shirts and giant heels, and women didn't mind dancing with those guys, and somebody's ego would get bruised, and it was on. Sometimes when a guy said he didn't want disco in his neighborhood, he was talking about more than the music.

Not that I'm saying race was a factor on the night of Disco Demolition. We were all there because we were fans of Dahl. I don't know that I even hated disco—the truth is, I loved Travolta in *Saturday Night Fever*, and I thought those Bee Gees songs were pretty damn good. I just wanted to be part of the scene that Dahl and Meier had been promoting on their show.

You have to remember the state of the Sox in 1979. It was another yawner of a year on the South Side. Concerned as always about money, Bill Veeck went with a youth movement, but the problem was that young players like Kevin Bell, Harry Chappas, Richard Wortham, Ross Baumgarten, and Marvis Foley were a lot better at being young than they were at the actual playing part of the equation. The Sox would finish in fifth place in the American League West, 14 games out. They averaged just over 16,000 fans per game.

"Disco Demolition Night" was the brainchild of Dahl and Mike Veeck, son of Bill and a madman promoter in his own right. They came up with the idea of literally blowing up a mountain of disco records between games of a Sox/Tigers doubleheader. Admission would be 98¢ (for the Loop's frequency, 97.9 FM) and a disco record.

As I recall, I used the Silver Convention's "Fly Robin Fly" as my golden ticket to the game. My buddies and I got to the park before Game 1, along with thousands and thousands of other fans who were lining up at the portable ticket booths rimming the park. At some point, the Sox stopped taking the records from fans. Bad decision. That meant that thousands of people were armed with round, sharp-edged pieces of vinyl that could fly like Frisbees. Hmm, wonder what these rock 'n' rollers were going to do with those records once they got inside the park and had a few beers?

We found ourselves in about the 15th row of the right field upper deck. The park wasn't quickly filling. There was a very definite and very different kind of buzz (along with the smell of pot) in the air. In those days they used to have rock concerts at Comiskey when the Sox were on the road: Journey, Santana, the Eagles, etc. The crowd at the "Disco Demolition" game looked and sounded more like a concert audience than a baseball crowd. I'd say the average age was close to Dahl's; he was 24 at the time.

It was Thursday, July 12, 1979. The Sox were actually on a bit of a high going into the game, having won four straight to get their record up to 40–46. They had no illusions about contending, but a .500 season seemed to be in reach.

In the first game of the doubleheader, the Sox went down in meek fashion, 4–1, with Pat Underwood of the Tigers outpitching the immortal Freddy Howard of the White Sox.

Not that half the fans could have told you what was happening on the field. They were too busy unfurling antidisco banners, chanting "Disco Sucks!," and hurling those disco records about. Between innings, grounds-keepers would race onto the field to scoop up records, along with beer cups, hot dogs, album covers, and all manner of debris. My friend Scott actually took a piece of vinyl to the cheek, drawing a small amount of blood. We told him to shake it off, and we ordered another round.

By the end of Game 1, Comiskey Park was the most crowded I'd seen it since the big weekend series against the Royals in 1977. There were at least 55,000 fans in the stands, in the walkways, and on the ramps, with maybe 20,000 more stranded outside.

Steve Dahl had drawn a bigger crowd to Comiskey Park than the Beatles.

As players from both teams took refuge in the clubhouse, a crate filled with disco records was hauled out onto center field.

Even before all hell broke loose, that container was evidence that this was not the most brilliantly conceived plan in the world. Where did they think the album shrapnel was going to go after it was "blown up"? Wasn't it kind of obvious that it would flutter back to the field, which might be a problem for Chet Lemon as he tried to patrol center field in Game 2?

When Dahl and Meier entered the arena, the crowd noise was deafening. Wearing a pseudomilitary outfit, Dahl led the crowd in a chant of "Disco Sucks!" and then started the countdown to the explosion. The crate was ignited with an explosive charge, and the place went nuts as shattered pieces of vinyl flew skyward and smoke billowed about.

After Dahl and Meier left the field, White Sox pitcher Ken Kravec went out to the mound to do some warm-up tosses. Behind him, fans were starting to trickle onto the field—sliding into second base, gathering around a bonfire in center field, scurrying about this way and that. As more and more fans streamed out, Kravec and his catcher gave up and headed for the Sox dugout.

Not for one second did my friends and I think about racing onto the field. We were just trying to figure out if we should try to squeeze through the throng and get the hell out of there, or if we should stay and watch the show, even if that meant Comiskey Park might go down in flames.

We stayed and watched the show.

Shirtless yahoos ripped up home plate and dug up pieces of turf. The batting cage was brought out to center field and demolished. *!@# was flying everywhere. It was apparent within minutes that the security force had no chance of clearing the field.

Bill Veeck hobbled onto the field, grabbed a microphone, and pleaded with fans to return to their seats. The Sox-o-Gram displayed the futile plea *PLEASE RETURN TO YOUR SEATS*. Some fans chanted, "Back to Your Seats!" while others countered with "Disco Sucks!"

In one of the most surreal scenes I've ever experienced, Nancy Faust started playing "Take Me Out to the Ball Game," with Veeck singing in a baritone voice while thousands of fans danced and partied all around him. In the meantime, WLUP-FM disc jockey Mitch Michaels was on the public address system, trying to start up a chant of "Back to your seats, back to your seats!"

Up in the broadcast booth, Jimmy Piersall ripped the fans for "following a jerk," said he'd rather swim than stand on a baseball field, and howled, "This garbage of demolishing a record has turned into a fiasco!"

Channel 44 stopped beaming the images to the stunned fans watching at home. Caray bellowed, "Holy Cow! Can you hear me?" and exhorted people to return to their seats, but he had little success.

Two things got the idiots to leave the field:

A. They wore themselves out. There's only so much running around you can do when you're drunk. The fourth time you round the bases with your shirt off, you start thinking about taking a seat and getting some liquid refreshment.

B. A serious show of force by the Chicago riot police with their shields, their nightsticks, and their powder-blue helmets. If they could run roughshod over the protesters at the 1968 Democratic

Convention, they could handle a bunch of Donna Summer–hating Coho Lips. It took about three minutes for the police to clear the field. They received a standing ovation from the 45,000 or so fans who hadn't stormed the field and had remained in our seats throughout the madness.

After the field was cleared, some of the Sox and Tigers players returned to loosen up, but it was quickly apparent that the field was unplayable. It was announced that the game was being postponed. Veeck told fans to hang on to their rain checks.

"Those weren't fans of baseball," said a pissed-off Piersall in the booth. "They were fans of far out."

A little perspective here: Disco Demolition was a debacle of epic proportions, but it wasn't a "riot." Los Angeles after Rodney King—THAT was a riot. Police arrested fewer than 40 people on the South Side that night, and there were no serious injuries. It could have been much worse.

Game 2 was called off. In those days I used to write the final score on ticket stubs. For July 12, 1979, it read, "Game One: Tigers 3, White Sox 1. Game Two: postponed, Disco Demolition."

The Sox said the game would be made up that Sunday, but Detroit manager Sparky Anderson said, "Only an act of God can cause a postponement. That was no act of God."

Guess it depends on how you felt about disco at the time.

In the record book, the "final score" of that second game is listed as 0–0, with Detroit declared the winner by forfeit. The Tigers finished far back in their division that year, but imagine if Disco Demolition Night had been the deciding factor in either team's fate that year. There are a lot of ways to lose or win a division title, but this would have been one for the ages. As it is, people still talk about Disco Demolition Night—and though there might have been 75,000 people in the vicinity that night, about 400,000 claim to have been there.

We Loved the '80s—Sort Of

November 17, 1981

The "Transactions" feature in the sports section of the *New York Times* contained three items:

> Mets (NL)—Named Bill Monbouquette pitching coach.
> California (AL)—Added Ricky Steirer, pitcher, to 40-man roster.
> Chicago (NL)—Signed Harry Caray to a two-year contract as
>   announcer of Cubs games for WGN radio and television.
>   Caray, in broadcasting for 37 years, had done the Chicago
>   White Sox games for the last decade.

I think we can say with reasonable confidence that item number three ended up having a slightly bigger impact on the game at large than the first two items.

Of course, Harry's move to the North Side was major news in Chicago. The headline from UPI: Holy Cow! Harry Caray Leaves Sox to Broadcast Cubs Games.

The story from Randy Minkoff: "Harry Caray, giving up the White Sox because of their commitment to cable television, said Monday he has signed a contract to broadcast Chicago Cubs games.

"'I would lose my people—cab drivers, bartenders and others who can't afford cable TV,' said Caray.

"The announcement was made by Jack Brickhouse, retired Cubs broadcaster . . .

"Sox owner Jerry Reinsdorf told the UPI, 'I just hope the White Sox fans realize that we made an effort to keep Harry. It was his choice. We wish him well and we'll be disappointed to lose him.'"

Just two years later, Reinsdorf would take time out from celebrating the AL West title to tell a live television audience that Caray and Jimmy Piersall were "scum," so it's debatable how disappointed he was to lose Harry before the 1982 season.

Not that anyone could have predicted just how *huge* Harry would become on the North Side, thanks in large part to WGN-TV's ascension as a superstation available coast to coast. Just as the Sox were trying a before-its-time cable experiment that shrunk their television base to nearly nothing for a considerable chunk of home games, Harry was becoming a fixture in homes all over the country.

You also have to consider Reinsdorf's side of the equation. Imagine taking over a team whose biggest stars were in the broadcast booth. In the late 1970s and early 1980s, Caray and Jimmy Piersall were more popular than anybody on the team—and more difficult to control. They pretty much said what they wanted about the players, the coaches, and the ownership as they did a two-man show that rivaled anything taking place at Second City. The fact that Piersall was a part-time coach for the outfielders didn't stop him from reaming manager Tony LaRussa and just about anyone else who didn't see things Piersall's way.

The Sox were a lousy team in 1980, LaRussa's first full year as manager. They finished 70–90, bad enough for fifth place in the American League West, and at times it seemed as if LaRussa and some of his players were more concerned with the barbs from Caray and Piersall than with improving the quality of play on the field. If you're ducking into the clubhouse during the game to listen to what the announcers are saying, you need a priority check. (After Piersall ripped Greg Luzinski for not running hard on a routine grounder, Luzinski threatened to leave the team via free agency if Piersall wasn't fired.)

After Bill Veeck's wife Mary Frances made a few mild comments about Piersall, he responded by calling her a "colossal bore" on a local talk show. The Sox fired Piersall from his coaching gig, but he remained in the broadcast booth.

In July 1980, *Daily Herald* reporter Rob Gallas asked Piersall about his recent troubles. Piersall responded by trying to choke Gallas.

Horny Broads

The full text of Jimmy Piersall's infamous "horny broads" quote:

> First of all they were horny broads that wanted to get married, and they wanted a little money, a little security and a big strong ballplayer. I traveled, I played the game. I got a load of those broads too.

A month later, the cash-strapped Veeck tried to sell the Sox to Edward DeBartolo, who had designs on moving the team, perhaps to New Orleans. But the American League refused to approve the sale because of questions about absentee ownership and DeBartolo's horse racing interests.

In January of 1981, a group headed by Reinsdorf and Eddie Einhorn bought the Sox—and they made a splash by signing Mr. Red Sox himself, Carlton Fisk, as well as Philadelphia slugger Greg Luzinski, who had the physique, beard, and last name of a guy who could have been playing left field in a South Side 16-inch beer league.

Nineteen eighty-one turned out to be one of strangest years in Sox history. The first few weeks of the season were filled with excitement as the team sprinted to a 10–3 start. Fisk immediately demonstrated his flair for the dramatic by hitting a home run and driving in three runs on Opening Day in Fenway Park. (The Boston fans didn't know whether to cheer or cry, so they did both—and then they talked about it for the next decade or so, because of course anything that happens to Red Sox fans is much more important than anything that happens to fans of any other team.) A few days later, nearly 52,000 fans at Comiskey Park went wild when Fisk hit a grand slam in his home debut with the White Sox.

With a lineup featuring Jim "Light My Fire" Morrison, Chet Lemon, a young slugger named Harold Baines, Wayne Nordhagen, Luzinski, and Fisk, this team had some clout. The pitching was on the rise as well, with young hurlers such as Richard Dotson, Dewey LaMarr Hoyt, Steve Trout (son of Dizzy and a native of South Holland), and Britt Burns.

The 1981 Cubs were a god-awful bunch, and at the time the area around Wrigley wasn't fully yuppified—so we were the bigger draw. Sox home attendance in '81 was nearly twice that of the Cubbies.

On June 12, the Sox were 31–22, just 2½ games behind the division-leading Oakland A's, when the players' union called a work stoppage due to an ongoing dispute over free agent compensation. When play resumed two months later, Major League Baseball announced that the season would be split into two, with the division leaders from each half meeting in a five-game series to determine the champion.

That didn't work out for the Sox, as they faded in September. The Royals won the second-half title with a record of 30–23.

In other words, if the Sox had managed that 31–22 mark in the second half of the season, they would have been in the playoffs. But, as would be the case in 1994, they were thwarted by a labor dispute.

♩   ♩   ♩

The 1982 Sox had more talent on the roster than any team since 1977. They won their first eight games and played solid ball all year long, finishing 87–75, six games out.

I was at Illinois State University and I was working at a lot of part-time jobs in the early 1980s, so my attendance at games was extremely limited. The rock 'n' roll days of the 1970s, when we were teenagers and we'd hit two or three games every home stand—gone. From 1980–82, I caught a total of maybe 10 games at Comiskey Park in person.

The summer of 1983 was a different story. I was out of college and doing some freelance writing. I can't say I couldn't find a job—I just didn't want the jobs that were coming my way. Armed with my mass communications degree from ISU and a wildly unrealistic sense of my value on the open market, I just couldn't accept entry-level jobs with advertising agencies, for technical manuals, or in public relations firms. I'd be sitting in the lobby of some downtown office, wondering if I'd get an offer, and if the offer would be for $14,500 or an even $15,000, and I'd see some 32-year-old guy in a Sears suit hustling past on his way to his cubicle or some meeting—and I'd have to resist the urge to jump out the window.

So I announced that I was a freelance writer, and the great thing about being a freelance writer is that all you have to do is decide that's what you want to be—and there you are. Nobody ever becomes a "freelance dentist" or a "freelance lawyer," but the world is filled with freelance writers, or, as they're known in the 21st century, bloggers.

Making money at it—that's the trick. In 1983, I made just enough to scrape by—and just enough to get to a fair number of Sox games.

The timing couldn't have been more perfect. For the first time in my life, the Sox were bound for the postseason.

When Texas Rangers manager Doug Rader inadvertently gave the Sox their rallying cry for the 1983 season by saying the team was "Winning Ugly," he wasn't trying to insult the team—he was making a very legitimate observation. The Sox weren't blowing away opponents, yet they always found a way to win.

Besides, the Sox WERE kind of ugly—and it went beyond their questionable defense. They had those horrible uniforms, with the double-knit, pullover jerseys and the supposedly modern-looking *SOX* spelled out across the chest. Like most fashion trends of the 1980s, this is not a look that has withstood the test of time.

As for the players, we're talking freaks and geeks. Marc "Booter" Hill? I'm sure he was a heckuva guy, but not a looker. Luzinski and Hoyt looked like bouncers at a bar in Calumet City. Vance Law and Scottie Fletcher could have been the accountant guys carrying the briefcases containing the vote tallies on Oscar night. Julio Cruz, Jerry Dybzinski, and Tony Bernazard looked like porn stars, and Dennis Lamp looked like he should be selling you a lamp in a furniture store. The only regal-looking guy on the whole team was Carlton Fisk—and as much as we all admired Fisk (who wound up living in the southwest suburbs with his family after his retirement), he would always be a Red Sox first, a White Sox second.

In April, Jimmy Piersall managed to get himself fired from his studio gig with the Sox. (He'd already been removed from play-by-play duties.) Rookie Ron Kittle got off to a fast start, but the defense was brutal, the pitchers were struggling, and the Sox were five games under .500 in mid-May. Tom Paciorek was bitching about lack of playing time ("This ain't exactly the 1927 Yankees"), Greg Luzinski was looking fat and tired, and the Sox owners considered firing LaRussa.

The Sox hosted the All-Star Game, but nobody from my neighborhood had the money or the clout to score tickets. We watched the game on TV in Dolton, cheering wildly as Fred Lynn hit the first grand slam in All-Star history and the American League stomped the National League 13–3.

To give you an idea of how mediocre the Sox were in the first half of the season, consider that their lone representative was the rookie Ron Kittle. Fisk, Luzinski, Baines, Hoyt, Dotson—none of these guys was having an All-Star year up to that point.

In the second half the Sox went nuts. The only hot streak to compare with the Sox in the second half of 1983 would be the Sox in the first half of 2005. It was just *W* after *W* after *W*.

LaMarr Hoyt went 15–2.

Richard "Nissan" Dotson went 14–2.

Floyd "The Barber" Bannister went 13–1.

When your Big Three starters go 42–5, it's time for the other teams to *fold up the tent and call it a season.*

The Sox were 22–9 in August and 22–6 in September. Seventeen years after I attended my first Sox game, they cruised to the division title with such ease that it was almost anticlimactic. The official clinching date was in mid-September, but by late August, it was all but over.

On Saturday, September 17, I got in a car with a bunch of buddies and we drove up to Comiskey Park, parking about four blocks away and hiking to the box office, where we managed to score some standing-room-only tickets for that night's game against the Mariners. It was raining, and the start of the game was delayed, but we knew the Bossards would have the field in shape. For the first time since 1959, the Sox were on the cusp of clinching a title—and this time they had the chance to do it in front of the home fans. There was no way this game was going to be rained out.

There were nearly 46,000 fans jammed into Comiskey Park, and we spent much of the game circling around, trying to find a good vantage point. Occasionally, one of my buddies would dash down and grab a seat until the rightful owner would show up and kick him out, but most of the time we just walked the aisles as slowly as possible, catching the game on the fly, buying a beer here and there. The main thing was to be in the park for *the* moment.

When Harold Baines smacked a solo shot to put the Sox up 3–1 in the bottom of the 8th, the crowd nearly drowned out the exploding scoreboard. Not since the summer of 1977 had there been such a buzz at Comiskey.

Workhorse reliever Denny Lamp took over for Jerry Koosman in the 9th—and promptly gave up two runs. Instead of mobbing each other on the mound, the Sox trotted off the field, tied at three with the Mariners.

Rather than being deflated, the crowd ratcheted it up about six notches. I could already feel my voice going as we roared at Mariners reliever Bill Caudill, who couldn't find the plate to save his life. He walked Julio Cruz, he walked Rudy Law—and when he walked Carlton Fisk to load the bases, we sensed the end was in sight.

The immortal Ed Vande Berg was brought in to face the ever-stoic Harold Baines. With one out and the bases loaded, Baines had an at-bat that personified his entire career with the White Sox. He didn't try to do too much, he didn't try to make history, he didn't get out of his comfort zone. He just waited for the right pitch and lofted a medium-deep fly— nothing dramatic, just another easy RBI that just happened to score the run that put the White Sox in the postseason for the first time in two dozen years.

Cruz raced home and did that little leap onto home plate, where he was quickly mobbed by his teammates. Fans streamed onto the field. The scoreboard exploded for what seemed like 10 full minutes.

In the stands, we hugged and high-fived and screamed our lungs out. Next year was here.

In 1983 there were just two divisions in each league and no wild card entries. Win a best-of-five series, and you were in the World Series.

As champions of the West, the Sox squared off against the Baltimore Orioles, with the first two games in Baltimore.

Weirdly enough, my strongest memory of Game 1 is taking out the garbage. I hosted a small party at my parents' house, and as soon as the game was over, I took a Hefty bag filled with beer cans and other trash out to the garbage cans behind my folks' garage. For some reason, I remember the moment as I was walking back to the house, which was still alive with the postgame buzz of a 2–1 White Sox victory, courtesy of a complete game, five-hit masterpiece from LaMarr Hoyt. A win on the road in Game 1 of a five-game series was huge. I thrust my fist into the air, thinking the White Sox are going to the World *!@#king Series.

After that, Winning Ugly gave way to Losing Ugly, as the Sox had one of the most devastating three-game losing streaks in franchise history. It was probably too much to expect them to win both games in Baltimore, so we weren't all that discouraged when Mike Boddicker threw a five-hit, 14-strikeout shutout at the Sox in Game 2. After all, there was going to be playoff baseball on the South Side for the first time in my lifetime—and though I couldn't afford tickets, I was going to be glued to the set for every pitch, as was everybody else in the neighborhood.

Game 3 was a disaster. On a Friday night in front of a raucous home crowd, the Orioles touched Richard Dotson for three runs in the first, immediately taking the fans out of the game. Dotson had nothing. Dick Tidrow was even worse. The O's kept circling the bases. After Mike Flanagan hit Ron Kittle in the knee in the 4th inning, the frustrated Sox got into a beanball war with Baltimore, losing their composure and looking nothing like the team that had won 99 games in the regular season.

Final score: Baltimore 11, White Sox 1.

Even then, we thought we had a chance. Hey, the Sox had blasted the Dodgers 11–0 in the opener of the 1959 World Series only to see the Dodgers come back to win it all; why couldn't we pull off a similar trick?

Britt Burns was on the mound for Game 4. He had been plagued by arm troubles the previous couple of years and he was the fourth starter in 1983, but the Sox were saving 24-game winner Hoyt for a potential deciding game. If they could find a way to win this one, they'd be sitting pretty for a one-game contest for the AL pennant.

Burns pitched the grittiest game of his career, but he was matched by first Storm Davis and then Tippy Martinez. (That's right: the three main pitchers in this game were named Britt, Storm, and Tippy.)

Heading into the bottom of the 7th it was 0–0.

Let's get some runs.

Greg Walker led off with a single, and Mike Squires was called on to pinch-run. Vance Law also singled, with Walker stopping at second.

Pandemonium at Comiskey. Runners on first and second, with nobody out.

Enter the Dibber—Jerry Dybzinski, a utility infielder, a solid bench presence, and a stand-up guy. He was also a career .234 hitter who managed to swat three home runs in six seasons.

The Dibber tried to lay down a sacrifice bunt, but the ball bounced straight up. O's catcher Rick Dempsey grabbed it and fired to third, forcing out Squires.

Runners on first and second, one out.

Julio Cruz hit a sharp single to left—so sharp that Vance Law had no chance of scoring. Law was held up at third—but to Vance's horror, Dybzinski rounded second and kept on coming, suddenly finding himself in no man's land. As the Dibber got caught in a rundown, Law made a break for the plate, but he had no chance. Dempsey was waiting for him, ball in hand, and Law's attempt to bowl him over failed miserably.

Runners on first and second, two outs.

Martinez balked the runners to second and third, but Rudy Law flied out to left, ending the inning. The Dibber's base running error had cost the Sox the chance to score at least one run. It is a gaffe that Sox fans will never forget—but to our credit, we don't blame Dybzinski for losing the 1983 playoffs, and we never obsessed over the play as did Red Sox fans with their constant moaning about Bill Buckner and the 1986 World Series. We knew that (as was the case with Buckner) there were a lot of other factors that had to be taken into account. The game was still tied after nine, and the Sox made the questionable decision of sending Burns to the mound for the 10th. He got the leadoff hitter, but light-hitting Tito Landrum snapped the scoreless tie with a home run into the left field upper deck. The Orioles scored twice more before the inning was over, effectively putting an end to the season. The Sox managed only a Harold Baines single in the 10th, going down quietly as the Orioles gathered on the Comiskey Park infield and celebrated their American League pennant.

Maybe the Sox would have held on to win Game 4 had they scratched out a run or two in the 7th. Even then, though, we don't know that they would have won Game 5. The Orioles won the 1983 playoffs three games to one, and it wasn't because of one base-running gaffe. It was because they performed at a higher level.

The 1983 Sox picked up far more individual decorations than the 2005 Sox. LaMarr Hoyt (24–10) was the American League Cy Young winner. Ron Kittle was named American League Rookie of the Year, and Greg Walker joined him on the All-Rookie team. Hoyt, Luzinski, and Fisk were named to at least one Major League All-Star team. Tony LaRussa was manager of the year, and Roland Hemond was executive of the year.

But it was the Baltimore Orioles who won the American League pennant and the 1983 World Series.

In the off-season, the Sox picked up the legendary Tom Seaver from the New York Mets. At the All-Star break, the Sox of 1984 were in first place. My buddies and I were starting to think the Sox had a chance to become one of the premium teams of the decade. In mid-July, we were certain there'd be playoff baseball in Chicago for the second year in a row.

And we were right. We just had the wrong damn side of town.

As the Sox faded badly in the second half and fell below .500, the Cubbies took the city by storm. One Saturday afternoon in June of 1984, my buddy Shemp—a six-foot-two, 300-plus pounder who lived in Calumet City and yet called himself a Cubs fan—had a bunch of us over to his apartment to watch the Game of the Week featuring the Cubs and the Cardinals. There were about eight of us there—a half-dozen Sox fans and two Cubs fans.

That was the day Ryne Sandberg made the Hall of Fame.

In 1984 Cardinals reliever Bruce Sutter (a former Cub) was nearly unhittable. He had 45 saves in more than 122 innings and an ERA of 1.54. Sutter's signature pitch was the split-fingered fastball, which looked like a fat pitch coming right down the middle until the last moment, when it would "drop off the table." The best hitters in the National League would tell themselves to lay off that pitch—but they couldn't do it. Sutter didn't just retire batters; he made them look silly.

Not Sandberg. Not on this afternoon.

In a game that will live forever on ESPN Classic, Sandberg went five for six with seven RBIs and twice homered off Sutter in dramatic fashion—once to tie the game in the 9th, and again to tie it in the 10th. After the Cubs won 12–11 in 12 innings, a dazed Whitey Herzog compared Sandberg to Babe Ruth.

The Coolest Defensive Play in White Sox History

Before every home game, when the Sox play their greatest hits montage to the sounds of "He's a Pirate" from *Pirates of the Caribbean*, there's one scene that never fails to raise chills: Carlton Fisk defending home plate, tagging out two Yankees in quick succession on the same play.

Here's how it went down. On Friday night, August 2, 1985, the Sox were in New York to take on the Yankees and Billy Martin, who had just returned to the team after being hospitalized with a collapsed lung.

What happened in the 7th inning could not have been good tonic for ol' Billy.

With the scored tied at 3, the Yankees had pinch runner Bobby Meachem at second base and Dale Berra on first. Rickey Henderson sent a long drive to the gap in left-center off Britt Burns—but Meachem hovered near second, waiting to see if Sox center fielder Luis Salazar (I don't remember him either) would be able to run it down.

Berra, in the meantime, had started running, figuring he had a chance to score from first on what looked to be a double or maybe even a triple, given Henderson's speed. But when Meachem finally started moving, he slipped on his way to third base. Third base coach Gene Michael was ready to hold Meachem at third and take the bases-loaded situation—but by that time Berra had already rounded second and was on his way to third. Michael had no choice but to wave Meachem home, even as shortstop Ozzie Guillen was taking Salazar's throw and relaying it to Fisk.

Meachem was a dead duck—but Berra compounded his mistake by running through Michael's stop sign and heading to the plate. Fisk tagged out Meachem, did a neat little side step, and tagged out Berra as well. If Martin or George Steinbrenner or a random Yankees fan had stormed the field, Carlton would have tagged them out too.

The White Sox ended up winning 6–5 in 11 innings.

According to the *New York Times* game report the next day, Martin was asked if he'd ever seen anything like the double tag.

"No, and I hope I never see [it] again," he replied. "I've never even seen one like that in grammar school."

Sandberg would go on to win the MVP in '84, with teammate Rick Sutcliffe earning the Cy Young Award for going a spectacular 16–1 for the Cubs after arriving in a mid-June trade. (A month before that, the Cubs had sent Bill Buckner to the Red Sox for Dennis Eckersley. And we never heard from Buckner again. Ahem.) On a crappy September night in Pittsburgh, the Cubs swept the Pirates and clinched the National League East.

This was a Sox fan's worst nightmare. In a span of just 12 months, we went from celebrating our own division title to watching the Cubbies spray champagne on each other.

Harry Caray was in heaven. (Though he refrained from saying, "Eat your heart out, Jerry Reinsdorf.") Mayor Harold Washington said it was a "great day for the city of Chicago." Vice-President George H. W. Bush, in Chicago on a campaign visit, told the Associated Press that he was "thrilled" for the Cubs and their long-suffering fans. *Tribune* columnist Mike Royko, a lifelong diehard Cubs fan—excepting a stunt when he pretended to switch allegiances—could hardly contain his glee.

"I'm elated!" Royko told the AP after watching the clinching game at the Billy Goat Tavern. "I'm bouncing off the ceiling. It's a remarkable moment. I'm also worried [about the playoffs]. My stomach's all knotted up. I'm sick to my stomach."

Maybe I've got that Sox fan chip on my shoulder, but as I remember it, the city and the media were more excited about the Cubs' win in 1984 than the Sox' win in 1983.

It got worse for Sox fans when the Cubbies took the first two games from the Padres in the National League Championship Series. Game 1 was a 13–0 shellacking; Game 2 a 4–2 victory. All they had to do was win one more game, and they'd be in the World Series for the first time since 1945.

"Oh boy, does it feel great," wrote Royko.

I thought about moving to Nebraska.

The Padres won the first two games in San Diego, but the Cubs jumped out to a 3–0 lead in Game 5, with ace Rick Sutcliffe on the mound. In the 6th, San Diego closed the gap to 3–2—and in the 7th, the Padres put up a four-spot in a rally that was greatly helped by a Leon Durham error. Former White Sox Rich "Goose" Gossage shut down the Cubbies in the 8th and the 9th, and just like that, the North Side dream was dead.

Most of Chicago went into mourning. On the Sox side of town, there was no attempt to hide our glee. Yes, it had been a disappointing season for the Sox, but, at least, we weren't going to have to endure the sight of the Cubs in the World Series.

♫ ♫ ♫

It says something about the generally sorry state of the franchise in the 1980s that the second biggest victory of the decade for Sox fans involved the Padres beating the Cubs. In 1985, Carlton Fisk tied Dick Allen's franchise mark with 37 home runs and Tom Seaver won his 300th game, and Sox fans showed both future Hall of Famers much respect—but it's not as if they had made their bones while members of the White Sox. Fisk wound up playing more years for the White Sox than the Red Sox, but Seaver was a New York Met (and to a lesser extent, a Cincinnati Red) who was just taking a curtain call with the White Sox—like Joe Namath spending his final days with the Rams, Joe Montana with the Kansas City Chiefs, or Bobby Orr with the Blackhawks.

From 1986 to 1989, the Sox pretty much sucked, and I pretty much concentrated on building a career. I'd still go to a half-dozen games a year, but it was just for the fun of being at the ballpark and bitching about the latest folly. The Cubs were taking control of the town, and the Sox were coming up with genius moves like naming Hawk Harrelson their general manager in 1986. These days as Sox announcer and head cheerleader, Harrelson sounds as if he's the foremost authority in the history of the game—but he never talks about his tenure as GM, which was highlighted by such moves as firing Tony LaRussa and trying to make a left fielder out of Carlton Fisk, who absolutely loathed the idea. Harrelson didn't last a single season. He stepped down in late September.

Sox ownership spent most of the late 1980s searching for funding for a new stadium in the suburbs—and barring that, a new home in Florida. The Sox lost 90 or more games in 1989 and in 1990, while the Cubs won another division title in 1989. (That time around, it was the Giants and Will Clark killing the World Series dream.)

In July of 1989, the Sox sent Harold Baines and second baseman Fred Manrique to the Texas Rangers for infielder Scott Fletcher, pitching prospect Wilson Alvarez—and a whippet-thin young outfielder named Sammy Sosa, who was said to have plenty of speed, a great arm, and a live bat, but not all that much home run power. Baines was only 30 years old and he played but 10 seasons for the Sox, but Jerry Reinsdorf retired Harold's number 3. Granted, Baines was a class act and he was the franchise home run leader at the time—but he hadn't even reached the 200–home runs mark. He had to be the least accomplished player ever to have his number retired—and the Sox had to "unretire" his number twice when he rejoined the club in later years. It was just silly.

But at least the Sox were going to stay in Chicago. I was working as a reporter for the *Sun-Times* in 1988 when the word came down through the newsroom that it was all over: the Sox were moving to Florida. "They're gone," said a veteran reporter who knew the inner workings of Chicago and Illinois government better than 99.9 percent of our elected officials. "There's no chance of the Sox staying."

I was sitting right next to this reporter, and I dared to question the assertion. "I can't believe they're going to become the St. Petersburg White Sox," I said. "I'll bet they'll work out a last-minute deal."

The veteran reporter told me I had no idea what I was talking about, and that it was all over. Our front-page story the next day reflected the reporter's sentiment.

Only it wasn't over. Thanks to some classic last-minute maneuvering by Illinois's Governor James Thompson, the Illinois House just beat a midnight deadline and approved a $150 million stadium package for the Sox that kept the team in Chicago. According to the official House journal, the bill was passed at 11:59 P.M.—but it was actually a few minutes past midnight when the bill was rammed through.

Little matter. The Sox would play out the 1988, 1989, and 1990 seasons at the crumbling old Comiskey Park, and a gleaming new ball yard would be ready in time for Opening Day of 1991.

Word was that it would be a state-of-the-art facility.

Stretch Drive

August 23, 2005

In mid-August I returned from a trip to Amsterdam, where the only news available about the White Sox was via the Internet and the *International Herald Tribune*. The sports bars in Amsterdam were filled with memorabilia of the Ajax soccer team, which has an unofficial slogan of "We are the Super Jews!" (Fans rooting against Ajax chant lovely things like "We're sending you to the gas chamber!" and "Off to Auschwitz!" It's a long story, but suffice to say that if you think American sports nuts are fanatical, we're like a bunch of 58-year-old ladies at a Clay Aiken concert compared to European soccer maniacs.) While in Amsterdam, I did the things you do in Amsterdam—except the two things most closely associated with Amsterdam. I don't smoke pot, and I have this funny phobia about having intimate relations with heavily rouged women who stand in doorways in their underwear, framed by red lights. But that's just me.

I returned home to dive back into the pennant chase with my fellow Sox fans. The Sox were home for a six-game set against the Twins and Yankees, and I was able to make it to three of those games.

In 27 innings of baseball, I saw the White Sox score four runs. Not an average of four runs per game—four runs, total. I felt as if I had a time machine parked outside and I was watching the 1968 Sox all over again.

The Sox were in the middle of a mediocre stretch that saw them go 12–16 in August while the Indians just kept winning and winning and winning. After gliding through the first four months of the season, the Sox were banged up and beat. Podsednik had a strained muscle in his left leg, El Duque looked tired, Konerko had a strained back, Hermanson's back was in much worse shape than Konerko's—and Frank Thomas was sidelined after toughing it out and hitting 12 home runs in 34 games, even though it was obvious he could barely make it around the bases. Thomas was never a particularly likable guy, but you had to feel for the best hitter in franchise history. After 15 years with the Sox, he was going to be sidelined for the most exciting season on the South Side in nearly half a century.

Longtime Sox watcher Jay Mariotti feared the worst.

"Someone scolded me for mentioning this slump suggests the early strains of 1969 on the North Side," he wrote on August 23, after the Sox had lost a 1–0 heartbreaker in Minnesota. "Nothing the Sox did in the Metrodome made me rethink things. . . . When Lew Ford and Nick Punto are beating you, the chances of beating the Red Sox and the Angels in the playoffs aren't good."

The following day, longtime Sox watcher Jay Mariotti continued to fear the worst:

"If I owned the Sox—and at this point, maybe I should—I'd remove those radio spots that promise tickets in October to fans who buy the 2006 packages . . . I wouldn't be tempting fate with quick-fix sales gimmicks. . . .

"The final, final, final trading deadline passed late Wednesday night without activity. . . . So the new in-house slogan becomes We Are What We Are. And what are they? A downwardly spiraling imposter that has little chance to win a postseason series, unless ominous patterns unexpectedly turn bright in coming weeks . . .

"It's only a natural part of Chicago life to wonder if this is a choke in progress."

I was hearing a similar chorus from Sox fans at the Cell, at my local taverns, and in my e-mails. Why didn't the Sox get Griffey? Is El Duque done? Is Frank coming back? What about Podsednik? *Why won't the Indians lose a game more than once a week!!!!*

That sort of thing.

Chicago Tribune columnist Rick Morrissey scolded Sox fans with the ultimate insult: "You're acting very Cub-fan like. You're acting as if the cosmic forecast calls for sunny skies most of the season followed by an F5 tornado in October."

I tried to throw a little positive energy on the pileup by writing a column in which I pointed out that the Sox were still in first place (though the lead had shrunk from 15 to 7½ at the time), and that the worst could be over. Maybe the Sox had gotten their minislump out of their system. The column ended with a hopeful prediction: "Meet you in October."

Hundreds of Sox and Cubs fans responded to that column. Most of the Sox fans were cautiously optimistic. Most of the Cubs fans demonstrated great creativity in finding all sorts of ways to use the word "choke."

In the broadcast booth, poor Hawk Harrelson seemed to be on the verge of a complete breakdown. All season long, Hawk had championed the Sox as the best team in baseball, and he had lauded 99.9 percent of the decisions made by Ozzie Guillen. You know how the contestants on *The Apprentice* suck up to Donald Trump, calling him Mr. Trump and speaking of him in tones usually reserved for deities? They're disrespectful punks compared to how the Hawk spoke of "Ozzeroo." If Ozzie had announced that he relaxed by kidnapping puppies from small children in his spare time, Hawk would have said, "That's just Ozzie being Ozzie."

Now, though, the Sox were finding all sorts of ways to lose—and Hawk was falling into more silent funks than Britney Spears coming home to find that K-Fed had left Cheetos dust all over the couch again. When Hawk wasn't brooding, he was blaming the umps. They were squeezing the plate on Sox pitchers, and giving the opposition anything that was *near* the strike zone. They were calling fair balls foul and foul balls fair, they were saying guys were safe when A.J. had clearly made the throw in time. They obviously had it in for the Sox. Hawk couldn't believe what the men in blue were doing to the good guys wearing black.

Grinder Rule #45: If the Sox blow this lead, there *will* be crying in baseball.

Take Me Out to the Mall Game

July 31, 1997

It was a flat-out surrender. Not since 1919 had the Sox been so brazen about throwing in the towel.

With two months remaining in the 1997 pennant race, the chairman of the White Sox effectively told his team and the fans that they should start thinking about next year—even though the Sox were just 3½ games behind the Cleveland Indians at the time.

Days before the July 31 trading deadline, the Sox shipped Harold "Can I Have My Number Back, I'm Not Done Using It" Baines to Baltimore for the ubiquitous Player to be Named Later—and if you're going to be named later you're not going to be much help to a franchise right now. The player later named was the immortal Juan Bautista, who never pitched for the Sox.

On trading deadline day, the Sox sent pitchers Wilson Alvarez, Roberto Hernandez, and Danny Darwin for six minor league prospects.

Two of those prospects were Bobby Howry and Keith Foulke. If they were the Bobby Howry and Keith Foulke of, say, 2004, you might say that's a pretty good deal. But at the time, they were just kids who were going to be assigned to the minor leagues, along with the other four nobodies the Giants had sent to the Sox for three established major league pitchers.

When your team is 3½ games behind with some 60 games to play, *you're* supposed to be the one trading prospects for extra arms and a veteran bat. You're not supposed to be dumping the season.

Respecting the Game

Carlton Fisk was a modern-age ballplayer who would have been at home playing in the 1920s, or for that matter the 1890s. Fisk was old school all the way—a strapping tough guy who respected his profession and knew that every game, every inning, every at-bat, was a privilege.

On May 22, 1990, the Sox were at Yankee Stadium, and two-sport phenom Deion Sanders was at the plate. Sanders hit a routine pop-up to shortstop Ozzie Guillen, started jogging—and abruptly quit about halfway down the line before Ozzie even made the catch.

Even though Sanders was on the opposing team, Fisk took umbrage at Neon Deion's lack of respect for the game. He pushed his facemask to the top of his head and barked at Sanders to run it out—to act like a professional. It was one of the great Baseball Pride moments in Sox lore.

Were the Indians a better team than the Sox in 1997? Yes—but they weren't *that* great. In fact, Cleveland won the division, but they were just 86–75, only 5½ games in front of Chicago.

Would the Sox have won the division if they had kept the veterans and maybe added a couple of solid players? Maybe not. We don't know. All we know is that the owner surrendered—and he didn't ask the fans if they'd like a refund of the tickets they had purchased for the remainder of the season.

"Anyone who thinks this White Sox team will catch Cleveland is crazy," said Reinsdorf. It's a statement that irks Sox fans to this day. Just three years after Reinsdorf had endorsed the strike that killed the 1994 season, he traded away veteran hurler Danny Darwin, Wilson Alvarez, who at the time had the fifth best ERA in the league, and Roberto Hernandez, who was third in the league in saves.

Sox fans weren't just disappointed. We were disgusted. The one thing we always asked of our players was the full effort. I've seen Sox fans applaud guys who *missed* foul balls, because the players hustled to try to make a play. I've seen them stand up and cheer for a base runner who tries to break up a double play with the Sox down by six. Yoda says, "Do or do not. There is no try." But Yoda's a little green puppet that never saw Carlton Fisk blocking the plate and bracing himself for a collision with a runner half his age, or Aaron Rowand running into walls in the outfield, or Brian Downing slamming his bat down after a strikeout. On the South Side, we appreciate winning, but we *respect* the never-say-die spirit.

Reinsdorf said die.

Of course, the local media ripped into Sox management—but baseball purists everywhere were offended.

REINSDORF IS SAD EXCEPTION TO TRADE RULE was the headline in the *Washington Post*. Veteran sportswriter Thomas Boswell wrote: "How can the White Sox trade the heart of their staff, All-Stars Wilson Alvarez and Roberto Hernandez, plus Danny Darwin?

"This week's booby prize goes to White Sox owner Jerry Reinsdorf. He's Mr. Baseball, isn't he? First, he orchestrated the strike. Then he destroyed the game's salary structure by signing Bad News [Albert] Belle for $2 million above the going market price. Now . . . he pouts and quits with two months of the regular season remaining."

REINSDORF GIVES UP WITHOUT A FIGHT was the headline in the *Cleveland Plain Dealer*. Writer Bud Shaw, noting that the Indians were hardly a juggernaut, noted, "Reinsdorf is far more popular these days in Cleveland than he is in Chicago." Shaw also wrote: "It's a good thing Reinsdorf's fighting spirit didn't show up in various points in America's history. . . . Had he come into power during the Revolutionary War . . . we'd all be drinking warm beer and singing 'God Save the Queen.'"

Being a Sox fan in the 1990s and the first half of the 2000s was like dating a supermodel who tells you that she loves you—and then slaps you when you try to kiss her. The Sox would spend tens of millions of dollars on big-name free agents such as Albert Belle and David Wells—but they'd make head-scratching trades and hire second-rate managers such as Terry Bevington and Jerry Manuel. They'd refuse to admit there were problems with Comiskey Park II—that the blue seats were atrocious and the upper deck was so high you could board a plane bound for Midway as it was actually bound for Midway—and then they'd announce plans to lose the top eight rows of the upper deck and replace the blue seats. They'd bring in washed-up head cases like Jose Canseco—but they'd also revitalize the career of a head case like A.J. Pierzynski. For the last 15 years, it's been a love-hate relationship. White Sox fans feel like Pacino in *Godfather III*—every time we're out, they pull us back in!

👟   👟   👟

By the late 1980s, Comiskey Park wasn't really the Baseball Palace of the World any more. It was more like the House-You-Keep-Painting-in-the-Hope-That-Nobody-Notices-It's-Falling-Apart. Soon after Reinsdorf and Co. purchased the Sox, they started making noises about a move to the suburbs, a move to Florida—or a new stadium in Chicago. It was clear that in order for the White Sox to stay on the South Side through the 21st century, they were going to have to build a new home. The grand old structure that had played host to everybody from Shoeless Joe Jackson to Babe Ruth to Joe Louis to Paul McCartney and John Lennon—it was time to shut it down.

It's kinda like when you go to Wrigley Field these days. Sure, the field itself is beautiful and the surrounding area is alive with excitement—but the place itself stinks, literally and figuratively. The facilities for the players are among the worst in the major leagues, and fans find themselves jammed into narrow concourses as they wait forever for the bathroom or line up at one of the below-par concession stands.

I loved going to Sox games—and Eagles concerts, among other events—at Comiskey Park, and I wrote the obligatory weeper of a column after I attended the last home game in 1990, but I was in favor of the Sox getting a new ballpark. For one thing, it would finally put a stop to the incessant chatter about the team's leaving town. Since I was a kid, I had heard that the Sox were moving to Seattle, Milwaukee, Florida, New Orleans, the western suburbs—every place but Wrigleyville itself.

After closing out the 1980s with a 69–92 record and one of the worst teams in baseball, the Sox surprised everyone by flying out of the gate with a 48–30 mark. They had all kinds of young talent, including Robin Ventura, Jack McDowell, Bobby Thigpen (who set a major league mark that year with 57 saves)—not to mention right fielder Sammy Sosa, and a late-season call-up named Frank Thomas, who hit .330 in 191 at-bats in the bigs. The Sox weren't deep enough to stay with the Oakland A's, but they finished 94–68—an amazing 25-game turnaround from the previous year.

July 1, 1990, was Comiskey Park's 80th birthday—and one of the strangest games in White Sox history. The Sox hosted the Yankees, and going into the bottom of the 8th it was a scoreless tie—with Andy Hawkins of the Yankees working on a no-hitter.

Here's the thing about no-hitters—they're extremely rare, like quality Paul Walker movies or proper uses of the word *irony*. I've experienced hundreds of baseball games in person, and the only no-hitters I've seen at any level were thrown by me, when I was 12 years old. So even when it's the other team's guy who has the no-hitter going, you start calling your friends around the 7th or 8th inning: "You watching the game? Yeah, he's got a no-hitter going." I don't expect my buddies to call me if they've just spotted Elvis at a White Castle, but I do expect a call if someone's got a no-hitter going.

I wasn't at this particular Sunday afternoon game—but I was working in the *Sun-Times* newsroom and I caught the unbelievable sequence of events on TV.

The bottom of the 8th started out with Ron Karkovice popping out to Steve Sax. (Karko was a tough defensive catcher, but he spent his life at the plate popping out and striking out. We used to call him "Karko the Magnificent." We were joking.) Scottie Fletcher also popped out, and it appeared as if the Sox were going to go down quietly in the 8th.

Sammy Sosa reached on an error and stole second. Now the Sox had the go-ahead run on second base. Still no hits, but all we needed was a single, and the fleet-footed Sammy would score.

Ozzie Guillen drew a walk. Lance Johnson also worked Hawkins for a walk. Now the bases were loaded. In a normal situation, the Yankees might have pulled Hawkins for a reliever—but he still had that no-hitter working, and the next man up was left-handed hitting Robin Ventura, so Hawkins was allowed to stay in the game.

It appeared as if Hawkins was going to work out of the jam when Ventura lifted a fairly deep but playable fly to left—but to the amazement of the crowd, Jim Leyritz dropped the ball. The runners had been moving on contact, and one, two, three runs scored.

Before the fans had even calmed down, Ivan Calderon hit a fly ball to right—and Jesse Barfield misplayed THAT easy out for another error, with Ventura scoring. Hawkins finally retired Dan Pasqua on a pop-up. It was basically the sixth out of the inning, given that the Yankees had committed three errors on easy plays.

Things I Miss About the Old Comiskey Park

The Picnic Area in left field

McCuddy's Tavern

The kid-height water fountain in left field

The original center field shower

The Sox Supporters

The Sox-o-Gram

Those awesome speakers mounted on the center field wall

The basket behind home plate that would pop up from the ground, giving the ump a fresh supply of baseballs

The original exploding scoreboard

Falstaff and Carta Blanca

Mack Trucks

The ELGIN OFFICIAL TIME clock in center field

Shards of sunlight shooting through the arched windows on a late afternoon

"Gold Box" seats

Bill Veeck's Patio, with the painting of Richard Daley the First looming over the city's skyline, a giant baseball, and a shamrock floating near his head

Things I Don't Miss About the Old Comiskey Park

Cigarette and cigar smoke forming an unnatural cloud above the field

Obstructed-view seating

The bathrooms

The artificial turf experiment in the infield

The temporary fences in the outfield

The Sox won 4–0. Hawkins was credited with a no-hitter—but it was later taken off the books, which makes no sense. He pitched a complete game and didn't give up any hits. That's a no-hitter.

Nearly 43,000 fans saw the final Sox game at Comiskey Park. By that time, construction was well under way on the future home of the Sox. You could tell by the foundation and the skeleton that Comiskey II was going to be a much larger structure. It was like watching some nouveau riche building a giant house on the beach, next to the charming but decrepit old cabin that's been there for decades.

The Sox beat the Mariners 2–1, with Bobby Thigpen getting the final out to record his 57th save. Sox players took their time leaving the field, with even the younger players respecting the history of the old palace. Perhaps they'd been there for just a year or two, but they knew that some of the fans in the stands had been coming to games since World War II. Carlton Fisk threw souvenirs into the stands. The scoreboard exploded. We sang a season-closing version of "Na Na Hey Hey" but with a different attitude. This time it was an affectionate good-bye.

I had to race back to the *Sun-Times* to write my column for Monday's paper. (Remember, this was 1990. It was a lot easier to drive back to the office and work on the big, old Atex computer system than it was to write from the ballpark.) Most of the crowd was still in the stands, still saying their final good-byes, as I exited Comiskey Park for the last time. The six-year-old who watched that Mickey Mantle homer in amazement; the 12-year-old who cheered wildly as Harry Caray nearly caught the Dick Allen shot to the bleachers; the 19-year-old who witnessed Disco Demolition firsthand; the 23-year-old who had a standing-room-only ticket for the clincher in 1983—I left them all behind.

There are times when Jerry Reinsdorf seems like the least sentimental human on the planet. I'm sure that's not true; I'm sure those who are close to him will tell you that he's a devoted family man who cries at United Airlines commercials and is prone to hugging the mailman.

Remember the victory rally, when Paulie pulled out the baseball from the last out of the World Series and handed it to Reinsdorf, and the chairman got all choked up? "This is the greatest moment of my life," said Reinsdorf, and you knew he meant it.

A lovely sentiment. Maybe not so much if you're one of Reinsdorf's sons and you've just heard your dad say that getting a souvenir baseball trumped the moment of your birth, but there you have it.

But I had to laugh when some of my fellow fans said Konerko was sure to return to the Sox after that moment. As if Reinsdorf would allow the admittedly touching moment at the World Series celebration to cloud his judgment come negotiation time. Yes, Konerko signed with the Sox—but he didn't gain any advantage, emotional or otherwise, by giving Jerry that baseball. We're talking about an owner who favored the cancellation of a season in '94, even though his team had World Series written all over it. A guy who didn't care that outgoing players Carlton Fisk, Ozzie Guillen, and Frank Thomas, among others, didn't appreciate the way they were shown the door. The man who waved good-bye to Phil Jackson, Scottie Pippen, and Michael Jordan when the Bulls still had another NBA championship or two left to win.

Reinsdorf enjoys talking about his beloved Ebbets Field, and there's no debating his passion for the game, which led to his infamous remark that he'd rather have one World Series trophy than six NBA championships. Still, there are times when he seems to just spit on the history of the very team he owns.

Sammy So-So

When the Sox traded Sammy Sosa to the Cubs for George Bell in March of 1992, I didn't think it was a bad move for either side. We were giving up a talented, underperforming, enigmatic young player for a proven slugger—and those are the kinds of deals that are made between contenders (the Sox) and rebuilding clubs (the Cubbies). Sosa had loads of potential, but he had struck out 150 times in one season for the Sox while walking just 33 times—and he followed that up with a .203 average in 1991.

He seemed a lot more like Buddy Bradford than Willie Mays.

Bell was a bit of a jerk and a flake, but he'd put up some impressive power numbers for Toronto before coming to the Cubs. The Sox seemed to be getting the better of this trade.

CUBS LIKE SOSA'S OUTFIELD DEFENSE was the headline in the *Tribune* after the trade. If you saw a headline like that 10 years later, it would have been in the *Onion*.

Jay Mariotti wrote that Sox GM Ron Schueler had hit a "grand slam," and wondered if Sosa's "head will ever catch up with his talent." He projected a 120-RBI season for Bell on the South Side—and Bell came close to doing just that, knocking in 112 runs in his first season with the Sox.

Of course, once Sammy added those Flintstones vitamins to his diet and his physique filled out, he turned into one of the greatest sluggers the game has ever known, while Bell drifted off into obscurity, reportedly working at a gas station after his retirement. Yet Sox fans never really bitched about that Sosa trade. For one thing, nobody expected Sosa to mature into a home run hitting machine. To blame Sox management would have been like blaming the Portland Trail Blazers for selecting Sam Bowie ahead of Michael Jordan in the NBA draft, even though Portland had two quality guards at the time and they needed a big man—and nobody knew Jordan was going to become the greatest player ever.

Anyway, Sammy turned out to be a one-dimensional, self-centered phony who never won a thing. We'd hear about the boom box in the clubhouse, we'd see him sprinting out to right field before games, doing that little home run hop or the love-tap for the cameras, and we'd think: *Ugh*. We laughed our heads off when Sammy's bat exploded and cork flew out. And once interleague play was instituted, it was *great* fun cheering against Sosa in the Cubs–Sox series. When Sammy walked out on his teammates in his final game as a Cub, he left behind a legacy as one of the greatest home run hitters of all time—and we were fine with that. For all of Sosa's talent and all the excitement he brought to the game, especially in the summer of '98, we never missed him all that much on the South Side.

Case in point: what the Sox did—or more accurately, what they *didn't* do—after Comiskey Park was torn down and paved over.

Fine, so they had to pave paradise and put up a parking lot. It only made sense to make use of the land that was just north of the new Comiskey.

But where's the tribute to the Baseball Palace of the World? A 12-year-old fan on his way to the Cell might not even notice the outline of the original home plate and batter's boxes in the parking lot. It's just a concrete etching. If you're in a hurry, you step right over it without pausing for the slightest moment to consider that you're standing on the spot where Gus Zernial, Minnie Minoso, and Nellie Fox took their cuts.

And what about McCuddy's, the legendary tavern where Babe Ruth reportedly stopped to quaff a beer or two—during games. When McCuddy's had to be torn down to make room for the new park, Governor James Thompson pledged that they'd find a spot for the tavern once the dust had settled. It never happened. And it's not even as if Reinsdorf got involved. For a neighborhood guy, he doesn't seem to have much feel for the neighborhood. You could call Reinsdorf the anti-Veeck, and I don't think he'd mind that.

Not that the Sox were completely without sentiment when it came to the destruction of Comiskey Park. Much of the infield dirt was preserved and was reinstalled at the new park—but a big mound of dirt was divided into razor-thin pieces slightly larger than postage stamps that were pressed into Lucite and sold to fans. You could also buy bricks from Comiskey as well. I never got a brick, but my preserved patch of infield dirt occupies a prime spot on a shelf at home, next to a slab of the original floor from the Lodge on Division Street.

We must preserve our history!

I first heard about the Comiskey Park bullet holes in 1990. A Chicago cop called and told me that residents of the housing projects near Comiskey Park were taking potshots at the brand-new upper deck.

"The construction crews are finding bullet holes in the seats," the cop told me. "They're afraid someone's going to shoot one of them. And what happens when the park opens next year? Someone could get killed."

In late December of 1990, I wrote a skeptical item about the so-called bullet holes. Mike Royko of the *Tribune* broached the same subject and dismissed it out of hand as an urban legend.

"[T]he story is going around like crazy," wrote Royko. "Every news desk in Chicago has dozens of calls about it. A few brainless disc jockeys have gone on the air and babbled as if it were fact. With variations, the story usually goes like this: 'The new Comiskey Park is built so that it faces the projects. So the gangs can get up there on one of the upper floors and shoot right into the place. They're already doing it. A construction worker out there told my brother's boss . . .'

"And so we have a new piece of what is known as 'urban folklore.'"

Rob Gallas, who had become the Sox vice-president of marketing after surviving Jimmy Piersall's attempt to choke him, told Royko the stories were untrue. Chicago Police Superintendent LeRoy Martin said it was all "nonsense."

Less than two weeks later, the headline in Royko's own paper told a different story: BULLET DAMAGE HITS NEW SOX PARK—REALLY.

"Bullet holes were found Thursday in the new Comiskey Park, and police wondered whether they were inspired by earlier media reports of rumors that the ballpark had been fired upon," reported the *Tribune*.

"White Sox management confirmed that a bullet hole was found in the center-field scoreboard. The discovery led to a check of seats, and three in the upper deck were also damaged."

We never found out whether the urban legend created the reality, or whether the reality existed first and we just thought it was an urban legend. In any case, after that one instance, we never again heard about any bullet holes at the new Comiskey. And as Sox shortstop Ozzie Guillen said at the time, "It's better to shoot at seats in the park than at human beings." As a piece of useful philosophy, that's right up there with "If you can dodge a wrench, you can dodge a ball."

Reinsdorf hired Ron Schueler to take the Sox from point B, a contending club, to point C, the World Series. Schueler made some aggressive moves heading into the 1991 season, including the signing of Bo Jackson, the phenomenal two-sport athlete who was battling a severely damaged hip and was thought to be done forever. The rehabbing Jackson returned on September 2 to drive in a run with a sacrifice fly for a White Sox win.

I got a tour of the new Comiskey Park several months before Opening Day—and even in its unfinished stages, it was obvious that the new facility was going to be a vast upgrade over a structure that had been built during the Taft administration. But I also felt that the field was facing in the "wrong" direction, the blue seats were awful, and the upper deck was insanely high. I warned Sox fans: If you were prone to nose bleeds or you were asthmatic, you were going to want to stay away from the upper deck.

For years the Sox were so defensive about the upper deck, they sounded like Britney Spears sticking up for Kevin Federline: "He really can dance and rap!" With the Sox it was "The upper deck is fine! The fans never complain about the upper deck, it's just you guys in the media! Why are you saying it's high? It's not that high!"

It was *that* high.

As the *Tribune* pointed out, in Old Comiskey Park the distance from home plate to the first row of the upper deck was an estimated 100 feet. The distance from home plate to the last row of the upper deck was 150 feet.

At New Comiskey Park the distance from home plate to the first row of the upper deck was 160 feet. So the *first* row in the new park was farther away than the *last* row in the old park! The distance from home plate to the last row of the upper deck in the new park: some 250 feet, a little less than the length of a football field.

It took more than a decade for the Sox to admit that the upper deck was a problem. After the 2003 season, they removed the top eight rows, eliminating more than 6,600 seats, and installed a flat roof. This was just one of the many vast improvements that the Sox would make during a five-year upgrade. (There was also a gradual phase-out of the blue seats. During the championship run of 2005, the seats were an unfortunate mixture of blue and green.)

On a scale of 1 to 10, the new Comiskey Park was about a 5 on the day of its debut. The U.S. Cellular Field of 2006 is about a 7.

Anybody sitting in the upper deck on Opening Day 1991 could have told you the upper deck was a problem. I walked all around Comiskey II on its first official day, talking to the fans and getting their instant reviews of the facilities. Everybody loved the gleaming new bathrooms, the wider concourses, the fantastic concessions, the beautiful new field. Pretty much everybody hated the upper deck, the blue seats, and the fact that the exterior looked like a department store.

There was plenty of time to check out the new bells and whistles, what with the Tigers handing the Sox a 16–0 whipping—probably the worst home opener for a new ballpark in the history of the major leagues. That's not even a close score for a football game.

The Sox had some decent teams in 1991 and 1992, finishing 12 and 10 games above .500, respectively—but they were never in serious contention.

It was a different story in 1993. Ten years after the "Winning Ugly" team, the Sox reached the postseason again as champions of the American League West. Their slogan that year was Good Guys Wear Black—but Robin Ventura was the villain when he charged Nolan Ryan on the mound at Texas and found himself on the embarrassing end of several "noogies" from a man 20 years his senior. And Sox management was cast in the familiar bad guy role when they released Carlton Fisk while the team was on a road trip, just days after Fisk had set the record for most games caught. The future Hall of Famer was batting less than .200 and, like a lot of greats, he was having a hard time letting go of the game—but there had to have been a better way for the thing to be handled. It would be years before the damage was repaired. If someone had told Fisk in the mid-1990s that he'd one day have his own statue on the South Side, he would have laughed his head off.

Those incidents notwithstanding, 1993 was a memorable year for Sox fans. This was the most talented White Sox team in memory. Over the years, I had seen guys like Reggie Jackson and Jim Rice come to Chicago and hit home runs that would have Sox fans wincing and ooohing. With the exception of Dick Allen's brief tenure with the Sox, we never had a player like that on our side—until Frank Thomas came along. In 1993 Thomas hit .317 with 41 home runs and 128 RBIs, easily one of the greatest offensive years in White Sox history. Thomas had such a perfect swing, such a combination of timing and power, that observers were comparing him to Babe Ruth and Ted Williams. He was the first White Sox player to win the MVP since Dick Allen.

We also had the Cy Young Award winner in "Blackjack" McDowell, a guitar-strumming free spirit who was a fierce competitor on the mound. McDowell won 22 games for the '93 Sox—but a lot of us thought he was the third- or fourth-best talent in a starting rotation that included Jason Bere, Alex Fernandez, and Wilson Alvarez.

As they had done 10 years earlier, the Sox clinched the division at home, against the Mariners.

The South Side was center stage once again.

♪   ♪   ♪

I'll never forget running into a fellow member of the media about an hour before Game 1 of the American League Championship Series between the Sox and the Blue Jays. (Remember, it was still a two-division setup in '93, with just one round of playoffs before the World Series.) He'd been at the park for hours, collecting quotes and making observations for a feature story about the first playoff game on the South Side in a decade. Now he had just learned that the city desk wanted him to stick around for the entire game, just in case something happened. (More on that something in a moment.) My colleague was cold, tired, and cranky, and all he wanted to do was go home. Yet his goddamn newspaper was making him stay.

He told me all this as we were standing on the concourse behind the left field stands. All around us, excited fans who had been fortunate enough to score tickets were buzzing about, counting down the minutes until the first pitch of Game 1.

"Let's run down your situation," I said to my friend, who was sipping a cold beer and munching a hot dog. "You drove down to the park, right?"

He nodded.

"Parked for free in the media lot. Had immediate access to the park."

He nodded again.

"You've got your media credentials that give you access to the field, the dugout—and the press box when it gets colder. You were able to wander around on the field while the Sox were taking batting practice."

"That's right," he said.

"And now you're eating a hot dog and drinking a beer, and you get to watch the game for free, *plus* you're getting paid overtime for working into the night shift. Does that about sum it up?"

"Uh, yeah."

"Dude. That's first prize in a radio station contest for most fans."

The Jordan Experiment

The only thing more stunning than Michael Jordan's first retirement from the Bulls was the revelation that the 30-year-old superstar wanted a second career in pro sports—as an outfielder with the White Sox.

Say what?

Jordan hadn't played baseball since he was a teenager. I had once played in a charity softball game with him, and he showed up in jeans (in jeans!), carrying a brand-new glove. For a 16-inch softball. Granted, the guy pounded the hell out of the ball in that game, and at one point he jumped *over* an infielder as he was rounding the bases—but come on. A major leaguer? I didn't see it, and I said as much in a column on January 4, 1994:

"Imagine [Jordan] falling down in the batter's box or flailing away at pitch after pitch, hitting nothing but air. That's what would happen."

A month later, I was among the throngs of reporters who watched Jordan conduct an indoor workout at the Illinois Institute of Technology.

"His bat speed is somewhat slower than that of Sean Burroughs, the portly child hero of last year's Little League World Series," I noted. (Burroughs, son of former major leaguer Jeff Burroughs, wound up playing in the bigs for the San Diego Padres.)

"He'd be the best guy on your softball team," I opined, "and the worst guy on the White Sox . . . [but] if the greatest ambassador Chicago has ever had wants to be the next Tim Nordbrook, who are we to deny his dream?"

Jordan spent a year at Double-A Birmingham and batted a robust .208. In March of 1995, Jordan fled the Sox rather than get caught up in a labor dispute. A couple of months later, he faxed a two-word statement to the media—"I'm back"—and he returned to the Bulls, who won three more NBA championships. On the "Superfans" on *Saturday Night Live*, the beer-swilling, sauce-stained Chicago guys used to talk confidently of an "eight-peat" for the Bulls. It was a joke—but if Jordan hadn't taken two years off, the Bulls might actually have won eight straight NBA crowns.

As an outfielder, Michael Jordan was a very good shooting guard.

At first the buzz was all about Michael Jordan, who had been spotted in Jerry Reinsdorf's suite before the game. Then the buzz was about *why* Jordan was at the game:

He was retiring from the Bulls.

The news crackled through Comiskey Park with more speed and impact than Dick Allen's home run to the center field bleachers in 1972. It seemed unfathomable that Jordan would be walking away from the game in his prime, with the Bulls having won three NBA championships in a row—but the story quickly went from rumor to serious rumor to you can put it on the board. It's not as if fans stopped paying attention to the game—but if Heather Locklear had been playing second base in the nude, it wouldn't have been a bigger distraction.

A crowd of more than 46,000 watched the Blue Jays' star-studded lineup pound McDowell for 13 hits. Toronto pitchers issued semi-intentional walks to Frank Thomas four times and dared the rest of the lineup to make them pay for it—a strategy that worked to perfection. The Blue Jays took Game 1, 7–3.

The Sox played uninspired ball in the second game, losing 3–1—and George Bell and Bo Jackson bitched about sitting on the bench. Heading to Toronto down 2–0 in the seven-game set, it seemed as if the Sox were dead—but they whipped the Blue Jays in the third and fourth games to even the series and regain the home field advantage. Now all they had to do was win two of the next three, and they'd be in the World Series.

In Game 5, the Jays scored four runs in the first off McDowell and held on for a 5–3 victory. Still, a lot of us were surprised that the Sox had managed to win those two games in Toronto and send the series back home. If we could win back-to-back home games on our own turf . . .

It never even got to a Game 7. Dave Stewart was just a little bit better than Alex Fernandez in Game 6, and the Blue Jays scored a 6–3 knockout and went on to win the World Series.

Still, the future looked bright. Going into the 1994 season, the Sox were on the shortlist of World Series contenders.

On August 10, 1994, the Sox beat the A's 2–1 in Oakland, as Jason "Raspberry" Bere raised his mark to 12–2. With 50 games left in the season, the Sox were 21 games over .500 and in first place in the American League Central. (This was the first year of the three-division format.)

For the first time in my life, the Sox were looking at a second straight postseason appearance.

Too bad that was the last game of the season.

Locked in a salary-cap dispute, owners and players allowed the unthinkable to happen: they canceled the season and then the World Series. The Major League Baseball Players Association authorized a strike, the players walked out—and there was no chance the thing was going to get settled in time to save the season. The Sox were screwed. (You know who else got screwed that year? The Montreal Expos. Believe it or not, the Expos had the best record in baseball at the time of the strike.)

With 10 or 12 more starts coming, Bere had an outside chance at 20 victories. Julio Franco and Robin Ventura would have reached the 100 RBI mark—and Frank Thomas would have had the biggest season of his career and one of the best seasons in White Sox history. Even with nearly a third of the season wiped out by the strike, Thomas had a monster year: a .353 average, 38 homers, 101 RBIs. He was named MVP of the American League for the second year in a row, but it was a bittersweet honor— like winning an Emmy for a TV show that has been canceled.

By the mid-1990s the new-car smell had faded from Comiskey Park, and the Cubs had a firm grip on the city. We had a nice little season going in '97 until the White Flag trade. The Indians then dominated the American League Central for the remainder of the decade.

In the spring of 2000, I marched up to a window at the Sports Book at the Venetian in Las Vegas and put $200 on the Sox to win the World Series, at odds of 40–1.

Six months later, it appeared as if I had a serious shot at the $8,000 payout. The Sox were a beast, setting team records for home runs (216), RBIs (926), hits (1,615), and runs scored (978). These guys were the real South Side Hit Men. As I pointed out in a column that September, the power figures for the starting lineup of the 2000 White Sox matched or bettered the top eight hitters for the 1927 Yankees, the 1955 Brooklyn Dodgers, and the 1961 Yankees.

The Sox faced the Mariners—the same Mariners who had been on the field when the Sox clinched in 1983 and 1993—in the American League Division Series. (Okay, technically they weren't the SAME Mariners, because those guys from 1983 would have all been in their 40s and 50s.) By this juncture I had season tickets, down the left field line, and my buddy and I squeezed in with the capacity crowd for Game 1, an afternoon affair. Seattle jumped out to a 3–0 lead, but we roared back and even went ahead briefly on an RBI triple by Magglio Ordonez.

"Oyeeeeoh, MAG-LIO!" roared the crowd.

But the Mariners sent the game into extra innings, and Keith Foulke yielded back-to-back homers to Edgar Martinez and John Olerud, and we were down 1–0 in the best-of-five series.

The Sox lost Game 2 by a 5–2 count, meaning they'd have to go to Seattle and sweep two games to force a fifth and deciding game back at Comiskey. No chance. The Mariners scored the winning run in Game 3 on a squeeze play in the bottom of the 9th, and the team with best record in the American League was gone. The Sox hit .185 for the series. Frank Thomas was all but invisible.

I was 40 years old. Between 1993 and 2003, I had seen the Sox play five postseason games in person.

They were 0–5 in those games.

After finishing third behind the Indians and Twins in 2001, the Sox settled into a second-place rut for three straight years. Every year it appeared as if the Sox had more talent on paper than Minnesota; every year the Twins played harder, smarter, faster, and better on defense, and left us in the dust.

Little wonder that virtually nobody was picking the Sox to do anything special in 2005.

The Curse Is Reversed

September 25, 2005

It might have been the biggest game of the season for the Sox—and they weren't even involved in it.

Cleveland had won 38 games out of 50. Heading into a Sunday afternoon game at Kansas City against the hapless Royals, the Indians were within 1½ games of the Sox.

The score was tied in the bottom of the 9th, and the Royals had a runner on second with one out when Paul Phillips lifted a high fly to center. Grady Sizemore drifted back, camped under the ball, set himself to make the catch . . . and lost the ball in the sun. It caromed off his leg as Angel Berroa raced home with the winning run.

The lead was back up to 2½ games. Even more important, the game seemed to knock the wind out of the Indians. Sure, they had that big three-game set with the Sox in Cleveland to close out the season—but could they hold their ground or make a move on the Sox during the week?

Even with the Sox stumbling at Detroit, the Indians couldn't mount that final charge. They lost two straight to lowly Tampa Bay, so by Thursday afternoon all the Sox had to do was beat the Tigers and they'd clinch the American League Central. Konerko hit his 40th homer, Freddy Garcia got the win—and the save went to Bobby Jenks, the wide-bodied kid who started the season in the minor leagues. In the spring nobody in Chicago had ever heard of Jenks. By October he was a folk hero.

♩   ♩   ♩

I watched the first two games of the White Sox–Red Sox American League Division Series from a cruise ship in the Bahamas, and I watched Game 3 while paralyzed from the waist down in a recovery room at Northwestern Memorial Hospital.

For real.

Every year, the Disney Cruise people hold an "Ebert & Roeper Film Festival at Sea." Hundreds of movie geeks join Roger Ebert and me for four days of watching and talking about films as the Disney Wonder makes its way from Port Canaveral to the Bahamas and back.

Usually the cruise is held in March. Due to circumstances beyond my control, the 2005 cruise was moved back to October. I was aware of this potential conflict by midsummer, and I must confess there were times when I thought it wouldn't be the worst thing in the world if the Sox didn't have home field advantage in the first round of the playoffs. No matter what, I was going to miss the first two games—but if the Sox were on the road, it wouldn't be as painful.

Of course, that's not how it played out. As the Sox geared up to host Game 1 in Chicago, I was on the Disney Wonder, talking movies and keeping one eye on the clock. As luck and the time difference would have it, I finished my movie duties just after the scheduled start time of the game.

Now, let me tell you about my favorite sports bar in the history of sports bars—and I've been going to sports bars since I was 16, I mean, 18, I mean, 21. On the Disney Wonder there's a lounge called Diversions, with multiple flat-screen television sets—and they were all tuned to Game 1, White Sox vs. Red Sox.

They knew I was coming. The waitress, who was from Bosnia—BOSNIA—had saved me a spot by placing a bottle of Stella Artois squarely in the center of a table that held a clear view of the biggest of the plasma TVs. As I entered the bar, a fellow Sox fan hollered, "You're not going to believe it, Rich!"

Before I could ask what that meant, I saw the score on the screen:

CHICAGO 5, BOSTON 0.

In the top of the second!

"A.J. hit a three-run homer," explained my fellow Sox fan.

I settled into my seat, shaking my head at the wonder of it all, and no, that's not a cheap plug for the Disney Wonder. Here I was on a cruise ship, the sky growing dark and ominous through the portholes—and I could still watch the Sox, in real time, in their first playoff game in five years.

Of course they were going to win. I wasn't there.

The final score was 13–2. It was *the worst postseason defeat in the history of the defending World Champion Red Sox*, and I cannot tell you how much I enjoyed that. I'd always kind of been a Red Sox fan. When I attended a game at Fenway Park in 2004 and saw Pedro twirl a masterpiece, I was impressed by the fans—their knowledge of the game, their passion for their Sox, their belief that this was finally going to be their year. But when it turned out that 2004 really was going to be their year— ugh. I thought we'd never hear the end of it. As the playoff picture clarified in the final weekend of the regular season, I really hoped that the White Sox would draw Boston, followed by the Yankees, and then the Cardinals in the World Series. I wanted them to beat the most storied franchises in the game. I didn't want to hear anything about how lucky they were to face off against some team with even less playoff experience.

Knocking off the defending champs seemed like a great way to start.

The temperature in Chicago was about the same as it was in the Bahamas as the Sox took the field for Game 2 against the Red Sox. We're talking 80 degrees in October.

Game 2 will always be remembered for Graffanino's Gaffe. The former White Sox infielder allowed a routine, double play grounder to roll through his legs in the 5th inning—and then Tadahito Iguchi ripped a three-run homer to give the Sox a 5–4 lead.

You gotta love Tadahito. For one thing, it's great fun to yell his name when he steps to the plate. Say it right now, you'll see what I mean: TADAHITO!

I was still on the cruise ship, cursing the stormy weather that occasionally froze the picture on the TVs in the Diversions bar—and loving the fact that my older brother and my father were at the game. My father had never seen the Sox in the postseason—and he'd been going to White Sox games since 1936.

You know, a loyal fan deserves to see a postseason victory in person every 70 years or so.

By Friday, the White Sox were in Boston and I was back in Chicago—and under the knife. (Let's just say that the surgery was necessary and it couldn't be put off, but it wasn't close to being near the neighborhood of something truly serious.) As I regained consciousness, a nurse wearing a skullcap with the White Sox logo told me I'd come through like a trooper, and it was perfectly normal for me to feel absolutely nothing from the waist down. That feeling of numbness would wear off in an hour or two—three or four at the most.

A while later, I was wheeled into a private recovery room, where my sister and my brother-in-law already had the game on for me. (As I've mentioned, my brother-in-law is a Cubs fan. It's not his fault. He was born that way.) The White Sox had a 4–2 lead in the 6th, courtesy of a Paul Konerko moon shot—but Manny Ramirez made it 4–3 with a blast of his own in the bottom of the 6th. Ozzie went to the bullpen and brought in the least popular pitcher on the White Sox staff: Damaso Marte.

A few years back, I thought Marte had just about the best stuff of any left-handed reliever in the game. He was filthy, as the players like to say. He was also a head case who turned into a marshmallow in key situations—so I wasn't the least bit surprised when he yielded a single followed by two walks, giving the Red Sox a bases-loaded situation with nobody out.

Ozzie then did something that made even less sense than calling on Marte. He brought in Orlando "El Duque" Hernandez, who had barely made the playoff roster after fading terribly down the stretch. I could just see the Jason Varitek grand slam, giving the Red Sox the victory and a ton of momentum heading into Game 4.

Varitek popped out to Konerko in foul territory.

Next up, Tony Graffanino, who worked the count full—and then popped out to Uribe.

Finally, Johnny Damon, the man they called Jesus in Boston. In all my years of following sports as a fan and covering sports as a reporter, I don't know that I'd ever seen fans worship a player the way they knelt at the altar of Johnny Damon in Boston. (They must be singing a different song in Boston after Johnny became a Yankee and cut his locks.) Damon also worked the count full, and El Duque threw him a pitch that would have been ball four—if only Damon had been able to lay off. Midswing Damon realized the ball was dipping down to the dirt, but it was too late to check. He didn't even argue when the ump ruled that he had swung around for strike three.

It was an astonishing performance by El Duque, and he followed that with two more scoreless innings. The White Sox tacked on an insurance run, and as Bobby Jenks took the mound for the 9th, I started to get the feeling back in my legs. It was a miracle!

Either that or the anesthesia was wearing off. But still.

The cameras showed shot after shot after shot after shot after friggin' shot of those diehard Red Sox fans looking on in disbelief as their season came to a close. This was it? After coming back from a three-games-to-none deficit against the Yankees in 2004, the Carmines weren't going to mount a charge against these, what do you call them, White Sox?

That's about right, baby. The final score was 5–3. As predicted by many experts, it was a Sox sweep in the first round.

They just picked the wrong Sox.

♪   ♪   ♪

The Sox were well rested for the American League Championship Series. While the Sox were enjoying three days off, the Anaheim Angels of Los Angeles had to fly from the West Coast to the East Coast, beat the Yankees in Game 5 of the ALDS, and then fly to Chicago, arriving at 6:30 A.M. on game day. Also, Angels ace Bartolo Colon had finally broken down, his shoulder too painful for him to be a factor in the ALCS.

You'd think all that would make the Sox heavy favorites for that first game, but there was a mitigating factor: me. I was going to be in the stands for the game, and, as I said earlier, I had a lifetime mark of 0–5 at Sox home playoff games.

Make that 0–6.

On a lovely October evening, the ghost of the Dibber seemed to loom above the Cell. Half the team seemed to be suffering from brain cramps. Scott Podsednik and A.J. Pierzynski were cut down on ill-advised attempts to steal; sPod, Rowand, and Dye failed to get down crucial sacrifice bunts; and Jose Contreras eschewed an easy out at home plate in favor of a double play attempt that didn't happen. The Angels scored a couple of cheap runs, and junk-baller Paul Byrd kept the Sox lineup in check.

Angels 3, White Sox 2.

So much for the home-field advantage. So much for taking advantage of a physically tired, battered, emotionally exhausted opponent.

If the Sox lost Game 2 at home, it would be Toronto and 1993 all over again. That would mean they'd have to win four of five from the Angels—with three of those games on the road.

In past years when the Sox contended but fell short, I'd write a little squib in October, noting the awful weather and trying to take some comfort in the fact that if the Sox had made the playoffs, we'd all be miserable watching the games. This year, with the Sox actually in the playoffs, the weather gods had been exceedingly generous. For the second night in a row, the game time temperature hovered around 60.

The crowd seemed a little edgy before the game. See? That Boston series had been too easy. Now, we were in a fight. Now, we knew that if we didn't pull this one out, the odds against a World Series appearance would be nearly astronomical. There was a lot of clapping and high-fiving and well-wishing in the stands before the game, but a lot of us were casting wary glances at the field, as if we feared something memorably awful might happen out there.

Enter the Lovehammers.

Not the entire band—just their guitarist, one Billy Sawilchik, who had been tapped to play the "Star-Spangled Banner." As Sawilchik ripped through a searing, heavy-metal version of the national anthem, the South Side crowd roared its approval and seemed to regain its footing. That's right—we're not about the Three Tenors or some *American Idol* second-place finisher or a Bobby Darin knockoff singing the national anthem. This version *rocked*.

Heading into the bottom of the 9th, the scored was tied, 1–1, and it looked like we were going into extra innings. I was still pretty pissed off about a Joey Cora mistake early in the game, when he needlessly sent Aaron Rowand home and Rowand was nailed at the plate. Cora had been doing that all year—the Hawkeroo loved it—but in the major leagues, and especially in the playoffs, if you treat third base like a revolving door and wave in every runner regardless of the situation, you're going to get burned. Sometimes Ozzie Ball was reckless ball.

With two outs and nobody on, I turned to my buddy and said, "They should reopen the beer stands when the games go into extra innings. Some of these fans are starting to sober up and get cranky."

A.J. Pierzynski was at the plate, and with two strikes he chased a pitch that was dropping quickly out of the strike zone. Umpire Doug Eddings seemed to call strike three—but after a moment's hesitation, A.J. started sprinting for first just as catcher Josh Paul rolled the ball to the mound.

Now, as God and the fans around me in Section 129 are my witnesses, I screamed, *"That's a live ball!"*

It wasn't that I was sure that the ball had scraped the dirt. I just knew that A.J. must have had a reason for taking off like that.

Bedlam ensued, with the Angels fiercely protesting the call. To this day when you see the replays, they're the very definition of inconclusive. Those of us who are sure the ball touched the ground point to the slow-motion replay as proof; those who are sure it was strike three use the same footage to prove their point.

Here's what really matters. Josh Paul—a local boy and a great guy— should have tagged Pierzynski, just to be safe. You see catchers do that several times a game. Better to be safe than a goat.

The other *huge* element, of course, was the Joe Crede at-bat that followed. With pinch runner Pablo Ozuma on second after a steal, Crede delivered the single most important White Sox hit of the year to that point—a rocket drive to left that we thought was a homer the minute it left Crede's bat. There was never any doubt that it would score Pablo. The only question was, did the Sox just win 2–1 or 3–1?

Turns out the ball stayed in the park, not that it mattered. The Sox had avoided going down two games to none, and the A-J-K became an instant part of Chicago baseball lore.

♪   ♪   ♪

Any chance the Angels had of retaking the momentum was killed in the very first inning of Game 3, when Paul Konerko blasted a two-run homer that gave the Sox and Jon Garland a quick 3–0 lead. The Angels fans just sat on their Thunderstix as the Sox won by scores of 5–2, 8–2, and 6–3—the clinching victory coming on a Sunday night in Anaheim, as thousands of Sox fans back home watched in taverns and in their living rooms. There were no air-raid sirens this time, but the streets of Chicago were filled with fans cheering and honking their horns.

I was with a group watching the game at the Kerryman, a relatively new, two-story Irish pub and restaurant in the River North neighborhood of Chicago. (I walked in one day shortly after they got their liquor license, ordered a Harp, glanced through the *Irish Times*, and gave the Irish bartender a quick word of advice: "You can't have all the TVs tuned to soccer matches if you're going to draw summertime crowds in Chicago.") We yelled at the TV throughout the game, and started lighting up cigars and ordering champagne as the outcome drew near. When it was over, we literally danced out of the bar and made our way to my place, where the party continued until the wee hours. I made phone calls to fellow Sox fans and engaged in sophisticated conversation that went along the lines of "WE'RE IN THE WORLD SERIES!" and "WE'RE IN THE $&#*^@! WORLD SERIES!" and "I CAN'T BELIEVE WE'RE IN THE *&$#^@! WORLD SERIES!" At one point, I took out my Dick Allen jersey and draped it over the shoulders of the one Cubs fan in our group, who was a good enough sport to pose for a few photos while muttering obscenities about how he was never, ever going to live this one down.

The last time the Sox were in the World Series, I was in Life's Waiting Room, just days from being born. Alaska and Hawaii had just become states, *Gunsmoke* was the most popular show in the country, and young John Kennedy had his eye on the presidency.

Well, gee. That didn't take too long.

♪   ♪   ♪

After I finished the round of media interviews before Game 1 of the World Series, I stayed on the field and walked around, soaking up every sight and sound—but it was almost like that feeling you have when you know you're dreaming and you're telling yourself to wake up, but you can't quite do it. It occurred to me that in the same year, I had been on the red carpet for the Academy Awards and now I was on the field before Game One of the World Series. I remembered the great exchange from *Broadcast News*, when William Hurt says, "What happens when your real life exceeds your dreams?" and Albert Brooks hisses, "*Keep it to yourself.*" But how can I do that? How can I not acknowledge that far more often than I deserve, I get to experience "radio contest winner" moments?

Most of the sports-media guys had left the field to make their way up to the press box, but the Fox camera guys and a host of photographers were gathered near home plate, snapping photos of 1959 White Sox greats, such as "Jungle" Jim Rivera, Bob Shaw, and Luis Aparicio, as they posed with that goofy green mascot, Southpaw. The old-timers wore Sox jerseys, modern Sox jerseys bearing their numbers, but they looked like somebody's dad or grandfather. It was hard to make the connection between the fellow wearing number 11 and Little Looie, the shortstop who had been my boyhood idol.

I snapped a few photos of the guys, and then aimed my camera at the Sox dugout. One of Ozzie's kids had a video camera, and he was shooting the guys, as if we were at a Little League game. You see that a lot these days at the World Series or the Super Bowl—pro athletes or their wives, or somebody involved with the team, shooting home video or snapping shots with a digital camera, as if there's not going to be miles of footage shot professionally. There's something endearing about that.

There was a bit of commotion when Ozzie stepped out of the dugout and greeted Mayor Daley, lifelong White Sox fan. As the two shook hands, I noticed that Daley was holding one of the Ozzie facemasks that had been handed to fans as they entered the park. With his trademark cackle, the mayor showed Ozzie the mask. *See what I've got? It's you!*

Only on the South Side.

I kept walking around, waiting for someone to tell me to leave the field. Instead, everybody just kept saying hi—including fans in the stands. We were all just kind of basking in the moment, knowing that even if heartbreak was around the corner, we'd made it. We'd made it to the World Series. As I said privately to just a few close friends and relatives, of course it would be fantastic if the Sox won it all—but just getting to the big dance, just getting the chance to see a World Series game on the South Side—that was awesome enough.

As I scanned the stands, I spotted Steve Dahl in the Scout Seats. The brash young deejay who had been the leader of the Anti-Disco Revolution now had three grown boys, including son Patrick, who was the same age as his father had been on Disco Demolition day. I waved to Steve, he threw his arm around Patrick, and I zoomed in and took a couple of photos.

A few moments after that, I spotted my father in the crowd. He was wearing his 1959 White Sox jacket and a Sox hat, and he didn't seem to care that the night was already turning harsh and cold. We were at a World Series game!

I waved. My dad tipped his cap.

What do you do when your real life exceeds your dreams? You thank the heavens for smiling on you, and you vow to never, ever take it for granted.

Epilogue: Coming Home

October 26, 2005

From my column in the *Chicago Sun-Times*:

Shoeless Joe has left the cornfield.

There's no need for him to linger in baseball purgatory any longer. Let the South Side ghosts sleep in peace, for the White Sox have won the World Series—I'll say that again, because it really hasn't sunk in: *the White Sox have won the World Series*—and all the sins and failures and miserable seasons of the past are forgiven.

Today, the 1919 Black Sox are paroled.

Today, Buck Weaver's good name is reinstated.

Today, the cup of beer misses Al Smith's head.

Today, the Dybber doesn't make that base-running blunder against the Orioles.

Today, the 1967 Pale Hose and the 1977 South Side Hit Men are winners, not also-rans.

Today, the playoff teams of 1983 and 1993 and 2000 are given a fond farewell and invited to move to the back of the scrapbook, so we can make room for the 2005 World Series champions.

From JD's first-inning, first game homer to Joe Crede's Graig Nettles imitation to Konerko's grand slam to sPod's walk-off homer in the freezing drizzle to the unlikely heroics of Geoff Blum, the Sox owned this Series.

They are the Road Warriors. They clinched in Detroit, they clinched in Boston, they clinched in Anaheim and they clinched in Houston. They've knocked 'em dead in more cities than U2 on a whirlwind tour.

In the postseason, the Sox dominated their foes like the Michael Jordan Bulls of the 1990s. Yes, luck was on their side. From Graffanino's Gaffe to the A-J-K dropped third strike to the phantom hit by pitch that struck Jermaine Dye's bat, the Sox were extremely fortunate throughout this playoff run—but they were also the best team, by far. They had great starting pitching, clutch hitting, stellar defensive play—and a crazy-genius manager who became the most beloved sideline figure in Chicago this side of Da Coach.

This is a city of deeply divided loyalties, where many die-hard fans of the Sox and the Cubs can tell you more about their baseball lineage than their family's history. They might not know the name of the town in Ireland or Germany or Poland or Mexico where their great-grandfather came from—but they can tell you who was pitching when their grandfather or their father took them to their very first game in 1956 or 1968 or 1985.

This is why it matters. When we root-root-root for the home team, we're rooting for our home as much as the team. We know the players aren't from Chicago—and we know many won't be back in a White Sox uniform for the 2006 season. (It's possible Paulie Konerko will be wearing an Angels uniform the next time he steps up to the plate at the Cell.)

The players come and go. We're the ones who stay—not so much out of loyalty to the owner or the manager or the players, but because we're loyal to our own family history. If your Dad was a Sox fan, and his Dad was a Sox fan, and *his* Dad was a Sox fan, and members of your family have been going to games on the South Side since Herbert Hoover was president, how can you not be a Sox fan? In that context, it's not irrational at all to get so swept up in the sporting fortunes of a bunch of millionaires (and future millionaires) who have the privilege of playing a game for a living.

It's all about sharing a common interest across generational lines.

If you're a Sox fan, you're in heaven today. If you're a Cubs fan, either you don't really care, or you're seething and simmering like the guy who gets left at the altar in a romantic comedy. Curses!

But even if you bleed Cubbie blue and you were rooting hard for the Astros to win this thing just so you wouldn't have to put up with all the gloating from your Sox fan friends, aren't you feeling just a little bit of Chicago pride today? Isn't it pretty cool that A-Rod and Manny and Vlad and Albert and the Rocket and all the other glamour kings ended up on the sidelines, watching the blue-collar Chicago guys doing the World Series Victory Scrum?

Neighborhood rivalries aside, they're not the South Side White Sox—they're the CHICAGO White Sox, and there's nothing wrong with everyone in the city feeling a touch of pride today. In Houston and St. Louis, in San Diego and Atlanta, in Boston and New York and Los Angeles, they're saying, "Wait til next year."

In Chicago, this year is here.

As the Sox celebrated their first World Series championship in 88 years, hundreds of thousands of Sox fans—here in Chicago and around the world—shouted themselves hoarse and hugged each other until they were out of breath. We also took time to think about that long-gone loved one. It's the oldest cliche in the scorebook—the teary-eyed toast to the dad or the brother or the mom or the grandma who passed away before the White Sox won the World Series—but so what. Go ahead and embrace all the cliches, and celebrate this victory with every ounce of your heart and soul.

White Sox.

World Series.

Champions.

Amen.

Afterword: Wait Till Last Year

May 22, 2006

Frank Thomas looks weird in green and yellow. Then again, who doesn't? Maybe Beyoncé can pull off that color combo. Maybe.

When a Hall of Fame player in any sport is traded away, or signs with another team at the tail end of his career, it's always startling to see him in a strange uniform. Think of Johnny Unitas with the San Diego Chargers, Joe Montana wearing the red of the Kansas City Chiefs, Bobby Orr with the Blackhawks, Michael Jordan as a Washington Wizard, Willie Mays with the Mets. It just doesn't look right.

So it is with the Big Hurt, who spent 16 productive and often tumultuous seasons on the South Side before leaving the organization in a messy divorce, with Thomas ripping the Sox for bidding him farewell via a phone message, and White Sox GM Kenny Williams countering by calling Thomas "an idiot," among other things. Even after the parting of the ways, the bad blood boiled over into a spring training parking lot confrontation between the two men, and I'm pretty sure they didn't hug and exchange e-mail addresses.

Now, on a brisk evening in May, we're 39,000 strong in the stands, bundled up in our World Champion sweatshirts and our World Champion jackets and our World Champion hats and probably our World Champion underwear in some cases, and we're feeling pretty good about things as Thomas steps to the plate in that funky A's uniform. Even though I don't know a single fan who felt the Sox should have kept Thomas for the 2006 season—we were all sick of his selfish ways and we didn't have much need for a designated hitter who wasn't doing that much hitting any more—we're collectively in a forgiving frame of mind. A pregame video tribute to the Big Hurt reminded us that despite his obsession with individual stats, his off-field misadventures, and his public whining about salary issues, the guy was a force at the plate—a two-time MVP, the greatest offensive presence in team history (with apologies to Bee Bee Richard).

We're also in a forgiving mood because we're the defending World Champions (as Hawk Harrelson will remind us approximately 57,000 times over the course of the season), and at this early juncture the prospects of a repeat appearance in the postseason seem strong. After a rocky 1–4 start in which the club seemed preoccupied with getting their rings and holding ceremony after ceremony after ceremony, the Sox got down to business and reeled off 12 wins in 13 games. That set the tone. Now, after taking two of three from the Cubs at Wrigley in a wild weekend series punctuated by Michael Barrett's sock to A. J. Pierzynski's jaw on a sunny Saturday on the North Side (the South Siders won that game 7–0), the Sox are 28–15. As for Frank, he's hobbling into town with an Oakland team that is probably already starting to wonder why they took a flyer on the aging, injury-riddled slugger.

We've known it for two years on the South Side: Frank is pretty much done. The injuries have taken their toll, and a one-dimensional player is now down to about a fifth of a dimension. (Insert your own "Up, Up and Away" or "One Less Bell to Answer" joke here.) Frank has seven homers, but he's hitting just .178 in his first 118 at-bats with his new team. Our new designated hitter, Jim "Mr. Incredible" Thome, is batting around .290, and he's among the league leaders in home runs and RBIs. Thome is also a class act who is constantly thanking the fans for their loyalty, encouraging and advising his young teammates, leading the cheers from the dugout, and accommodating the media's requests for his time.

In other words, he's the anti-Frank.

When Thomas is introduced on the PA system, there's a smattering of boos and a few catcalls, but about 90 percent of the fans stand and cheer respectfully, with several holding signs thanking Frank for his years of service on the South Side as the Big Hurt steps out of the box and raises his helmet in appreciation. (After the game, Williams had this to say about the warm reception from the fans: "They don't know what I know about him.")

Me? I take a Switzerland approach. I remain seated and put my hands together a few times, but then I remember all that whining and all that me-first stuff from Frank, and I focus my attention on Sox pitcher Jon Garland, urging him to bear down and strike this guy out.

Bam!

Thomas launches a 400-foot bomb into the left field stands and begins a slow trot around the bases—and to my surprise, the fans keep cheering him, as if he'd done it for our side.

Wrong! It's one thing to welcome a guy back to town for his first appearance, but once the game is on, he's the enemy.

When Thomas steps to the plate for his second at-bat, there's about a 50/50 mix of boos and cheers.

Bam!

Home run number two. What year does this guy think it is, 1993?

This time, there's some clapping, but also quite a bit of restless boo-ing. I'm not sure if we've had enough of Frank's homecoming, or if we're worried that Garland is reverting to his 2004 form after a breakout season in '05.

The boos grow louder with each successive appearance by Thomas, while the Sox go to work on a comeback. Home runs by local boy Rob Mackowiak and Jermaine Dye send the game into extra innings. In the 10th, Thomas comes to bat with two on and one out, but he pops out, and the Sox win the game in the bottom of the inning when Pablo Ozuma lays down a two-out bunt single, scoring A. J. Pierzynski—and who the hell lays down a two-out bunt single in the year 2006?

Grinder Rule #146: Find new and interesting ways to win.

Sox win, Sox win. Let Frank have his two home runs. It's not as if he's going to stay healthy all season and hit 35 or 40 dingers, right?

And let the Detroit Tigers have their little one-game lead over the Sox with a little more than a quarter of the season gone. This is a team that lost 119 games in 2003. They were just 71–91 in 2005.

It's not as if the friggin' Tigers are going to be close to the Sox by August, right?

Well, right. The Tigers *weren't* close to the Sox in August—they were so far ahead we could barely make out the Olde English "D" on their uniforms. Going into the 2006 season, nearly every baseball expert in the country had the Sox repeating as American League Central Division champs. If you wanted to be too clever by half, you went with the Indians, who had mounted that late-season threat against the Sox in 2005 before fading in the last week.

The Tigers? They were slated for fourth, behind the Sox and the Indians and the Twins, just barely ahead of the woeful Royals.

Nobody foresaw a 1968 flashback—a Tigers/Cardinals World Series—for 2006. That's why they actually play the games.

All season long, whenever I talked about the Sox, I urged my fellow fans not to expect a repeat. Live in the moment! Ask fans of the Diamondbacks, Marlins, Angels, and Red Sox how difficult it is to win the World Series, or even make it to the Series, two years in a row. The Yankees were the last great minidynasty in baseball. Since they won four pennants and three World Series in a row from 1998 to 2001, it's been one single-season wonder after another. Sure, the 2006 Sox had as much talent as any team in baseball—but you also need a little bit of luck and a lot of hunger to repeat. Whether I was talking to my fellow season ticket holders in Section 129, writing columns for the *Chicago Sun-Times*, giving interviews in conjunction with the release of the hardcover version of this book, or engaging in pregame telephone strategy sessions with my father, I kept repeating the same mantra: we have to enjoy this victory lap, because there's no guarantee we'll be there again in October 2006. Did Chicago sports fans learn nothing from the ultimate one-hit wonder, the 1985 Bears?

It was one of the strangest seasons in the history of the White Sox.

The madness had started well before the regular season. In November 2005, a lot of diehard Sox fans expressed their disappointment to me when the club traded the popular, hard-nosed Aaron Rowand to the Phillies for Jim Thome, who had experienced his share of injury problems in recent seasons. Why would they get rid of one of the key elements of the magical 2005 season?

Because that's how you make a run for a second title: by refusing to stand pat. On November 29, 2005, I wrote: "If Thome stays healthy, he's going to hit 46 homers and knock in 126 runs for the Sox, all the while looking and playing like some 1930s slugger who's hitting behind Roy Hobbs in the lineup. As I said last summer, Rowand plays baseball like a football player—but he's never going to be any better than he was last year. He'll hit .270 with 16 home runs and 68 RBI, he'll steal a dozen bases, and he'll run through walls to make plays in the outfield."

For the record, Thome hit 42 homers and had 109 RBIs. Rowand had 12 homers and 47 RBIs, stole 10 bases—and played in just 109 games because he tried to run through a wall, but it broke his nose instead. I still love Aaron Rowand and I was disappointed by Thome's performance in the last two months of the season (even as Frank Thomas was hitting so many clutch homers for the A's that some were touting him as an MVP candidate), but it was a strong trade for the Sox.

But there were other problems on the horizon. Ozzie Guillen had been a crazy genius in 2005, but in 2006 he was heavy on the crazy and not so much with the genius. Just a partial list of Ozzie's news-making activities in 2006:

February

Ozzie says he plans to quiz his players with questions from his recent immigration test—but he's not going to bother going to the White House to meet with President Bush.

In a *Sports Illustrated* piece, Ozzie calls Alex Rodriguez a hypocrite because A-Rod had mixed feelings about which country he should represent in the World Baseball Classic.

April

Ozzie is the subject of the *Playboy* interview and drops more than two dozen variations on the f-word. Among the choicer quotes:

- On the worst thing he's said to an umpire: "I hope your mother is still alive, because you're a f------ m-----------."
- On the legendary Sparky Anderson: "He managed the Detroit Tigers for 17 f------ years, and he lost almost every year."

- On photos of former Sox greats Frank Thomas and Magglio
  Ordonez in the Sox clubhouse in spring training: "I told Jerry
  Reinsdorf that I didn't want any pictures . . . of any former f------
  players. F--- the former players."

June

After Rangers pitcher Vicente Padilla hits A. J. Pierzynski in consecutive
at-bats, Guillen orders Sox rookie pitcher Sean Tracey to exact revenge.
Tracey tries to comply but fails to hit a Rangers batter, prompting Ozzie
to dress down Tracey in the dugout. After the game, Tracey is sent back
to the minors.

After former pitcher Jason Grimsley makes claims about steroid use
among major league players, Guillen says he'd like to "shoot" Grimsley.

Guillen claims Houston Astros manager Phil Garner snubbed him
at the World Series by refusing to shake his hand. Garner produces photos showing the two men shaking hands, and says Guillen "needs professional help."

Ozzie calls *Sun-Times* columnist Jay Mariotti a "f------ fag," setting off
a controversy that drags on for weeks. Major League Baseball fines Ozzie
$20,000 and orders him to undergo "sensitivity training."

July

Guillen yells at Jon Garland in the dugout after Garland fails to hit one
of the Texas Rangers.

August

Asked about claims by some National Leaguers that the Sox stole signs,
Guillen says, "If we played National League teams . . . we might win 150
games. They think I cheat? We faced two good pitchers in [the National
League]."

September

As Thomas leads the A's to a three-game sweep of the Sox in Oakland in
a series the Sox had to win, Guillen bitches about the ban on beer in the
clubhouse.

And all year long, Guillen's man Joey Cora kept waving runners home, even though most of the guys on the Sox are slower than the statue of Carlton Fisk in the outfield concourse.

♪   ♪   ♪

There were other distractions, and early signs that it could be a difficult year. Five games into the preseason, Guillen lamented the happy-fat-contented atmosphere in camp and said, "I'm embarrassed by the way we're playing."

Tadahito Iguchi, a natural RBI guy who had sacrificed his individual stats in 2005 as the No. 2 hitter, was moved to the No. 7 spot, but floundered so badly in spring training that the experiment was abandoned. Juan Uribe was not happy about being booted from the No. 2 slot back to the very bottom of the order.

And there was concern that starting hurlers Javier Vasquez and Freddy Garcia had burned up some valuable fuel by pitching in the World Baseball Classic. (Nearly every Sox hurler, including Vasquez and Garcia, seemed about 5 mph slower to the plate in '06.)

Early in the regular season, Sox chairman Jerry Reinsdorf sent word he wasn't pleased with the shaggy mops sported by Pierzynski, Garcia, and Joe Crede. Chicago sports-talk morning man Mike North engineered a stunt in which Joe and A. J. got their locks snipped live on the radio— and a huge media contingent turned out to observe the historic moment. (A year earlier, if Crede and Pierzynski had wandered into Supercuts, they probably wouldn't have received a celebrity discount, because nobody would have recognized them.) This left former Soxer Magglio Ordonez with the worst long-haired look in the league.

In another minor distraction, Mark Buehrle wasn't pleased when the Sox told him to knock it off with the sliding-on-the-tarp routine during rain delays. (A move I advocated in the first edition of this book.)

All the while, the Sox were playing . . . OK. They were hitting a lot of home runs, but the concept of Ozzie Ball (if it ever existed) was dead. This was a station-to-station team, filled with slow-footed sluggers who struck out a lot. Scott Podsednik had a miserable year in the lead-off position, Brian Anderson looked absolutely overmatched at the plate for much of the year, and Juan Uribe was inconsistent at the plate and maddeningly aggressive in the field, repeatedly calling off outfielders who should have been calling *him* off.

Then there was the pitching. Were the starters worn out from all those innings they pitched in 2005, or were they just not that great in the first place? Prior to the 2006 season, the consensus was the Sox had the best and deepest starting staff in the major leagues—but maybe it was more accurate to say they had a couple of No. 2 starters and three No. 3 guys, but no real aces. Jon Garland overcame his early-season troubles to become the most consistent member of the staff, and Freddy Garcia finished strong, but Jose Contreras, Vasquez, and Buehrle were consistently inconsistent. Buehrle in particular had a rough year, looking like the oldest, most tired 27-year-old starter in the game.

As for the bullpen: deadly. With a 7–1 record and a 2.00 ERA in 2005, Cliff Politte had been one of the premiere middle relievers in all of baseball—but in 2006 he was so bad that the Sox had no choice but to release him in mid-season. (At the time Politte's ERA was a brutal 8.70.) Neal Cotts had an ERA of over 5.00, and Brandon "The Future" McCarthy struggled in relief. If not for Bobby Jenks, who might well have been the MVP of the team, the bullpen would have been one of the worst in baseball.

Still, there was that ferocious lineup, and just enough good outings from the starting staff to make you believe that at any moment, the Sox were going to shift into a higher gear and blow away the surprising Twins, who were dubbed "the piranhas" by the admiring Ozzie (how come he couldn't come up with a catchy nickname for his own team?)—and overtake the Tigers as well. Up in the booth, Hawk Harrelson would take a break from his Mariotti-bashing long enough to say, "I like our club right here," or "I still like our chances to win this whole thing," or "The Sox are in the best division in baseball, but we match up *very* well against the Tigers and Twins."

With all the distractions and disappointments, the Sox were still 56–29 after sweeping the Orioles over the Fourth of July weekend. They were on pace to win more than 100 games, and once they got into the postseason, they'd have to be considered the favorites given their experience as champions.

It was going to be a great summer.

And then it all fell apart. Over a 19-day period in July, the Sox lost two out of three to the Red Sox, were swept by the Yankees, lost two of three to the Tigers, lost two of three to the Rangers, and were swept by the Twins. They went from 56–29 to 59–41, and though they'd have a spurt here or a ministreak there over the final two months of the season, they never put together the 10-game winning streak we'd all hoped for and pretty much expected.

In late June, I wrote a column reassuring Sox fans that "there will be playoff baseball on the South Side in 2006." As for Detroit, I said we could "expect them to fade in the stretch, with the Sox winning the division by seven games."

Well, the Tigers *did* fade in the stretch, but it was the Twins who put together the huge run, to not only leave the Sox choking on their dust but also capture the American League Central. (Not that it mattered in the playoffs, when the Twins were quickly felled by Thomas and the A's, while the Tigers stunned the Yankees and then went on to manhandle Oakland, looking a lot like the 2005 Sox until they were flattened by the Cards in the World Series.)

Before the first Sox/Cubs series of 2006, I had noted that the so-called Crosstown Classic just didn't seem to matter as much any more. After all, the White Sox were World Champions and they were riding high, and the Cubs—well, how could you not feel sorry for the Cubs and their fans?

In the second half of the season, we didn't have the luxury of pitying anybody. After the All-Star break, the Cubs were 32–42, but the Sox were just one game better at 33–41.

That's what made things so frustrating. The Sox didn't have to be great in the last two months to get into the playoffs; they had to be average. They played hard, but they seemed to be lacking a sense of fire and urgency. When the Twins or Tigers would win a game with a late comeback, they'd mob each other on the field. When the Sox won, they were all business, shaking hands and high-fiving one another. Maybe that's the way you're supposed to conduct yourselves when you're the

World Champions, but sometimes you want to see a reminder that these men are playing a kids' game. Why not go a little goofy from time to time?

Jermaine Dye is a great player and a true role model. Paul Konerko is a world-class pro. But these guys are never going to be called "fun-loving."

From a personal standpoint, the 2006 season was one of the most frustrating of my life, and one of the most rewarding. When *Sox and the City* was released in June, the response from fans in Chicago and around the world was overwhelming. I heard from former Chicagoans living in Alaska, New Zealand, Australia, Ireland, England, Germany, and a dozen other countries. I heard from Chicago-area soldiers based in Iraq. I heard from 12-year-old minifans, and 80-year-old warhorses who had waited a lifetime for a World Series. Hundreds of fans e-mailed or told me first-hand what the Sox meant to them and their families. I've written a half-dozen books, more than 3,000 newspaper columns, and dozens of magazine articles, but nothing else I've done has elicited such passionate, personal, sincere responses from readers. Every time someone asked me to sign a book for a dad or a fiancé or a brother, it reinforced my belief that while the Sox may never have as many fans as the Cubs or the Yankees or the Red Sox, the fans they have care as much as anyone, anywhere.

That's why we were so disappointed by the third-place finish in 2006. Not because we expected another World Series championship, but because we didn't want to wake up from the dream.

Index